Best Wishes

Stephen D. Wike

STEPHEN

Isaiah 40:31

But those who hope in the Lord will renew their strength.
They will soar on wings like eagles;
They will run and not grow weary;
They will walk and not be faint.

G-DAY

Rendezvous with Eagles

D. WIEHE

G-Day, Rendezvous With Eagles, by Stephen D. Wiehe
www.gdayrendezvouswitheagles.com

First Edition, June 2011

Author services by Pedernales Publishing, LLC.
www.pedernalespublishing.com

The use of the shoulder sleeve insignia of the 101st Airborne Division, by permission of The Department of the Army.

For information, address:

    Eagle-FO Publishing Company
    P.O. Box 200921
    Austin, Texas 78720-0921

Special pricing available direct from the publisher for veteran's organizations, non-profits, and fund raising events.

ISBN 978-0-9834361-0-2

Printed in The United States of America

DEDICATION

The soldiers and veterans of the 101st Airborne Division (Air Assault)

My wife, Sue

Kristen and Clay

Mom and Dad

My Brother, Don, and Sister, Angela

G-DAY

RENDEZVOUS WITH EAGLES

Contents

Introduction

When I started my research, the twenty plus years that had passed began to shrink. By the end of the project, the events that changed my life two decades ago seemed like yesterday. The reconnection with old friends was well worth the time it took to put the book together.

In working on our unit history, I found very little about our important missions and objectives during Operations Desert Shield and Desert Storm. I was amazed that the units themselves had very little information regarding our objectives and the reasons for them. In a day when the internet and cell phones are everywhere, including the front lines of combat, there is a rich and living commentary written by the troops as they live it. But, just a few decades ago during Desert Storm, there were no blogs, satellite radio or internet. When it comes to Desert Storm there is a void in the written history. Our children would be hard pressed to put all of the pieces together.

My goal when I started writing G-Day was to create a factual, historical document that all of us could be proud of and that could be used as a reference for future generations.

When visiting with Dr. John O'Brien, Chief Historian at the Don F. Pratt Museum at Fort Campbell, I told him I didn't want this to turn into a book of "fish stories" or a compilation of war tales that are told so many times over the years that they gradually become the truth.

There are some great books written by accomplished authors who give us a great view of the "big picture" in Operations Desert Shield and Desert Storm. In writing this book, my hope is that it will help you see, and appreciate, the day to day activities of the soldiers who were there and how they fit into the "bigger picture."

Stephen D. Wiehe

Prologue

I grew up in Texas and was the oldest son of educators. After graduating from high school in 1972, I joined the Army. I just wasn't ready for college and the Vietnam War was drawing to a close. I went into the Army on the buddy plan with a good high school friend and we enlisted as Military Policemen. After serving three years, I got out of the Army and began working as an Assistant Manager in a family owned retail business. In 1977 I got married and in the same year I was offered a position in a local bank. At 22 years old, I began working as a teller and assisting the Vice President of Operations with his duties. Being a quick study and a hard worker, it was not long before I was rapidly promoted at work and had established myself as a well respected community leader. I spent a great deal of my time volunteering in the community, including civic clubs and the Chamber of Commerce. At 27 years old, I was promoted to Bank Vice President and a year later was offered and accepted an Executive Vice President's job in a small town near Houston. Along with the executive level responsibility, I became a bank director. As my leadership expanded at work, my civic responsibilities followed suit and I was elected President of the Chamber of Commerce. During this period, my wife and I moved from a small apartment, to a townhome, and then to a two story home at the local country club.

Meanwhile, in the Middle East during the Iranian Revolution in 1979, oil production was curtailed and exports were suspended, causing the price of oil to rise dramatically in the ensuing three years. Sensing weakness and taking an opportunity to settle long-standing disputes, long-time enemy Iraq invaded Iran in 1980 resulting in even more cuts in Middle East oil production and exports. Saudi Arabia and oil producing countries throughout the world stepped up production to offset the Iran-Iraq losses. During this period of unrest and conflict in the Middle East, Texas experienced an "oil boom." Money was flowing and there was an influx of people coming into the state to fill jobs. Closer to home, our bank customers who were in the oil and gas industry were working hard to provide needed services. To fund the expansion, many leveraged real estate and other assets for capital expenditures.

And then the valley came. From 1981 to 1987 oil prices began to plummet due to worldwide, excess production. Many oil and gas related customers would come through the doors of the bank complaining about oil prices. Known as the Crude Oil Collapse of 1986, the price of OPEC crude oil plummeted from $23.29 a barrel in December of 1985 to $9.85 by July 1986. As the price approached a twelve year low, we would hear, "If oil would only go back up to $18.00 per barrel, everything would be ok." The year 1986 was an emotional roller coaster of a year. Our daughter Kristen was born, creating a mind numbing high, and simultaneously, the Texas banking industry took a nose dive. Excessive and over-leveraged lending in real estate and the oil and gas industry brought banking to its knees. Overextension of bank credit to commercial real estate ventures caused the majority of the damage. Despite an increase in vacancy rates in offices and retail shopping centers, Texas banks threw caution to the wind and continued to lend money all the way through 1987. Seven of the ten largest banks in Texas failed during the period as bad loans grew from 1.75 percent in 1982 to 6.6 percent of the total outstanding loans in 1987.

It wasn't only the banks that were negatively impacted. Savings and Loans (S&Ls) had been deregulated (bad loans and poorly structured "joint ventures" began to rear their ugly heads, throwing more gasoline on an already unstable banking environment). S&Ls had grown quickly since the 1970s with minimal supervision. The Depository Institutions Deregulation and Monetary Control Act of 1980 encouraged competition, thus increasing the services thrifts could provide, placing them in direct competition with the banks. Historically, thrifts had limited power and concentrated on home loans, but with the new legislation they moved into uncharted ground. Expanding haphazardly into real estate development and other real estate lending, combined with lower capital requirements and inadequate supervision and regulatory oversight, was a recipe for disaster.

As losses continued to rise in the banking industry, banking regulators came down hard. State regulators demanded an increase in capital reserve and an increase in reserves for bad loans. The rules had changed for our management team in mid-stream. In the years before my time with the bank, there were several large bad loans. Being part of a new management team, we took control of those bad loans that were now classified assets and, with very few exceptions, all new loans made were sound ones. Even with the poor quality of some large loans that were inherited, the bank always remained profitable.

The President of our bank worked out millions of dollars worth of the inherited bad paper through restructures and sales of other assets. At the regulator's request, he also was successful in raising additional capital for the bank, but after changing the rules yet again the state regulators came back and said it wasn't enough. I thought my friend and President had done a magnificent job with the pile of garbage that was dumped on him. However, capital reserves were still insufficient and couldn't keep up with the newest requirements, so the regulators required the bank to be sold. Seeing the handwriting on the wall, I reluctantly (but voluntarily) exited. The fact is that once new ownership groups come in, so come their managers.

The time was both devastating and demoralizing for us. To have worked so hard for over ten years moving up the ladder, only to have the top rung taken away, was heart breaking. It was one of those times in life when events that unfolded were out of my control. I had done everything I had known and been taught to do. There were no banking jobs at the time in the Houston area, as our bank wasn't the only one with problems. I spent months searching and trying to open myself up to other possibilities to no avail. I was never one to give up on anything, but I quickly figured out I needed to look in another direction.

During this hardship I never lost my faith in God or blamed him for my problems. I just kept praying that I would be led in the right direction. As a result, I never lost peace and always knew we would be taken care of. And then a thought came to me, thinking I was crazy. I was in the Army before banking and enjoyed it. The Army was good to me, and I loved the structure and culture. It's peace-time, and there hadn't been a war for thirteen years, though I darn sure felt like I just left a combat zone. I thought to myself, maybe I'll run down to the recruiter and see what they have to offer. I had exhausted my job search in Houston. Maybe this would be my third career.

Chapter 1

Back to Basics

As I walked into the Army recruiter's office in Houston, I immediately noticed a difference. Unlike the last time I walked through the Army recruiter's doors in Austin some sixteen years earlier, I wasn't 18 anymore. I might have been considered a young man in the banking industry, but I suddenly felt a lot older once inside those doors. The sergeant on duty asked, "So, what brings you here today, sir?" Being 34 years old, I thought I was older than the recruiter. I told him I was interested in going back into the Army. After hearing my story, he said, "Now sir, you know there are some physical requirements that you'll be tested on." I said of course, what are they? The young staff sergeant began going down the list of height and weight requirements, push-ups, sit-ups, 2-mile run. "How long will it take before you can do all of this?" he asked. I thought a minute and said, "Oh about 3 months." He went on to tell me that "if" I could meet the physical requirements, my college and prior service would give me some rank when I reentered the service. After visiting with him a little while longer, I thanked him for his time, and walked out. While I knew I had some hard work ahead of me to get ready, I knew equally well he thought he would never see me again. I decided on that day that I would be going back in the Army.

I began my preparations with a simple prayer: "GOD HELP ME." From that day on, I began thinking about the Army and nothing else. I had to quickly clear my head from the banking days. I told myself, "Those days are gone. I can't think about my losses and there is no time to feel sorry for myself." I had to get over it and move on. I went home and started a strict training regimen that day. Every day for three months, I did an APFT (Army physical fitness test). I ran 2 to 4 miles a day, did push-ups and sit-ups, and I lost my banquet gut in the process. My goal wasn't to go back into the Army just meeting the basic physical requirement for enlistment. My goal was to go back in meeting or exceeding the basic training graduation requirement.

Because of my prior service as an Army soldier, I had a jump start on my renewed military career. The Army grants credit for the active and inactive reserve time a person accumulates during previous tours, and that "time in service" is important for advancement and pay purposes. My first tour was in the early 1970s during Vietnam, and at that time my Military Occupational Specialty (MOS) was Military Policeman. Now that I was reenlisting in the relative peaceful time in 1988, I didn't think twice about selecting Fire Support Specialist (forward observer) as my new MOS. Placing myself in harm's way was the farthest thing from my mind. There hadn't been an Army-wide conflict since Vietnam, so choosing a "combat arms" MOS didn't *seem* overly dangerous. But, the job offered one of the best possibilities of making rank due to it being one of the more dangerous MOSs. If I was going to make this a career, I sure didn't want to stagnate at a low rank for an extended period of time.

As I joined my basic training unit at Ft. Sill, Oklahoma, I knew what was coming. PURE HELL!! Being an older guy with prior service, the drill sergeants knew who I was before I got off the "cattle truck" with all the young recruits. We didn't even have a chance to make it to the foyer of the barracks before they had us in the front leaning rest position. Two of them were dedicated just for me. Shoot, they even knew my name. We were doing push-ups, sit-ups, and then made to stop and drink a whole canteen of water. I remember thinking: "Oh, I get it. They are trying to make us throw up." Then we would go through the whole process again. I was sure glad I spent some time at home working up to this or I would be heaving. I never felt that urge, but quite a few younger guys did. There was a lot of yelling with two drill sergeants barking orders over me; however, there was no contact between the drill sergeants and the new recruits. That was surprising. I remember a lot of contact during my first basic training when I was 18 years old at Ft. Polk, Louisiana. When I first went into the Army, Fort Polk was nicknamed "Little Vietnam." Many soldiers who went to Vietnam had gone through basic and Infantry AIT (Advanced Individual Training) there. The climate resembled that of Southeast Asia, and the humidity was stifling. While the drill sergeants at Sill were going through their well-rehearsed drills, I remembered the senior drill sergeant at Ft. Polk lining us up in a company formation and giving the 1st and 3rd ranks an order to "about face." After that order, we had the 1st and 2nd ranks looking at each other and the 3rd and 4th ranks looking at each other. We all thought that was pretty funny until he gave the order to start beating the crap out of the soldier in front of us. Before he put us back at attention, there were fifty fights going on. The recruits weren't laughing anymore, but the drill sergeants sure were.

At Ft. Sill, my platoon's senior drill sergeant promoted me to platoon guide on day one. I knew from the past that a platoon guide would work his butt off trying his best to lead the platoon, and then be replaced. Another recruit would be appointed only to be replaced, and so on and so on until the end of the training cycle. I sure didn't let the appointment go to my head knowing I was going to be replaced in a couple days. I thought I would rather just be one of the recruits for the nine week cycle, graduate, and go to AIT (Advanced Individual Training). Being one of the "old guys" in the training unit at Ft. Sill, the young recruits nicknamed me "Pops." I was lucky that I didn't receive grief from any of the recruits in my platoon, but I made darn sure I never exercised authority over them unless it was necessary. They knew I would work for them whenever possible, so they supported me.

Everyone, including platoon guides, did "KP" (kitchen police) duty. I was on my knees in the kitchen scrubbing the floor at the end of the day when the Senior Drill Sergeant stopped by. He leaned over and said, "This is a lot different than banking, isn't it, Herr Wiehe?" always addressing me by the German pronunciation of my last name. I looked up at him and grinned, but didn't answer. I just smiled and kept working. I was actually thinking this was much easier than what I had left behind in Texas, but I sure didn't want to stick my foot in my mouth and tell him that.

Fort Sill, Oklahoma in October and November ended up being a heck of a lot easier than Ft. Polk in August and September. At the end of the training cycle, the Senior Drill Sergeant asked me if I wanted to go to the NCO (Non-Commissioned Officers) Club for a beer. How can you tell a Senior Drill Sergeant, "no"? After we got to the club, he told me that I had been one of only a few that had ever led a platoon for an entire training cycle. He shared with me his Vietnam experience and some words of guidance and support for my career in the Army. Near the end of our visit he said it had been a long time since our Army had been in Vietnam and quipped, "You know the only thing we need now is a little war." Of course I smiled and agreed. The following day, I graduated as "Distinguished Graduate" and was promoted to Specialist Fourth Class. As a result of this promotion and graduating number one in the class, I was able to meet face to face with Colonel Robert H. Scales, Jr., Commander of The U.S. Army Field Artillery Training Center at Fort Sill, Oklahoma in his office. He was very kind and supportive. After hearing of my background, he had some great, fatherly advice for me as I pursued my career in the Army.

Fort Lewis, Washington, home of the 9th Infantry Division (Motorized) was my first permanent duty assignment. In fact, the Fort Lewis assignment was not just a fluke, it was a choice. The quality of life for families was very nice. Having Seattle and Mt. Ranier in my back-yard would be like living in a post card, plus there would always be something to do in my off time. Years earlier, I made a trip to Seattle and Vancouver when I was in banking and fell in love with the area. It was late in the summer and brutally hot in Texas, so the low 80 degree temperatures were a wonderful change. I flew into Seattle from Texas, rented a car, and drove the area taking pictures and enjoying the magnificent scenery that the Northwest has to offer. The choice for that assignment came with a bonus. I had a buddy named Dave, about my age that I had gone through Army schools with who would be at Ft. Lewis with the 2/75th Rangers.

The 9th Infantry Division had a storied history, and since its reactivation in 1972 the Department of the Army was using the division as a test bed for new equipment and ideas. In the event of a conflict, the motorized division's mission was to quickly deploy all of its vehicles and equipment anywhere in the world. Once on the ground, a motorized division could quickly self deploy to hot spots within their area of operations.

After getting settled into the 3rd Battalion, 11th Field Artillery Regiment at Fort Lewis, it was get to work time. There was always something going on. Besides the normal training day, which always included physical training and running, we were busy in the motor pool working on our HUMMVs (high-mobility, multi-purpose, wheeled vehicles). Our unit was also involved in training others in the division.

The summer of 1989 we taught ROTC cadets from various parts of the country. We set up three M198, 155mm howitzers with an FO (forward observer) bunker nearby. All day we would teach the cadets how to call different missions and then let them call for fire. Teaching was a great way to reinforce my AIT training. The next teaching opportunity came when we taught our infantrymen how to "call for fire", an element of their earning the Expert Infantryman's Badge.

With my background in management, the unit used me as coordinator for the division's upcoming senior leadership M-16 range. In my early years as an MP, I was the top marksman in the 519th Military Police Battalion. As a result, I attended counter-sniper "urban" (select marksman) training at Ft. Meade, Maryland. It was a great opportunity for a Texas boy to burn up some government ammo. I loved shooting and shooting sports, so putting me in a position as coordinator for the division's "Commanding General Senior Leadership Range" would be a blast. It took several weeks to coordinate, plan, and then execute the range, but it all came off without a hitch with the 3/11th receiving some kudos.

Fire Support Specialist AIT (Advanced Individual Training) School at Ft. Sill was just the beginning of my learning process as an FO (forward observer). Teaching call for fire missions to the cadets and infantry was fun, but it was just the basics. The next level for me was learning how to apply the skills I had learned at Ft. Sill.

Through the process of learning more about my job, I found the forward observer to be a different breed of soldier. An FO was a graduate from an artillery school, but also fought with the infantry. He was with the infantry, but he was not of the infantry. The FO had to know howitzers, mortars, and ordnance, with a firm grasp on how fire control worked, and also know how to prepare a fire plan for the maneuver commander. He had to know how the infantry moved as well as be the best at map reading and navigation skills. The FO was assigned and housed with the artillery unit in garrison (home base or fort), and attached to and lived with the infantry in war. It was much more independent than I had ever thought, and I liked it.

My buddy Dave at 2/75th also had prior service and was also in his thirties. He was a smart, educated, pro-military guy that was on a mission to become an FO with the elite U.S. Army Rangers. Through basic and AIT, we flip-flopped as to who was the best of the class. I graduated as "distinguished graduate" in basic, with Dave right behind me; and in AIT, Dave finished in the number one position, with me close behind him. Dave was in top shape physically and even in his thirties "dusted" the younger soldiers. I was in shape, but nothing compared to my buddy who could drive the "babies" into the ground on runs, push-ups, and sit-ups. He pushed me, and it was great having someone closer to my age that was a hard driver both mentally and physically. After Dave completed Airborne School and RIP (Ranger Indoctrination Program), he was assigned as an FO to the 2/75th Rangers at Ft. Lewis. With both of us at Lewis, our families shared some off time together.

Dave Gurley and my daughter Kristen

On 20 December 1989, the 2/75th was part of Operation Just Cause, a daring overthrow of General Manuel Noriega in Panama. The 2nd and 3rd Ranger Battalions conducted a parachute assault onto the Rio Hato Airport. Their mission was to neutralize the PDF (Panamanian Defense Force) rifle companies at the airport with follow-on missions after seizing the initial objective. Minutes before the 500 foot parachute drop, F-117s dropped two bombs which would help suppress the 2 companies of the PDF including a unit of Noriega's elite, "Macho de Montes." During the drop, Dave's parachute got hung up in a tree and began taking fire. As he was releasing himself from his parachute harness, an AC-130H Spectre was on station and Rangers called for its support. Spectre circled the target showering down death and

7

destruction onto the PDF companies and armored vehicles from its two 20mm guns, one 40mm gun and 105mm howitzer. With help from the gunship, Dave made it to the rally point and the Rangers were able to neutralize the PDF.

On the morning of 20 December, after President Bush announced Operation Just Cause to the Nation, I called Dave's wife. The only thing she knew was that Dave had been deployed, and assumed through the television reports that the 2/75th was involved in the operation. Even Army Ranger wives were in the dark, and as far as they knew, the unit had deployed on another training exercise. I remained glued to the TV and the initial reports coming out of Panama. This Panama story had suddenly become a story about one of my friends. I was proud to be Dave's friend, but concerned about the outcome. As the story unfolded, the Rangers were instrumental in the success in Panama. Noriega was found and confined, and the rightfully elected president took his place running the government. The United States no longer had to worry about Americans living in Panama being harassed or killed. Upon Dave's and the 2/75 Ranger Battalion's return to Ft. Lewis, it was like welcoming home the Super Bowl Champions. Everyone at Lewis was proud of what they had done, but sad the Rangers had lost five of their comrades and sustained forty-two wounded in the operation. Following their return, there were memorial services for those that were killed in action.

Ft. Lewis was a busy place for me. In addition to the daily activities of the 3/11th, I was going to Pierce College at night working on college credit and working on Army correspondence courses trying to accumulate promotion points. I had to turn down many invites to go out with my buddies because of this self-inflicted, hectic schedule. Focused on making this a career, I took advantage of any opportunity to better myself.

I started honing my skills as an FO in our field training exercises at the artillery range at Ft. Lewis and at Yakima. The Yakima Training Center (YTC) also known as Yakima Firing Center (YFC) was my first exercise away from Ft. Lewis. The 3/11th FA

(Field Artillery) convoyed from Ft. Lewis to Yakima. The training center was located about 170 miles east of Ft. Lewis. The convoy had to cross the Cascade Mountain range through snow covered passes. Getting there was a slow and arduous journey that took about five hours. YTC was a high desert range with temperatures as low as 0 degrees in the winter and 100 degrees in the summer. We were going in late fall, so during our three week stay, we could experience about any weather condition. The battalion was going to the National Training Center (NTC) at Ft. Irwin, California in February 1990, so the trip to Yakima was intended to get us all up to speed, hopefully revealing shortcomings before we were tested at a higher level.

Once we arrived at YTC, we settled into some temporary barracks for the night. One of the advantages of being an FO and having a vehicle was having stoves and food. We packed our one-burner stoves and brought a separate bag of Asian noodles and granola bars to supplement the MREs (Meals Ready to Eat). I thought this was great. These guys have figured out ways to "really" survive in the field. I knew I had picked the right duty assignment, and it sure beat the heck out of those light infantry divisions that had to hump their rucks (carrying a heavy backpack). Though it was a far cry from the way Dave and the 2/75th Rangers had to operate, this motorized division was the way to go, baby.

Those responsible for teaching me the finer points of being an FO were competent and willing to teach and assist in my growth. My fire support officer (FSO) was a hard charging 1st Lieutenant out of West Point who was a "by the book", no-nonsense kind of guy that demanded perfection. If I were to grow as an FO, I couldn't have been under a better guy. Then there was Sergeant Davis, who was responsible for teaching me directly. Sgt. Davis knew his stuff and knew how to FO. Not only did he know the fire support specialist job and its equipment inside and out, but he knew how to communicate with CAS (close air support). As a result of his knowledge, Davis volunteered us to work with the Air Force.

It seemed that the Air Force wanted to analyze the Army's ability to laze (paint) targets for their A-10s (Warthogs). In the past, the Army had been unable to maximize the use of the Warthog using the laser designator. Our job was to prove that it could be done efficiently using the existing equipment. After linking up with the Air Force FAC (forward air controller), we set up our position and laser designator over looking the range. Sgt. Davis was relaxed, but didn't let a minute go by without instructing. Not only did he teach me about the Air Force but, in addition, other FO nuances that would be important.

Lazing targets for Warthogs – Yakima Firing Center, Washington

The next morning, an Air Force colonel, along with his forward air controllers, arrived at our location. After a brief, we made sure our designator and radio were on the correct frequency. We were instructed to direct the aircraft and laze some abandoned tanks about 1200 meters in front of us. The A-10s would be directed by us to the target from our location. We would orient the pilots to the target, laze the target, and they would shoot. The first run of two A-10s went well. We lazed a target, the pilots were "cleared hot", and they destroyed the tanks. Once their nose pointed to the target and pulled the trigger, the only thing we could hear was the hum of the gatling-gun. The A-10 was built around the GAU-8 Avenger, 30mm gatling-gun and could spit out 3,900 rounds per minute of depleted uranium, armor piercing projectiles. Once the guns fired, the sound was a continuous hum. After seeing the destructive power of the Warthog, I was thankful they were on our side, and more thankful they were in a close air support role for the Army.

A-10 on a target run – Yakima Firing Center, Washington

After a couple passes by the A-10s, we got cocky and felt we could actually laze two targets on one run. After all, there were two aircraft coming in. The only thing we would have to do is stagger the aircraft a few more seconds. After discussing the idea with the Air Force, we gave it a try. We directed the aircraft into the PUP (pull up point) and designated for the first aircraft, then quickly re-trained the laser onto the second target. It worked well. Both targets were designated on one run and both were destroyed. The colonel was happy because now they could destroy multiple targets and expose their planes and pilots less to a SAM (surface to air missile) attack. The exercise was a success.

At the conclusion of the exercise, we had a chance to visit with them about the A-10 and its CAS (close air support) mission. They said the Warthog was on its way out and it wouldn't be long until the CAS mission would be passed onto another aircraft. Though they gave no time table for the phase out, it was sad news for me. After seeing the destructive power of the airplane against armor, I couldn't think of a better option in support of our Army.

After we concluded our Air Force exercise, we linked back up with the 3/11th for a day movement of our battalion. The firing batteries (as well as fire support) moved, communicated, and conducted fire missions well. Then there were the night-time exercises. In the dark, we had a lot of trouble finding objectives and targets because the area had very few terrain features I could see. It was tough operating, and though I was never lost, I definitely became "mis-oriented" (mis-orientation to an FO meant he was LOST). At times, the best thing we could do was to stop and listen to the radio. To be lost wasn't very HOOAH. I was an FO that was "out of the battle." Oh, to have the Army's new "slugger" (global positioning system) which would tell me to the meter where I was, even at night.

Our last night at YFC was extremely cold. We had linked up with the battalion and had an opportunity to sleep a few hours. I had trouble sleeping sitting up in my vehicle, so I threw my sleeping bag out on the ground next to it. By the next morning, I had a couple inches of snow on my bag and, after peeking out, I noticed nothing but white on top of me and the vehicles. I was glad we didn't have to endure any more of that. I left Yakima with my tail between my legs knowing what I needed to work on to get better.

One of the best field training exercises was held at the NTC (National Training Center) at Ft. Irwin, California. In February, we participated in desert warfare training at that facility. NTC offered a much larger training area where units could work on their desert and anti-armor war fighting capabilities. In our case, we could see OPFOR (opposition forces) in large columns of tanks and armored personnel carriers moving toward our locations. We had to correctly call for fire on those enemy columns and were evaluated on our accuracy. In calling for a fire mission, it was critical that we learned to identify every military vehicle operating on the planet. We had to know our targets. As FOs, we were issued a deck of armored vehicle recognition cards and kept them on us most of the time. When we had a little down time, we would get the cards out and test our RTOs (radio-telephone-operators), then we would switch and they would test us. The deck had friendly and enemy vehicles and differences were noted for the vehicles that could be mistaken. Also, notations were on the cards relating to armament and ranges. We had to know them all.

In one exercise at NTC, we were simulating "Copperhead" missions on a large column of OPFOR tanks moving through the desert. "Copperhead" was a one shot – one kill, laser guided missile launched from an M198 artillery piece. The exercises were stopped in midstream for President George H.W. Bush to land in his helicopter and observe the training. He came over the net (radio) and voiced his appreciation for what we were doing. After his short radio address, the tanks started rolling again and the battle simulation resumed. I was impressed that the President of the United States had taken an interest in what we were doing and dropped in on our training.

In the 9th Infantry Division (Motorized), the FO was in a HUMMV and had to learn the art of fire support on the move. When planning support, I had to not only know the terrain that I was on, but the terrain that was ahead of us. Map reading and navigation skills were sharpened both in daylight and more importantly at night. NTC and YFC had helped those nocturnal navigation skills tremendously. Another critical component in my learning curve was working with the infantry. Once you showed your infantry commander that you knew your stuff and could competently assist him with his target plan, you became a valuable asset. And once you showed your infantry sergeants that you could operate and assist them without slowing them down, you became one of them.

Upon returning from NTC, the 3/11th would not be going back to the field for a long time. The battalion was in a cycle of doing "other stuff." No FOs in the unit would be doing their job because of outside tasking orders handed down to the battalion from division HQ (headquarters). During this cycle, NCOs scrambled to find suitable non-FO positions, and after the cycle, everyone would go back to their "real jobs."

During that cycle, I was asked if I would be interested in working in Operations, and I immediately said yes. I couldn't think of a better opportunity during this cycle than to work as an assistant to the S-3 NCOIC (Non-Commissioned Officer in Charge), Master Sergeant David Martin. They knew from my history I had a great deal of experience in the private sector with organization and operations. That skill set was very appealing to the officers and senior enlisted personnel at the 3/11th as there were not many people in the unit who had the experience to do a good job at that level.

I worked hard in the S-3 shop and got along great with MSG Martin. I got to see how operations and plans worked at a battalion level. David was the kind of guy that appreciated the hard work, but also knew how important it was not to stagnate and encouraged me to keep working on my job. David could have kept me under thumb and at a desk, but that wasn't the way he was. After a short four months in S-3, he rewarded my hard work with a BNCOC (Basic Non-Commissioned Officers) School slot. The BNCOC slots were hard to get and David, along with other senior NCOs in the battalion, made it happen for me. The school was coming up in the summer of 1990, and the school would enhance my FO and leadership skills, preparing me to be a Staff Sergeant (E-6).

In July of 1990, I reported to BNCOC. I was blessed and very fortunate that the Fire Support NCO School was right there at Fort Lewis. Had it not been at Ft. Lewis, it would have been more difficult to get the slot. Some say a "mere coincidence." I say it was just another one of those places where I was supposed to be. I was convinced the place and timing was directed by God and the encouraging senior enlisted personnel at 3/11.

At BNCOC, we learned to sharpen our skills as a Forward Observer (Fire Support NCO) and improve our leadership skills so we could guide and teach subordinates. We learned advanced "call for fire" techniques as it related to close air support, naval gunfire, as well as advanced artillery missions and target planning. It wasn't a difficult school, but was extremely important in my growth. One of the finer points I learned at BNCOC was how the forward observer was a primary target for the Russians and Soviet taught countries. If the enemy could take out the FO, less fire would be directed at them. They were willing to expend a tremendous amount of ordnance attempting to kill the FO.

One of those countries using the Soviet doctrine was Iraq. At the direction of Saddam Hussein, troops crossed the border and invaded Kuwait on August 2, 1990. The events unfolding in Kuwait gave the BNCOC instructors a live training scenario as we started to receive briefings on the Southwest Asia Theatre of Operations and the nuances of fighting in the desert. When we weren't in class, we were in the day room glued to the television trying to get the latest reports from Kuwait. We graduated from BNCOC on August 17, 1990, one week early so everyone could get back to their units. We would normally graduate in our "Dress Greens", but since The United States had committed troops to theatre, and there was a high probability of going to war we graduated in our BDUs (Battle Dress Uniforms).

I reported back to the 3/11 FA after graduation and everything appeared to be "business as usual." The 9th Infantry Division's mission would make it an "unlikely" candidate to participate in a campaign against Iraq. We did pay close attention to the news and to the units that were being deployed. It looked like the 18th Airborne Corps (the 24th Infantry Division, the 82nd Airborne Division, and the 101st Airborne Division) would take the lead in establishing a defense of Saudi Arabia. Within days, a ready brigade from the 82nd Airborne Division had already been deployed, establishing the President's "line in the sand" with the 101st and 24th ID moving into theatre.

On Saturday, 1 September 1990, I was performing duty as NCO of DIVARTY HQ (Division Artillery). It was a weekend, so it was just me answering the phone and a runner. I received a call from higher headquarters that the following NCOs from 3-11 FA were to report to a briefing on Sunday, 2 September: Sgt Rosado, Sgt Mroz, Sgt Berry, Sgt Garrett, and you know who. The instructions for the Sunday briefing included family members. I didn't know specifically what the briefing would be about, but I felt like I knew. I was going to war.

During the briefing the next day, my suspicions became "reality." There were 27 of us that would be leaving Ft. Lewis to support the 101st Airborne Division. Our five NCOs from 3-11 FA (Field Artillery) along with two NCOs from DIVARTY (Division Artillery), four NCOs from 1-84 FA, and the majority of sixteen NCOs would come from 1-11 FA. I was proud to be in the meeting, but noticed quite a few that were getting their ears bent by their wives. I heard some of the wives saying, "No way, you aren't going" and "We just had the baby, you can't leave me here by myself." And then there were some single guys that just didn't want to go. I was amazed. This is the Army. I didn't think there was an option if you were called. As divisions were being called, jobs had to be filled to get those divisions up to battle strength. Our small group was one of hundreds throughout the United States transitioning to fill those necessary spots.

The days leading up to my departure were filled with continuous briefings about the host country, getting immunizations, updating wills, and the usual POM (preparation for overseas movement). It was a busy time at the office and at home as I prepared to leave.

Visiting with friends and walking the hallways of the 3-11 FA prior to our departure to Campbell, I couldn't help but notice one of the Sandfill 27 NCOs standing outside LTC Reitz's office waiting to go in. I asked him what was going on and he said that he, as well as others did not want to be deployed. After he left, I reported to LTC Reitz. He asked me to have a seat after some formalities. I told him that I didn't want anyone else speaking on my behalf about the deployment, and that "I did" want to go. He smiled and said he knew that was the way I felt even without talking to me. He went on to share with me about his deployment to Vietnam and the family support group that his wife would coordinate for the families left at Ft. Lewis in our absence. He also said we were on loan to the 101st and that orders would be cut after it was over for my return to the 3-11th. After our visit I felt better about the situation as I didn't want anyone to be confused as to my intentions. I was proud to serve and proud to go.

I spent as much time as I could just calling friends and family, filling them in about my deployment. One of the phone calls was to my friend in Arkansas, Jimmy Lile. He was a real patriot, following the crisis in the desert closely and wanting to hear all about my deployment to the 101st. Jimmy was the "Arkansas Knifemaker" and was famous in custom knife making circles, creating the Rambo knife for Sylvester Stallone in the movies. I owned a couple of his knives, and he asked if I was going to take them. I told him "of course" they would be with me. One was a sturdy knife that he made especially for Airborne and Special Operations. It was a great tool with finger grooves and a micarta handle that would be impossible to break. I never tried it, but I am convinced you could drive it into a tree and stand on it without bending. Jimmy told me he named the knife after his own nickname, "Gray Ghost." I would also be taking a small, fixed blade utility knife of his. Because of our friendship, it was important that they were with me, and both of us wanted to know "first hand" how the knives would perform in a real-life scenario. I told Jimmy I would report back to him when I returned.

After saying my family goodbyes, I signed out of the 3/11 FA on September 11, 1990. I departed Sea-Tac airport in Seattle on Saturday, 15 September and made a quick one day stop to see my family in Dallas before proceeding on to Nashville and Fort

Campbell, Kentucky. While visiting my parents, my sister and her husband, I made a trip to a school track to start getting acclimated to running with a ruck sack on my back. It was warm at the track, and with the added weight on my back, it didn't take long until I felt the burn. After running with the ruck, I knew I would have to get up to speed quickly. Now I wasn't so thrilled about the easy life I had enjoyed while riding around in vehicles with the 9th. The next stop would be with a division that would require much more.

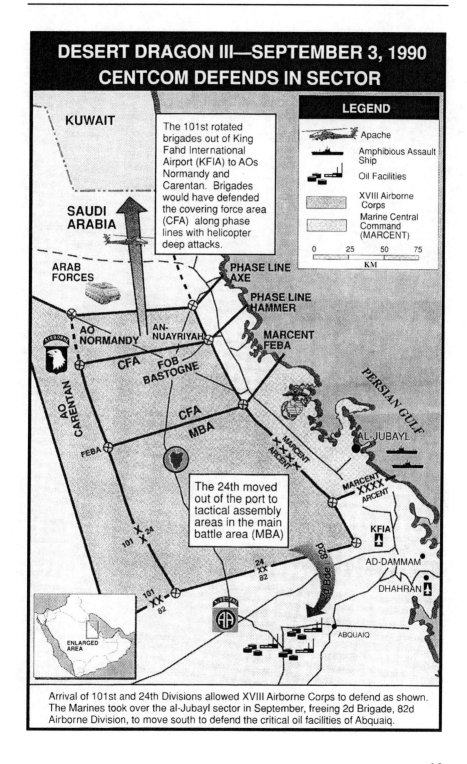

DESERT DRAGON III—SEPTEMBER 3, 1990
CENTCOM DEFENDS IN SECTOR

KUWAIT

The 101st rotated brigades out of King Fahd International Airport (KFIA) to AOs Normandy and Carentan. Brigades would have defended the covering force area (CFA) along phase lines with helicopter deep attacks.

SAUDI ARABIA

LEGEND
Apache
Amphibious Assault Ship
Oil Facilities
XVIII Airborne Corps
Marine Central Command (MARCENT)

0   25   50   75
KM

ARAB FORCES

PHASE LINE AXE
PHASE LINE HAMMER

AO NORMANDY
AN-NUAYRIYAH
MARCENT FEBA

CFA
FOB BASTOGNE

AO CARENTAN

CFA
MBA

PERSIAN GULF

FEBA

AL-JUBAYL

MARCENT XXX ARCENT

The 24th moved out of the port to tactical assembly areas in the main battle area (MBA)

MARCENT XXXX ARCENT

KFIA

101 X 24

AD-DAMMAM

24 XX 82

DHAHRAN

2d Bde 82d

101 XX 82

ENLARGED AREA

ABQUAIQ

Arrival of 101st and 24th Divisions allowed XVIII Airborne Corps to defend as shown. The Marines took over the al-Jubayl sector in September, freeing 2d Brigade, 82d Airborne Division, to move south to defend the critical oil facilities of Abquaiq.

18 soldiers of Sandfill 27, Fort Campbell, Kentucky, October, 1990

Chapter 2

Fort Campbell, Kentucky

I flew to Nashville, Tennessee on 17 September 1990. I was happy that I got to see my parents, sister, and her husband during the layover in Dallas. On the flight, I couldn't help reflecting on the 101st Airborne Division's history and my visit to the Omaha Beach Cemetery in 1986. When I was a young boy I became interested in WWII history and was in awe of the 101st Airborne Division and its sister division, the 82nd Airborne Division. My father was in the All American Division during the occupation of Germany following WWII, and I always enjoyed the stories about the division and his jumps as a paratrooper. I recalled the story of his last parachute jump, where he landed in a tree and was gently laid on the ground. He was a lucky guy. When I played "Army" with my friends in Big Spring, Texas, many times we were acting like paratroopers as we fought our wars in the valleys and hills behind our house. I also reflected on my time as a banker in Texas, and how the economy had forced me to find another career. Just three years earlier, if someone told me I would be flying off to war with the 101st Airborne Division, I would have chuckled and called them insane (albeit from behind my mahogany desk while smoking a fine cigar). I felt like I had just been through a war in banking, and now I am flying off to another. I recalled stories from a banker friend, who was with the 101st in Vietnam, remembering his talks to the Chamber of Commerce and Rotary Club luncheons about his near death experiences fighting the Viet Cong. I was startled when the announcement from the crew came over the cabin loud speaker to secure our seat-belts. We were about to land in Nashville.

I took ground transportation from the Nashville Airport to Ft. Campbell and once I went through the main gate at Ft. Campbell, Kentucky, it was like a dream. I was now with one of the most storied divisions in the world. After arriving at the 20th Replacement Center barracks, I linked up with other NCOs from Ft. Lewis. Since there were 27 of us from Lewis, we named ourselves "Sandfill 27" and took a picture of as many as we could. The 101st Airborne Division had many gaps in their personnel, and key jobs had to be filled to go to war. Many of those spots were forward observer positions. With the 9th Infantry Division drawing down, many fire support NCOs from Ft. Lewis were called and assigned to the 101st because of the war. We were told by our battalion officers and NCOs before we left Ft. Lewis that we would be coming back. However, my orders (as well as the others in Sandfill 27) read, "ASSIGNED" to the 101st. It took a few days to in-process, and it looked like some of us would be assigned to the 1/320th Field Artillery Battalion (supporting the 502nd Infantry Regiment). Some in our group were assigned to other Battalions in the 320th Field Artillery Regiment supporting either the 1st or 3rd Infantry Brigades.

We were all in the same replacement barracks, and some of the Sandfill 27 NCOs were working feverishly on ways to get out of the deployment. The excuses were mind boggling. If the truth were to be known, most did not want to go because they had left young wives and children back at Lewis, and many of these young Army families were away from home for the first time. The wives were convinced (as well as some of the soldiers), that their tours in the Army were just for the education benefits (GI Bill) and not to go to war. The pressure was unbearable for some as they were more threatened at home than from the Iraqi Army (the fourth largest Army in the world). Some of the guys thought it was cowardice (and this may have been the case for a couple), but the majority of the guys I talked to said it was the wives and in-laws resisting their deployment. When this started back at Ft. Lewis, I was shocked because the guys in question were competent NCOs and great forward observers.

Since recruiting began, young men just out of high school were sold on military life, not thinking about the risks of going to war. They then made the same sales pitch to their girlfriends or fiancés. After their short enlistments in a peace-time Army, they and their families could enjoy the GI Bill and go on with their lives. Other guys like me were fully aware of the risk when signing on the bottom line. I wanted to finish a career, even with the possibility of going to war.

Ft. Campbell, Kentucky and adjacent Clarksville, Tennessee were bustling with activity. Even though the division had vacated the month prior, families were left behind and had to go on with their lives. FORSCOM (United States Army Forces Command) had issued its deployment order to the 101st on the 10th of August, just eight days after Iraq invaded Kuwait. For the first time since Vietnam, the 101st Airborne Division was going to war. The 101st had its units spread out all over the place when the orders came down. They had an aviation unit supporting the U.S. Southern Command with Joint Task Force Bravo in Honduras, the 2-187th Infantry task force was at the Jungle Operations Training Center in Panama, the 3-327th Infantry task force was training cadets at the United States Military Academy, and the 2-502nd Infantry was preparing to deploy to the Sinai as part of the United Nations' peacekeeping force. In addition, the ADA (Air Defense Artillery) had soldiers at Ft. Knox, Kentucky training West Point cadets.

Shortly before Iraq invaded Kuwait, the division staff returned to Ft. Campbell from Ft. Bragg, North Carolina following the post exercise, "Internal Look." The U.S. Central Command based its annual exercise on a scenario in which Iraq invaded Saudi Arabia. It was not by accident that these exercises were based on an Iraqi threat. For many years, Central Command and leaders in Washington envisioned an attack by the Soviet Union through the Zagros Mountains in Iran. With the fall of Communism, the newly appointed Commander in Chief of Central Command, General H. Norman Schwarzkopf saw a different threat. With his first hand experience in the Middle East, he saw a threat which came from a disgruntled Saddam Hussein. As the exercise "Internal Look" played out, Iraq was moving its troops according to the war game they were playing. Schwarzkopf had correctly identified and foreseen the real threat to the Middle East which gave the participants of Internal Look, including the 101st Airborne Division, an idea of what was to come.

On 15 August 1990, the first Screaming Eagles arrived in Dhahran, Saudi Arabia, and the first elements of the combat force left Ft. Campbell on 17 August. The Division Ready Brigade (DRB-1), made up of the Second Air Assault Brigade Task Force (the 1-502nd and 1-320th Field Artillery were in the DRB-1) and an aviation task force made the trip by fifty-six C141s and forty-nine C5A transport planes. The 1-320th FA flight by C5 had a layover at Westover Air Force Base, where they were served a steak meal at the base dining facility. They were there about eight hours before making the trans-Atlantic flight to Rota, Spain. Once they arrived in Rota, reality set in that they were going to war because of the non-stop food and the availabiltity of cots to make the soldiers comfortable. After the long, twelve hour stop, the C5 took off for Saudi-Arabia.

It took thirteen days to transport the DRB-1's 2,742 soldiers, 117 helicopters, 487 vehicles and 123 equipment pallets into theatre. Once the Division Ready Brigade closed into theatre, the 101st officially assumed control of FOB Bastogne 4 September from the 82nd Airborne Division which had established the "line in the sand."

While the DRB-1 was moving their equipment and personnel to Saudi Arabia by air, the rest of the division began moving vehicles and aircraft to the port at Jacksonville, Florida. En-route to Jacksonville, the division's convoys were greeted by thousands of on-lookers and supporters waiving banners of support and American flags. Once the equipment arrived at the port, over 5,000 pieces of equipment were loaded onto ten ships. The American Eagle was one of the ships tasked with transporting division material to Saudi Arabia, and it was one that had also transported equipment for the division during the Vietnam war. The ten ships crossed the Atlantic, moved through the Mediterranean Sea, and moved through the Suez Canal into the Red Sea. After clearing the Arabian Peninsula, the final leg was through the Persian Gulf to the Port of Ad Dammam. It took an average of twenty-three days for the ships to make the journey to Saudi Arabia. The majority of the division's soldiers flew from Campbell Army Airfield to Saudi Arabia in thirty-six lifts of commercial aircraft between 5 to 25 September. Over the twenty day period, the Civil Reserve Air Fleet (CRAF) moved over 13,500 soldiers.

For those of us who arrived at Ft. Campbell in the middle of September, we got to see one big party in Clarksville. I had the misconception that all of the wives and girlfriends would be at home watching the news, sitting at home in small support groups agonizing over their soldier that had just deployed. I am sure that was the case for most, but then there were the "others." I have never seen so many girls in one place "painting the town." It was like one big bachelorette party. I know those ladies that were out on the town were in a weakened state, but I was sure that none of the Sandfill 27 NCOs would have taken advantage of the situation, or should I say, opportunity. They were Army professionals.

After days of in-processing, we finally began training. We had to get up to air assault standard in a short period of time. Day one of our training was M-16 issue from the arms room and weapons qualification. I loved shooting and took pride in those perfect 40 out of 40 hits. This day I must have been a little off as I only scored a 38. Even though it was in the expert category, I fell short of my personal standard. Day two, we spent the day on General Order number one which covered customs and culture of the host country, and also first aid. We were given strict orders that no alcohol and no pornography would be taken into country. When I say no pornography, I am talking about no "girlie magazines" that would show a woman in less than full dress.

We were issued a small booklet titled, "Winning in the Desert", a newsletter outlining the difficulties we would have fighting in the desert. The first section, Saudi Arabia geography and climate, gave us a map of the Arabian Peninsula and described the climate we would be working in. My eyes scanned the page and immediately fell on the temperatures we would be fighting in. "Saudi Arabia has a desert climate characterized by extremely high temperatures during the day and sharp drops in temperatures at night." And, "The temperature can reach as high as 130 degrees Fahrenheit and the almost nonexistent humidity of the central plateaus and deserts, combined with relatively low temperatures, can make nights on the Arabian Peninsula seem bitterly cold." Turning to the next page on Iraq, my concentration focused on the wadis, the dry river beds that ran "400 kilometers or longer carrying brief, but torrential floods during the winter rains, most of the rains occurring from December through March." It went on to say it was not uncommon to see up to ten feet of water moving through these wadis during a heavy rain, and warned us not to set up camp in those low lying areas.

I found the booklet humorous when it started talking about spiders, scorpions, and snakes. And, I found myself chuckling when it said, "DON'T PLAY WITH SNAKES." I remembered when I was young in Big Spring, Texas chasing rattlesnakes and thought, "Wow I'm going to war in West Texas where I grew up." When we got to that section of the book, I couldn't help but notice the fearful, wide-eyed reactions from the guys who had grown up in the cities. They wanted nothing to do with the critters, and the thought of snakes snuggling up to them at night had their skin crawling. After reading this section, I felt more at ease because of the flood of fond childhood memories.

The next section in the book was about water, sanitation, and diseases that were prevalent, including plague, typhus, malaria, dengue fever, dysentery, cholera, and typhoid. I read where proper sanitation and "personal cleanliness" can help prevent typhus and the plague. Water was the most important, because without water you die. Without enough water, upper respiratory problems also occur. I recalled playing on the football team when our coaches thought water would make you throw up, and they insisted on feeding us salt tablets instead.

The following day, we took an APFT (Army Physical Fitness Test). The standard for all soldiers in the 101st Airborne Division was the same for everyone, regardless of age. Even though I had just turned 36, I had to successfully pass the 17-21 age group standards. I passed the sit-ups and push-ups, but failed the 2 mile run by 30 seconds. I would have to take it again in two days. I was pissed.

The day was getting worse by the minute, as that afternoon we had to go into the gas chamber to see if the chemical mask they had issued us was working. The process is simple. You stand in a long line waiting to go into a building that is billowing with CS Gas (Tear Gas). You watch as others come out of the building gagging and throwing up, and then it's your turn. You move into the small shack with the gas mask on, forming a circle on the inside of the small building. Once inside, the door shuts and you are instructed to check the seals on the mask. When the NBC (Nuclear Biological and Chemical) NCOIC says, "remove your mask", you do so promptly. No running out. Oh no. The NCOIC ensures that you breathe and your lungs are full of the toxic gas. Only after he is confident that you have taken in the CS are you instructed to leave. I always thought those guys were a little sadistic.

As uncomfortable as it was, this was one time I really wanted to know if the mask worked. We were going to war with a country that was not afraid to use chemical weapons. Saddam had used the weapons on the Iranians during the Iran-Iraq war, and even more disturbing, he used them on his own people, killing tens of thousands. My only question was, how were we going to fight wearing protective masks in that intense heat? When we left the

NBC area, we road marched several miles back to our barracks with our gas masks on. After about a mile, heat and sweat built up in the mask and it became hard to take a breath. You had to literally suck oxygen through the filters of the mask to feed your starved lungs. They were testing our ability (under stress) to use the mask effectively in a chemical environment. Though the road-march only lasted about 30-40 minutes, we were all sucking wind. I could only imagine what it would be like on the battlefield.

The next day of training was a break from the previous, and the concentration was on one of my favorite topics: map-reading and land navigation. I loved to study maps and navigation by the stars, and was thinking I would probably use the stars in Saudi Arabia because there was minimal light interference from nearby cities. As we were reviewing map reading, I was confused as to how we would orient ourselves because of the lack of terrain features such as mountains, valleys, and roads. The maps were looking pretty flat to me, and the possibility of "mis-orientation" seemed a real possibility without using a slugger.

We had just one more block of instruction before starting the Air Assault School, and that was a refresher course on the AT-4 and LAW (light anti-tank weapons). Both would be important if we engaged enemy armored formations invading the Arabian Peninsula from Iraq. I was hoping and praying that we wouldn't be using either of these against a T-72 Russian made tank. It seemed like shooting a pea-shooter at an elephant to me. Oh well, if that was my only hope, I would sure take dead aim and hope for the best, but the last thing I wanted was to be a speed bump for a tank. After anti-tank training, I had some unfinished business on my PT test, needing to meet that 17-21 age group standard for the two-mile run. There must have been some adrenaline pumping because I met the standard with a half-minute to spare. Also, anger probably helped because the run felt easy.

The next day we would be starting Air Assault School, Day "0", so everyone hit the rack early that night. One more push of serious training and we would be heading to Saudi Arabia. I embraced the physical exercise because desert warfare and the 101st required it. This was not just another field training exercise. For two years I had been training to fight and provide fire support. After seven more days of intense, physically demanding work, I would be given the opportunity to put it all together in the desert.

Air Assault School was one of the most demanding training opportunities that the Army had to offer, only surpassed by Ranger and Special Operations Schools. The 101st Airborne Division (Air Assault) required all of its soldiers to go through the course to be familiar with the way the Screaming Eagles fought. The Air Assault doctrine was different than the Airmobile one from the Vietnam War. "Airmobile was the ability to move soldiers from one secure area to another. After insertion, the helicopters depart the area of operations. In air assault operations, aircraft are integrated with ground forces and generally make insertions and extractions under hostile conditions."

"Air Assault operations are deliberate, precisely planned, and vigorously executed combat operations designed to allow friendly forces to strike over extended distances and terrain barriers to attack the enemy when and where he is most vulnerable."

We would be going through a high-speed, low drag six day course that trained us on all of the elements. The school was normally 10 days long. On 3 October 1990, we were up at 0400 and made our way in formation to the obstacle course. All was going well with me until I had to climb a rope. I have never been able to climb a rope and still couldn't even if someone were holding a gun to my head. As hard as I tried, I couldn't get my 200 lb frame up the fricking rope. I was strong and could lift a set of 300 pounds on the bench press, but this one thing nailed me. If there was any consolation (and there wasn't), the rest of the course was easy. Many had trouble scaling the 30 ft ladder with the cross members getting further and further apart as they climbed. Some would get about 20ft in the air and could not figure out how to grab that next board 5 feet further up. When there were about 10 soldiers on the ladder, and it was shaking, the climb was made even more difficult (there were quite a few that bombed the "ladder"). After the O Course, we ran 2 miles in formation in our combat boots.

On Friday, 5 October 1990, the Air Assault School was again up at 0400 hrs with the two hundred soldiers running two miles in formation with rucksacks. As we made our run in the cool early morning hours, you could see steam coming off of the large group as it ran under the street-lights. A school instructor ran beside us singing a loud airborne cadence which kept the formation in step as we ran. After eating breakfast, we began Team 1 training. This was all classroom instruction, and it was hard staying awake during the lectures which lasted till 2030 hrs. I don't think I remember lying down, but I'm sure I did because we were up at 0400 the next day making the same run before going back to school. We started the morning by testing on the previous day's material, and then began Team II – Sling-load training. The day ended at 2000 hrs. The third day we again started the day with an early morning ruck run and hands-on testing on sling-loads. We were finished at 1600 hrs that day, and it felt like a day off.

We were off on Monday, 8 October 1990, for Columbus Day, and on the 9th we began two days of rappelling. We learned how to prepare a Swiss Seat out of rope and rappelled off of the 30 ft tower. After attaching ourselves to the carabineer and being checked by a rappel-master, the commands, "on rappel" for the one rappelling, and "on belay" for the one securing the rope on the ground rang out all day. We made the rappel tower trip many times, and then Australian rappelled with our face to the ground. After doing that for a day, we were evaluated and tested. All of the instruction was done for a reason, and it was all done very safely. We even got to "fast rope", making the trip down without being attached to anything. Just wearing gloves and using the hands and feet as a brake, one could make it down a wider diameter thirty foot rope without freefalling. I thought rappelling was fun and didn't have any trouble at all "going down" a rope. Just don't ask me to climb back up. At the end of the rappel days, we prepared ourselves for the conclusion of Air Assault School and the 12 mile road march.

In the early morning hours of 11 October 1990, we packed our rucks, drew our weapons from the arms room, and made our way to the road-march course in formation. The course would be a timed, 12 mile event which we would run and walk with a full ruck sack and an M-16. In order to finish in the required time, I would have to run more than walk. It was a cool morning, and after the six mile mark I felt like I had it licked. When I started passing other, younger soldiers I felt my energy level rise. I would run down the hills and walk at a fast pace going up. It felt like the hills and valleys I had run as a boy in Texas. Quite a few struggled with the course, but my strategy had worked and I finished the twelve miles well under the time limit. We were happy the school was over, and it was all about celebrating for the next few days.

We were kept on a short leash after Air Assault School. Now that we had completed all of the required training, preparation, and equipment issue, it was up to 20th Replacement to get us manifested on a flight to Saudi Arabia so we could link up with the division. There were no passes allowed outside a fifty mile radius of Ft. Campbell. They gave us passes for 12-14 October allowing soldiers to visit family members. For those of us who didn't have family in the area, we used the time to shop at the PX, see a movie, and go to the NCO Club. Some of the guys just went on a drinking binge over the three days, and because of the 'late-nighters' there was little or no sleeping in the barracks. It was a non-stop party. With no drinking in Saudi Arabia, I think some of the guys wanted to store booze like camels store water. There were a lot of hangovers that weekend. We went into some of the clubs "off post" and the bachelorette parties were still going on. Whatever business these places lost when the 101st was deployed was made up by female party goers. They were having a blast.

On Monday, 15 October, we had manifest formations beginning at 0800 and were finally given Wednesday as our "go" date. We would be flying to Saudi Arabia by an American Airlines

DC-10, leaving on the morning of the 17th. We had manifest formations throughout the day. Our second was at 1100 hrs and our third, and final of the day, was at 1600 hrs. I think they wanted to know how many would actually make it to Wednesday morning. On 16 October 1990, we had our formation at 0730 and were taken over to CIF (central issue facility) for flak vest issue. The flak vest was not the desert camouflage issue; it was jungle green. I personally thought it would stand out like a sore thumb in the desert. It was just me thinking though, "Yeah sure."

Everyone thought we had been at Campbell long enough to miss the war. I know I was thinking that anyway. I had arrived in Nashville on 17 September and would be flying to Saudi on 17 October. I was ready to go and I know the majority of the other NCOs felt the same. Truthfully, I was a little sick and tired of barracks life and the boisterous drunks coming in at all hours. You know it's bad when you would rather go to war.

On Wednesday 17 October 1990, we were wakened for the last time in the United States. The normal ruckus group of NCOs got up, showered, shaved and got into their desert BDUs. Everyone was quiet as we moved to the mess hall to have our last meal. Some looked like they were eating their "last meal" before an execution, probably because they were hung-over. I was ready to go and as strange as it may sound, excited. After eating, we made our way to the arms room to draw our M-16s that we would be living with 24/7 until our return. The moment was surreal as I thought about this world stage being set with all eyes glued on Iraq, Kuwait, and the United States of America, and we would be in the middle of it. And a more sobering thought entered my mind. I would not be coming back until this confrontation was resolved, I was wounded, or worse yet, was killed. I caught a glimpse of Screaming Eagles past who were sent off to war not knowing what the future held.

As the American Airlines DC-10 took off from Campbell Army Airfield, the cabin was quiet. It wasn't until we left Ft. Campbell airspace that I heard muffled voices throughout the plane. The airline looked like any other, with two exceptions: one, the door to the cockpit was open, and two, all passengers were carrying M-16s. True, they weren't loaded, but it was an unusual sight on a commercial aircraft. After just a short while in the air we began our descent into Boston's Logan International Airport. We would have two refueling stops along the way, one in Boston, and the other in Rome before proceeding to King Fahd International Airport in Saudi Arabia.

The flight was long as we traversed the Atlantic to Europe. Those that wanted could watch a movie or talk to friends. I couldn't stay focused on the movie thing, so my time was spent visiting with friends and drinking coffee. Occasionally, we would have a meal, the typical in-flight airline food. I thought we had it made going commercial, because the DRB-1 soldiers who had gone before made the trip in cold C5As or C141s eating box lunches (two sandwiches, cookies, and fruit) or MREs. I thought this was one heck of a way to go to war. I remember my Dad telling me about the arduous journey that took days by ship transport, and how many wanted to die because of sea sickness. This journey to Saudi Arabia would take less than 24 hours.

When we landed in Rome for refueling, I thought it would be great to finally walk around and stretch my legs. As we made our final descent, I peered out the window onto the lights of this historic European city. Wow, it would be great to spend a few days here taking in the Coliseum and other ancient sites. When the plane landed, the DC-10 made its way to the gate and after parking, we got the bad news: no one would be allowed off the plane during the refuel. As ground personnel came on board, it was like they had seen a ghost. Wild-eyed support crews quietly came on board going about their business cleaning and re-supplying the aircraft. It was like they had never witnessed anything like it. I am sure they hadn't. Obviously, the M-16s made them nervous because there were as many weapons on board as soldiers.

After refueling, the DC-10 taxied back to the runway and took off. The next stop was Saudi Arabia. I tried to nap as much as possible, because I didn't know what to expect when we arrived. I did know it was going to be hot. The sleep was sporadic as flight attendants made their way up the aisles and soldiers were talking, but I did the best I could.

The flight to Saudi Arabia took as much time or longer than the one from Boston to Rome. After we were in the air a couple hours, it started to get light. My internal clock was now messed up because it was only 2200 hrs at Campbell. With the nine hour difference in time, I felt like I should be going to sleep, but the brightness coming through the windows told me I should be getting up. "Oh well, I'll get up." The flight attendants came through the cabin offering us breakfast and coffee. Everyone on board ate because who knew when we would have a meal like this again. After breakfast, we all looked out the windows at the Mediterranean Sea, straining to see a coastline. After a couple hours it appeared: a land that looked as desolate as it has throughout time. There was nothing to see except sand.

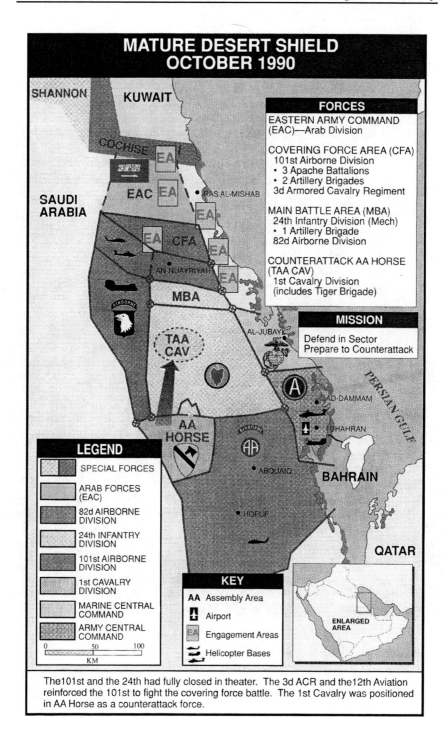

MATURE DESERT SHIELD
OCTOBER 1990

SHANNON

KUWAIT

COCHISE

SAUDI ARABIA

EAC

RAS AL-MISHAB

CFA

AN NUAYRIYAH

MBA

TAA CAV

AL-JUBAYL

AA HORSE

AD-DAMMAM

DHAHRAN

BAHRAIN

ABQAIQ

HOFUF

QATAR

PERSIAN GULF

FORCES

EASTERN ARMY COMMAND (EAC)—Arab Division

COVERING FORCE AREA (CFA)
101st Airborne Division
• 3 Apache Battalions
• 2 Artillery Brigades
3d Armored Cavalry Regiment

MAIN BATTLE AREA (MBA)
24th Infantry Division (Mech)
• 1 Artillery Brigade
82d Airborne Division

COUNTERATTACK AA HORSE (TAA CAV)
1st Cavalry Division
(includes Tiger Brigade)

MISSION

Defend in Sector
Prepare to Counterattack

LEGEND

SPECIAL FORCES

ARAB FORCES (EAC)

82d AIRBORNE DIVISION

24th INFANTRY DIVISION

101st AIRBORNE DIVISION

1st CAVALRY DIVISION

MARINE CENTRAL COMMAND

ARMY CENTRAL COMMAND

0   50   100
KM

KEY

AA   Assembly Area

Airport

EA   Engagement Areas

Helicopter Bases

ENLARGED AREA

The 101st and the 24th had fully closed in theater. The 3d ACR and the 12th Aviation reinforced the 101st to fight the covering force battle. The 1st Cavalry was positioned in AA Horse as a counterattack force.

American Airlines DC-10. Sandfill 27 ride to Saudi Arabia arrived October 18, 1990

Chapter 3

Camp Eagle II
"The Saudi Country Club"

"Hell could not compete with the heat in Saudi Arabia."
General Hugh Shelton
Assistant Division Commander
101st Airborne Division (Air Assault)

About an hour out from our destination in Saudi Arabia, our kind DC-10 flight attendants walked up and down the aisles asking us if they could fill our canteens. This was a reality check for what was to come. Not the war, but the heat which was the other enemy for which we had been preparing and training to face. The attendants did not appear as jovial as they normally would on commercial flights, but instead were solemn and concerned as new friends would be, knowing the reality of our monumental, dangerous task at hand. Upon final approach, the occupants of our plane became deathly silent as we looked out the windows and onto the desolate desert terrain. At 1200 hrs on the 18 October 1990, we finally arrived at King Fahd International Airport (KFIA), Saudi Arabia.

The airport was a massive construction site located about thirty-five miles from Dhahran along the highway to Riyadh. After seven years, the construction at KFIA was about seventy percent complete. Once the massive construction site was complete, it would be the largest airport in the world, spanning more square miles than the country of Bahrain. My mind ran wild with thoughts like, "Why such a large airport and why would so many people want to come here?" Money was obviously no object. There would even be a separate terminal just for royals. We filed off of the comfortable, climate controlled American Airlines DC-10, and if it weren't for all of us wearing desert BDUs (battle dress uniforms) and carrying M-16s, it would have been like any other trans-Atlantic flight. We left our last connection to home with the crew wishing us luck and God Speed as we stepped on the tarmac from hell. I have no idea how hot it was, but it wasn't long until I felt my feet burning through the bottom of my combat boots, a far cry from the mild temperatures at Ft. Lewis I had left the month before. We made our way about 100 yards or so off the tarmac onto a dirt holding area. As soon as our duffle bags were off loaded, the DC-10 closed the doors, taxied, and took off, presumably to fly the same trip again after crew rest. Shortly after the airplane's departure, we filed onto buses and made our way in a small caravan destined for Camp Eagle II.

General J.H. Binford Peay III:

"The soldiers stepped off of the aircraft into intense heat. Temperatures ranged from 120 to 140 degrees Fahrenheit on the airfield surface during the hottest part of the day."

Shortly after his arrival in August, Brigadier General Hugh Shelton laid claim to the spot for the 101st Airborne Division. Camp Eagle II (so named in recognition of Camp Eagle in Vietnam) was located close to KFIA, and the Arab tents set up by 101st soldiers before our arrival seemed to go on forever. In between long rows of tents were wide, white powdery roads that divided the regiments and units in the division. I was amazed at this massive camp and what an undertaking it must have been to build.

SP4 Matt Huff, C-Battery 1-320th FA:

"When we first arrived we began to set up these tents. The problem was the tents were to be placed on a surface like concrete. We had no drills! So,

that means we used sledge hammers. It was like taking a 24" stake and trying to hammer it into a concrete sidewalk. You see, they were building an airport in the middle of the desert. A strong base was needed and this was their way of making a foundation strong enough for their construction project. We made do with what we had and put up Camp Eagle II. Well, at least our battalion.

"I believe the toilets were made for creating a bonding experience with the guys. Each latrine had 4 seats, no partitions, and a nice view. These were nothing more than 10' x 6' boxes made of plywood. The top half was open to view the public walking by. This was great if you wanted to hold a conversation with the guys hanging out by your tent. Our tent was the first row of tents in the entire camp and the latrines were 15' outside the tent flap. This was conveniently located until the heat of the day when we needed to burn the crap. Fortunately, we only had to burn it for a short time. We had septic sucker trucks A.K.A. s-suckers visit daily to suck the latrines clean and spray them down. Guys from Nam tell me we had it good compared to their living conditions. I would say we did.

"The showers were a great addition, because prior to those all we could do before was pour a little water in a tub and wipe down. This was the same way we did our laundry. The only issue was that the showers were out doors. The water was so cold, I could only wash one limb at a time and then jump in to rinse off. I wonder if we had anyone get hypothermia in the desert."

Camp Eagle II was critical to the support of the division and provided a connection to logistics for the 101st. The tent city was strategically located to provide a defense of the airport and a camp for brigades to rest and refit after returning from one month stints in the desert. It was also used for soldiers entering the country, allowing for the critical acclimatization process. If necessary, soldiers had the ability to hit the ground fighting from Camp Eagle II. Soldiers and equipment poured in from the Port of Dammam, the airfield at Dhahran, and KFIA.

I don't really know what I was expecting when we hit the ground in Saudi Arabia, but it wasn't this. There had obviously been a lot of planning and a tremendous amount of work that went into this camp. Other than the heat and the powdery sand that seemed to cling to you, the camp itself was well thought out. My initial concern was security of the perimeter since it was housing so many troops, but the tent city appeared to be secure and well guarded.

Upon our arrival to Camp Eagle II, we went into a briefing with Command Sergeant Major (CSM) Dulin, the DIVARTY (Division Artillery) Command Sergeant Major. Dulin gave us a situation brief about the 1-320th Field Artillery and the 502nd Infantry Regiment it supports, along with what to expect in the harsh desert where we would be fighting. In the SITREP (situation report), the CSM also brought us up to date on the threat at the Saudi Arabian-Iraqi border. Saddam had massed several divisions and could cross at any time. After his briefing, we were pointed in the direction of the 1-320th FA tents. The heat was stifling, and my first night at "tent city" was a sleepless one. Sweat poured off of me all night long. With King Fahd International Airport (KFIA) just a short distance from us, the heat and the non-stop take-offs and landings of A-10s and helicopters kept me from sleeping.

We were told if Saddam didn't decide to cross the border and invade Saudi Arabia in 48-72 hours, the next few days would be for adjustment and acclimatization. We wouldn't have very much to do other than drink water, wash clothes, and attend briefings until the 1-320th FA's return. Our artillery unit and the 502nd were in the desert performing a covering force mission and would not return from FOB (forward operating base) Oasis until the 24th. I saw an immediate need to get used to this heat, and even though it wasn't required, I made some runs through the camp. Due to its massive size, about one lap around tent city was all I could take.

After our unit's return, I met with CSM Kalub Duggins, the Command Sergeant Major of 1-320th FA. The Sergeant Major looked to be in his early 40s of medium height and build, with a seasoned, senior enlisted soldiers' attitude. My eyes glanced at the shoulder insignia of the 1st Cavalry Division on his right sleeve, indicating he was a Vietnam War veteran. The only soldiers that wore anything on the right sleeve of the uniform were war vets, whom I always held in high esteem. In my mind we were going to war, and having a war veteran as a leader gave me confidence. He told me I would be assigned to A Battery 1-320th FA, which supports the 1-502nd Infantry, and my job would be one of Charlie Company's fire support sergeants (FO). I then met with Sergeant First Class Bone, the 1-502nd FSNCO (Battalion Fire Support NCO) and Staff Sergeant Vernon Sizemore, who was the Charlie Company's FSNCO.

Being a fire support sergeant, I was assigned to a field artillery unit, but would have very little contact with the artillery in war. The field artillery battalion attached their forward observers or fire support teams (FIST) to the infantry to call in artillery and air support for those units. Forward observers would be in the infantry, but not of the infantry so to speak. It was very confusing to civilians outside the military. They would say, "I thought you go to war with the infantry." Yes, that is right. "But you are assigned to an artillery unit." Yes, that is right. In all of my training at Ft. Lewis, we interfaced very little with the infantry. The FTXs (field training exercises) were all controlled by the artillery, and I was with them the entire time. Once attached to my unit with the 502nd, I probably wouldn't meet with the artillery guys again until I got back to tent city or at the end of the war.

After receiving my assignment from the 1-320th, SSG Vernon Sizemore and I went to the other end of tent city where 2nd Brigade, 1-502nd was located to be introduced to the infantry unit I would be supporting. My reception at Charlie Company was very business-like, and I could tell that the unit was drained physically from their deployment to FOB Oasis. Their uniforms were dirty and the soldiers were exhausted. I was first introduced to the First Sergeant of Charlie Company, William K. Batie, and then to the platoon sergeant, Sergeant First Class, Dunn whom I would be working with directly. The platoon sergeant was a "just out of a war novel", airborne, air assault infantry NCO. In his late 30s, gruff with no smile, he was a no-nonsense, Army Sergeant First Class that looked older than his years because of the recent desert wear and tear. He gave me a professional brief which included their recent deployment to Oasis and the squad leaders I would be working with in 2nd platoon. At the end of that initial meeting, I felt confident I was with a good, competent group.

SSG Sizemore also introduced to me my new FO/RTO (forward observer, radio telephone operator) PFC Martin McPherson. Martin had been with the 101st a while, and if he knew his job, would be a valuable asset for me. Marty had come over to Saudi Arabia by C5 transport the month before with the 1-320th and had already been to Oasis. He knew "first hand" the area we would be defending, had been exposed to the personalities of 2nd platoon, and could get me up to speed quickly. He briefed me on some of the infantry NCOs' quirks and tendencies, and in his opinion, which ones were strong and those that weren't. Marty and I would be working very close, and if I were to become a casualty, Marty would have to take over the fire support role for the platoon. During infantry operations, Marty would be responsible for my PRC-77 radio, keeping up with its frequencies (that changed daily) used by the artillery, attack helicopters, and the Air Force.

While interviewing Marty, I also found out he had come into the Army on the buddy plan, and both of them ended up at Ft. Campbell as forward observers. He had joined the Army for the college benefits, which was typical for a nineteen year old Private First Class. At least, he was typical of the guys who had worked for me at Ft. Lewis. It was hard finding young PFCs that had already figured out what they wanted to do in life, much less finding one that wanted to make the Army a career. However, I wasn't as interested in those answers as much as: can he do his job, can he keep up, and is he a whiner? If he could carry my radio, perform as a forward observer without slowing me down, and doesn't cry, I would be able to work with him. His music tastes were pretty typical of a 19 year old: Guns n' Roses, Motley Crue, Def Leppard, Van Halen, and Whitesnake seemed to be what he listened to. I was impressed with Marty and couldn't wait to see how he performed in the desert. Hopefully we would have a chance to work together before the war started.

After getting settled in with 2nd platoon, I met up with Sergeant Frank Giger and Staff Sergeant Ernie Swindle at the 502nd mess tent. Catching up on their assignments to infantry units and drinking some of the old coffee at the tent became normal during our off times. Frank, Ernie and I had developed a friendship, having all come out of Ft. Lewis, and tried to get together when we could. Ernie would be the Bravo Company 1/502nd FSNCO and Frank would be attached to Charlie Company 3/502nd. During one of these high level forward observer meetings, I think it was Frank who gave Camp Eagle II our own name, "The Saudi Country Club."

Sergeant Frank Giger, 2nd Platoon, C. Co, 3rd Bn., 502nd Infantry Regiment FO:

"The mess tent was this huge circus sized affair that could seat 200 or more, and it served as a community center of sorts. If one could master the art of wheedling, a not-quite-cold left over cup of coffee could be had and it had tables out of the wind – a very good feature if one wanted to play spades (the never ending tournaments and scores were closely tracked the entire time I was there). It was also where us Fort Lewis Sandfill people met up, having been farmed out to different infantry units and spread around the camp. The downside was that one could hear the stupid chemical gas alarms and had to respond appropriately. Why they put chemical sensors where the latrines could occasionally waft methane and other nice irritants over them is beyond me."

In the evenings, SSG Ian Berkowitz, a squad leader from our infantry platoon, and some of my FO buddies would sometimes slip out of Camp Eagle II. We would venture out of tent city and walk to some of the temporary housing facilities that housed the KFIA construction workers from other countries. There was one Egyptian who had figured out how to make a buck off of soldiers by letting them use his phone. There were no phones yet at Camp Eagle II. The guy really raked it in because very few could actually make a connection. Just another one of those GI scams, we thought. There was also a recreation center in the area where we could play pool and ping pong. We could pretty much take over the recreation center while the construction workers were in the adjacent mosque praying.

Letter writing and receiving was a big deal for all of the soldiers at APO New York 09309 (which was Camp Eagle II). The camp and its vicinity had several names that soldiers were using when writing friends and loved ones back home, creating some confusion for them thinking we were at different locations. Locations like King Fahd International Airport (KFIA), Camp Eagle II, and nicknames like Ft. Camel, Tent City, and our own The Saudi Country Club were actually one in the same. I am sure when families compared notes, some thought we were moving around. We spent some of our time writing letters to friends and loved ones and, with no postage required, there was no excuse for not dropping a letter back home. All we had to do was write FREE where the usual postage stamp would go. It was one of those evenings of letter writing at the mess tent that we even cranked out letters of support to President Bush, never thinking for a moment that it would actually get to the White House, but it did make us feel good that we were supporting the cause.

Mail was pretty slow on the receiving end, as all mail had to go through our Army screening process and the Saudi censorship police. The Saudi Arabian government would screen all mail for pornography, and what they deemed as illicit materials were destroyed. Many a box filled with cookies and good wishes would get crushed or burned before it reached the soldier at Camp Eagle II because of the process. Units would get bags of letters addressed to "any soldier" that would come by the thousands from caring citizens back in the States, and many of the guys would send reply letters back to the sender. I never picked up any of those "any soldier" letters as I was getting plenty from family, friends, and students from back home.

When a box from home showed up, it was like a feast. Simple things like a hand drawn picture from my 3 yr old daughter Kristen and homemade cookies kept the connection to home. I was adopted by two elementary schools while I was there. My Mom was a music teacher at Bess Brannen Elementary in Lake Jackson, Texas, and the wife of a dear friend of mine, Marguerite Naiser, was an elementary school teacher at Wild Peach Elementary in Brazoria, Texas. I received regular mail from the kids. If we got a box with homemade cookies or treats, they would always be shared with the guys. Included in the care packages was a variety of what we thought were necessities like baby wipes, batteries, sun block, foot powder, toilet paper, writing paper, and games.

It wasn't all off time and letter writing at Camp Eagle II. The camp was packed with soldiers and military equipment, offering terrorists a target of opportunity on a large scale. A timely mortar attack, a car bomber, or perimeter infiltrator could have a devastating affect on the densely packed division. As a result, the camp was heavily sand bagged and diligently guarded. All soldiers at Camp Eagle II pulled guard duty shifts, even the 101st Airborne Division Band. I didn't know when the band was guarding, but I was in hopes it was a tuba player familiar with an M-60 machine gun and not a flutist studying his sheet music for the next concert or ceremony. The entrances and exits to the camp were heavily fortified as were all tactical operation centers (TOC). I am sure the camp was scoped out for an attack, but a terrorist would have a hard time coming up with a plan that would have succeeded due to the division's diligence.

We continued to train hard physically at Camp Eagle II. The physical exercise became easier and easier as we became acclimated to the harsh, hot conditions. We would run a couple miles around the camp, and then road march in the sand northeast of the camp. Top physical conditioning was the only way we could fight and live in the desert.

We made a trip south of Camp Eagle II about forty miles out in the desert to do a live fire exercise with the 1-320th field artillery. Marty and I got to call for fire and do our jobs. The exercise was uneventful until camels came over the horizon into our target area. Check fires were yelled over the radio as we didn't want to kill the camels and cost the Army money. None of us wanted to answer to that. Stories ran rampant about soldiers who had intentionally killed some camels.

Later that day, several of our soldiers became mysteriously ill with abdominal cramps and nausea, with some passing out. We had to call in medivac Blackhawk helicopters to have the soldiers flown to one of our Army hospitals located in Dhahran. We never did find out what that mysterious illness was.

On September 11, 1990, the same day I signed out of my unit at Ft. Lewis, the division issued its first operation plan for Desert Shield, OPLAN 90-1 (Eagle Defense). The mission statement read, "When directed, 101st Airborne Division (Air Assault) defends King Fahd International Airport (KFIA) to protect the airport and key facilities." General Peay's proposed plan of action was that the division would defend with its Aviation Brigade, the Second Air Assault Brigade Task Force would conduct a delay with one battalion, and an infantry brigade would set up anti-armor positions along likely avenues of approach. Another infantry brigade would establish blocking positions along the main highway leading to KFIA.

OPLAN 90-1 also directed that the division's troops in Forward Operating Base Bastogne would conduct covering force operations with the Aviation Brigade prepared to attack in support of the defense. Each unit at Camp Eagle II would prepare to augment the base defense. Each brigade arriving in Saudi Arabia was to be prepared to establish anti-armor ambushes along the avenues of approach to KFIA.

According to General Peay's Command report, we would have been hard pressed to execute this plan because of inadequate ammunition supply from Corps. The late arrival of corps assets to theatre would have strained our ability to fight and sustain ourselves during the first few months. The Division Ready Brigade ammunition stockpile maintained at Fort Campbell would not sustain the whole division.

As more and more division assets and troops arrived in theatre, the division developed OPLAN 90-2 for the covering force mission at An Nuayriyah (FOB Bastogne) in AO (area of operation)

Apache, and to provide helicopter and fire support for forces between the 101ˢᵗ and the Kuwaiti border. The plan also called for the division to disrupt and delay Iraqi forces and assist in passage of lines. On order, the 101ˢᵗ would screen the west flank of the XVIII Airborne Corps and prepare to defend KFIA. OPLAN 90-2 made the assumption that the division would be at full strength by 6 October and that the division would have at least eight to twelve hours warning prior to the initiation of hostilities. This plan was never published but served in formulating OPLAN 90-3.

Camp Eagle II was right in the way and sitting on top of enemy objectives. KFIA and the Saudi Arabian Industrial Complex were right there and could be easily defended by the camp's occupying brigade and the 101ˢᵗ Aviation Brigade. It was brilliant planning that Camp Eagle II could house a brigade in rest and if the necessity arose, defend critical enemy objectives with the same troops. At KFIA, the division had large parking spaces for its helicopters on the tarmac. The parking garage at KFIA housed troops from the 101ˢᵗ Aviation Brigade including one of my longtime friends' son, Marc (a new private in the Army and a Chinook mechanic).

Camp Eagle II had to feed thousands of soldiers at a time and did so using the T-Ration. The T-Ration was a large tray of food in a can that could be easily heated up with boiling water and quickly served to the troops. The downside to that fast food was that no one knew how old the food was and there was a limited variety. Fresh food was not in plentiful supply for the troops. As an alternative, some of the locals surrounded Camp Eagle II with burger and chicken shacks.

SPC Matt Huff, 1-320ᵗʰ FA:

"At Camp Eagle II, we had some fine chow. A mess hall was set up and we had all we could eat of the T-Rats. Fortunately, many of the local entrepreneurs set up shop and started selling chicken. We think it was chicken. Adams says it was cat. It sure was good cat if that were the case. MMMM Good ! The hamburger joint popped up just across the road. Or maybe it was camel burger. No one will ever really know. At formation one day we were instructed not to eat at the local establishments. Our health and safety

47

could not be protected. Look at it this way. We could have freshly cooked cat or food that has been stored for 20+ years in metal containers and boiled to perfection. You make the choice. I did. Give me the cat, baby!

"*Over time, American business caught up with us. We had companies shipping tons of food and drinks to us. There are two things I remember best-Pepsi and Hershey's. Pepsi provided cases of soda to us weekly. We had been in country for maybe 2 months or so and had not seen a soda of any kind. One day chief showed up with Pepsi. We decided that we would ice it down prior to consumption. Where the heck did he get the ice? We chilled it for hours and when we finally did partake in soda enjoyment, it was absolutely the best soda I ever had. Thanks PEPSI!*"

One of the unusual happenings at Camp Eagle II was a brigade change of command ceremony for the 2nd Brigade (502nd Infantry), to which I was attached. I found it odd that here we are in war, probably pretty close to going on the offense to expel Saddam Hussein from Kuwait, and we are replacing our brigade commander. I had no knowledge of either colonel or their abilities, but knew that if there was a colonel serving as brigade commander in this division, he would have to be among the best. I asked one of our officers about the command change, and he just said, "It was time," meaning it was time for the change of commanders, war or no war. The outgoing brigade commander was Colonel Greg Gile, and he was to be the chief of staff for the 10th Mountain Division at Ft. Drum, New York. The incoming commander was Colonel Theodore (Ted) J. Purdom.

After 3 weeks at Camp Eagle II, I was fully acclimated to the dry, harsh, heat of Saudi Arabia. We were now running 4 miles in our company runs and everyone was fired up. Charlie Company was rested from their last tour at FOB Oasis and everyone seemed ready to go back to the desert.

1/320th Field Artillery – Camp Eagle II, October 1990

Tent City – Corner of Guns of Glory and Balls of the Eagle

Saudi Country Club – Sergeant Frank Giger, FO meeting at the mess tent

Camp Eagle II – Sergeant Fred Baskin, FO. Courtesy of Ernie Swindle

2nd Platoon doing PT. Camp Eagle II – October, 1990
Courtesy of Ian Berkowitz

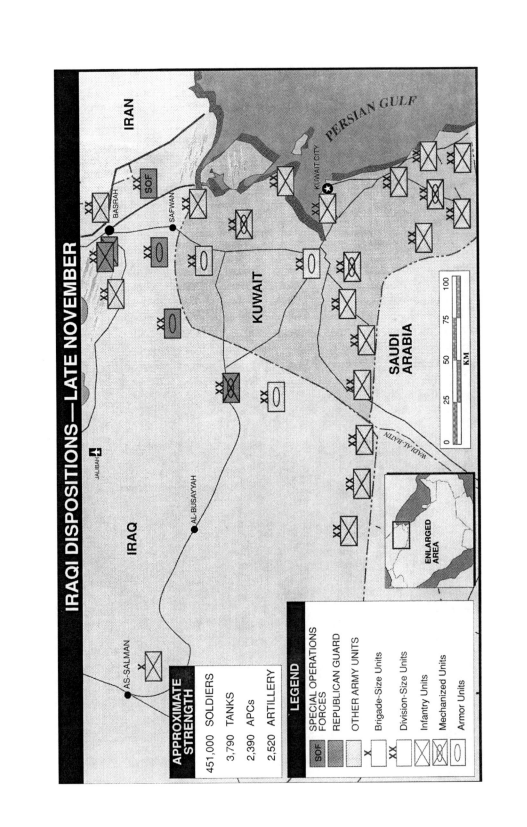

IRAQI DISPOSITIONS—LATE NOVEMBER

Chapter 4

The FOBs
Bastogne and Oasis

On 16 November 1990, after what seemed to be an eternity at the "Saudi Country Club" (Camp Eagle II), the 1-502nd was in PZ (pick up zone) posture on a road adjacent to KFIA and Camp Eagle II. I was with the 2nd platoon of Charlie Company as we positioned ourselves along the road with the rest of the battalion. It was impressive to see all of these soldiers waiting for the lift. After thirty minutes in PZ posture, the CH-47 Chinook helicopters came in one behind the other, landing on the road to pick us up. It took only a minute or so to load up, and in unison, the row of tandem rotor heavy lift Chinook helicopters took off.

The 1-502 and 1-320 FA had already been to Forward Operating Base (FOB) Bastogne and Oasis in AO (Area of Operation) Normandy, but this was my first trip. After almost a month of boredom, training, and waiting, I was finally being carried to an important first objective. We were going to an area south of Kuwait the 82nd Airborne Division held by their Ready Brigade at the beginning of the campaign and was known as President Bush's "line in the sand." It is also where 82nd soldiers nicknamed themselves "Iraqi speed-bumps." The 101st officially took control of the area on 4 September 1990 and renamed the FOB (Forward

Operating Base), Bastogne. The town had an important road junction to Dhahran and Riyadh similar to the one in Bastogne, Belgium during WWII (The FOB in Saudi Arabia received its name from General Peay). Most of our aviation brigade was in an attack position in support of the defense.

As we made our way northwest, throughout the loud, vibrating ride, I looked out a window. The sand dunes below reminded me of my youth growing up in Texas, when our family would take two hour road trips from Big Spring to Crane to visit grandparents. It took us almost an hour to reach the FOB which was located at An Nuayriyah. Bastogne was along Pipeline Road and south of the Kuwaiti border. If Iraqi divisions attacked across the border and moved south into Saudi Arabia, we would be in the gap with the 24th Infantry Division behind us to counter-attack.

The enemy attack formations poised across the border had us significantly outnumbered, and the force ratios put us in a bad position if we were forced to defend our position. The Iraqis had 836 tanks compared to our 123 and 198 artillery pieces compared to our 76. The great equalizer for us was the 101st Aviation's attack helicopters and the Air Force's A-10s. If Iraqi formations were to come across, it would be like a shooting gallery for the Cobras, Apaches, and Warthogs.

By this time, OPLAN 90-3 was in force for the defense of Saudi Arabia. The plan was based on intelligence predictions that Iraq would attack across the Kuwaiti border and lead with the same divisions that initially invaded Kuwait. Those same Iraqi divisions were amassing along the southern border of Kuwait along with six others. Their objective would be to seize key petroleum facilities in Dhahran and Abqaiq. Intelligence had nine Iraqi divisions in forward positions, with six of those divisions to be in the initial assault. The 101st was expected to be hit head-on by one division followed by a flanking attack from a second. Our division's mission was to disrupt and delay the attack.

When we arrived at FOB Bastogne, our platoon's mission was to guard the ammo supply point (ASP). It was a pretty relaxed duty, and we slept in some old deserted buildings at the site. I shared guard duty with the rest of the platoon, so when I wasn't on guard duty I was working with PFC Martin McPherson, my new RTO (radio telephone operator). Some of the guys had Gameboys and were "hard at it" playing Tetris. A lot of Gameboys sent from the U.S. by family and friends never made it to theatre (they were either blown up, crushed, or burned by mailroom soldiers or Saudi censors who thought there might be bombs or porn in the packages). AA batteries went for a premium price because of the game. I would always include batteries in my wish list from home as my shortwave radio, mini-maglite and my battery-operated razor used them. I always had spare batteries that I shared with the guys.

After five days at Bastogne, our unit moved to FOB Oasis. Oasis was a ghost town named Qaryat Al Ulya. The ancient town had been abandoned many years before and offered us an opportunity to train on urban terrain and how to survive in the desert. This was my first taste of living in a hole in the ground. Our home in the desert was an individual fighting position dug below the ground a couple feet. After initially digging the hole, the loose sand kept falling back into it, and this kept me digging the same sand over and over. After doing this a while, I figured out that by creating a lip around the hole, the sand wouldn't keep coming in. After digging our holes, we stretched our semi-waterproof panchos over the holes flat so they would not give away our positions to the Iraqis. The cover also provided us with a barrier against the morning desert moisture and sand storms. Those that slept in the holes just wrapped in their panchos without the cover would wake up the next morning soaked.

McPherson and I dug holes adjacent to each other so that we could share radio watch at night. Radio watch kept us up on alternate watches all night long. If there was an attack across the border, we needed to know and respond immediately. We would alternate watch every two hours. Deep sleep wasn't possible as we always had one ear to the radio in case the other fell asleep. During these vigils, the desert got very cold. We didn't have field jackets, just the night-time light weight desert cammo and a pancho liner (the infantry lives and travels light with their home on their backs). I used my bullet-proof vest as a pillow and would wrap up in the pancho liner. To help me stay awake, I would turn on my small shortwave radio and listen to the news from the BBC or Voice of America. That little shortwave radio turned out to be a blessing for not only me, but our whole platoon as well. Getting news is a big deal when you are isolated from the rest of the world.

Of course, when you are living in the desert, your concerns are the extreme temperature variations from night to day, eating, sleeping, and you know…taking a dump. The fact that there are no bathrooms in the desert was not a problem. The world is your bathroom, and we didn't have to concern ourselves with girls. My entrenching tool and I would walk a comfortable distance from the rest of the guys, dig a hole, pull my pants down around my combat boots, place one butt cheek on the e-tool I just used to dig the hole, and take a dump. After doing my business, I would cover the hole up with the e-tool and was off and running.

Eating was also a simple process, and the decision on what to eat went like this. Do I want to have that chicken and rice MRE or the spaghetti MRE? Humm, I think I'll have the spaghetti MRE and save the chicken and rice for tonight. The MRE came with Tabasco Sauce which seemed to make it all taste better by numbing the taste buds. When we ate, flies would come in by the thousands, okay, maybe fifty or so every time you started eating. One of the team leaders, SSG Ian Berkowitz shared a little trick with me. He said, "Before you start eating your MRE, take off your boots." Berkowitz was a big cut-up and always had a joke, so I carefully digested his words. He went on, "When you take your boots off, the flies will go to your feet instead of the food." Ok, I thought. I was willing to give anything a try to keep these darn flies away from me while I ate. I slipped into my hole, and with no one looking took my boots off, opened my MRE, and I'll be if it didn't work. Sometimes, we had to eat on the run, so taking your boots off wasn't an option, but when I could, I used Berk's trick. I never found a solution to eating an MRE in a sandstorm. I wished Berkowitz had a trick for that because the MRE got a little crunchy during a shamal.

The desert floor at Oasis was covered in goat crap, camel crap, donkey crap, and the associated dung beetles, scorpions, and snakes. Once you got past all of that, you felt right at home. At night, your sleep partner might be any one of these that would either fall in the hole with you, or you could hear them crawling on the stretched pancho above your hooch. It was a common occurrence to throw the unwanted guests out of my desert home at night. The next morning I would recall evicting something, cringing at the thought.

We lived with sand. It would get into the smallest of places, so the maintenance of our M-16 rifle was ongoing and critical. We spent many hours cleaning our weapons because we never knew when we would have to use them. We would have had a "bad day" if our weapon jammed. Many a time I thought about the guys in Nam that had their weapons jam at the wrong time costing soldiers' lives. The M-16 was modified during Vietnam with the forward assist that eliminated some of the jamming, but the weapon could be finicky when it came to malfunctions (unlike the enemy's AK-47 that would seemingly never malfunction). Our boots always had sand in them. They were the OD Green, jungle combat and they had air vents that would suck sand when we walked. We were always cleaning out our boots. The infantry always figures out a way to use duct-tape (100 mph tape), so it wasn't long until we taped up the boot vents to keep the sand out. We also used tape on our binoculars to minimize the reflection off of the objective lens. As a forward observer, the last thing we wanted was to give away our position by reflecting sunlight back to the enemy.

We trained every day at Oasis, and it made us desert tough. We trained day and night coordinating platoon raids, communicating with hand signals, and moving in a platoon formation. Living and working together 24 hours a day, 7 days a week in the harsh desert climate bonded us together. As a result, our platoon was taken to a higher operating level. This training was different. We were training in the same place where we would be fighting, and this gave us an advantage. We knew every inch of our AO. Working and living with the infantry was valuable for me as I had never worked that closely with them. At Ft. Lewis, I was used to the comfort of my Hummer and never had to hump a ruck sack with the infantry. Now, here I was with the 101st Airborne Division, one of the most mobile, fit divisions in the Army. Even with all of the running I had been accustomed to, it took me a few days to feel like I was up to speed carrying an extra 100 pounds on my back.

Bonding with 2nd platoon and my RTO McPherson was valuable since it usually takes months, not days, to build trust on all sides. The platoon sergeant and platoon leader had a limited amount of time to get their platoon up to fighting speed. They had to make sure that I, being new to the platoon, was capable of meeting their standards and that they could depend on me if the time came. I wanted to know the same about them. I had already sized them up at Camp Eagle II as being professional, competent soldiers, and this trip to Oasis was verifying that. I could not have been placed in a better position than I was with 2nd platoon. It was a revelation to me at Oasis that all of the guys in the platoon were really fine soldiers. I'm sure the competence just didn't magically happen, as it takes weeks and months to get everyone up to standard. After seeing how these guys worked, I knew the platoon sergeant and platoon leader had done a fine job training the platoon back at Ft. Campbell.

Thanksgiving Day, 1990 was spent at the Oasis. It was rumored that President George Bush could make an appearance so we spent the day prior cleaning up the best way we could. We made a long road-march to a mess tent set up in the desert just to serve us the usual Thanksgiving fare. Turkey and dressing never tasted so good. The only thing we had eaten for weeks had been MREs and T-Rations. I was taken aback by those guys in the mess tent and how hard they had worked to give us a Thanksgiving

Feast. We thanked them for all they did to pull that off. President Bush didn't show up at our remote location, but he did make an appearance with many units showing his gratitude and support for the troops.

Over the next few days, our platoon conducted training exercises and was given the duty of FOB Oasis guard. With the vast amount of space we were defending, the possibility of a small unit of infiltrators and terrorists from the north kept us alert. At any time a vehicle could make a detour off of Tapline (Trans Arabia Pipeline) Road and head for unsuspecting units. Tapline Road was a narrow, two lane super highway that ran from the northwest to the southeast corner of our AO that paralleled the Saudi Arabian border with Iraq and Kuwait. Our platoon took guard duty seriously as lives could depend on it. We were used to doing guard duty and setting up security perimeters during field training exercises, but this was war. In a FTX back home, we would try to sneak up on each other throwing smoke bombs, artillery simulators, and firing our dud M-16 rounds. If that happened here, there would be no duds or simulators. A breach in security would cost lives.

The starlit nights were awesome in Saudi Arabia as there were no lights from towns close by to compete with the stars. It was easy to pick out constellations in the sky. The Lazy W, The North Star, and the Big Dipper were huge and breathtaking. I also was amazed at how vast this desert was and how small I felt in comparison. There were many days and nights when I felt like I was taken back in time thousands of years because of this seemingly untouched land.

After concluding our unit's guard duty, we spent a day maintaining our equipment, cleaning our M-16s and relaxing at "Wally World." Wally World was where we enjoyed the Thanksgiving feast a couple weeks before. This time, we had the opportunity to take showers like those that had been set up at Camp Eagle II, eat a hot T-Ration meal, and enjoy a day off from training. We also got to take a dump sitting down on the wooden boxes they had constructed and have a mail call. After living and working hard in the desert, Wally World wasn't like going to Disneyland, but it was a nice break.

SSG Berkowitz at Wally World – FOB Oasis
Courtesy of Ian Berkowitz

Mail calls in the desert were few and far between. It was difficult to get mail out to us and wasn't a priority. My first mail call in the desert was a special one. The Company Commander came strolling up to my hole one evening after dark holding a large brown envelope. He said, "Who are you?" as he handed me the envelope. I had no clue about what he meant until I looked at the envelope. It was from The White House, Washington, D.C. I looked at him and said, "Oh sir, it must be from my friend." After turning on my little flash-light with the blue lens on it, I opened the envelope and sure enough, it was from The President of the United States. The letter, written on 7"x9" White House stationary, was signed by the President. Amazingly enough, the President had responded to the personal note of support I had written back at Camp Eagle II.

THE WHITE HOUSE

WASHINGTON

November 26, 1990

Dear Sergeant Wiehe:

Thank you for your good letter about our policy in the Persian Gulf. Receiving such words of support from members of Operation Desert Shield means a great deal to me.

I speak for all Americans when I tell you how proud we are of the work you and your comrades are doing in Saudi Arabia and the surrounding waters of the Persian Gulf. I remember how difficult it was to leave loved ones and venture into harm's way. I salute you for all you are doing on the front lines of freedom and hope you will let the others in your unit know of my sincere appreciation for all your efforts.

Barbara and I are keeping you in our thoughts and prayers. God bless you.

Sincerely,

Gg Bush

Sergeant Stephen D. Wiehe, USA

C Company, 1/502 INF, (FIST)
2 BDE, 101st ABN DIV (AASLT)
APO New York 09309

After reading the letter, I shared it with the Captain. He said, "That is one special letter there, Sergeant." I agreed. As per the President's instructions, I shared the letter with the rest of the platoon and got comments like, "How did you get the President of the United States to write you a letter." It was a special note from him, and I was truthful when I sent him my letter of support.

With the division expecting Iraqi armored and infantry divisions to cross the border at any time, we trained for the possibility of meeting Iraqi armored formations head on. We conducted an anti-tank ambush on the night of 7 December 1990 with Charlie Company. We had to move and navigate at night to a designated ambush site and begin no later than 0001 hrs on 8 December. We made our way ten or so kilometers to the ambush site well in advance of our ambush time. Once we arrived, our uniforms were soaked with sweat, and the temperatures dropped quickly in the desert night. Setting up an ambush meant being motionless and quiet for long periods of time. With no field jackets, the only thing you could do to keep warm was to lie in a prone position in the sand, arms underneath the body and hands catching your breath to warm your face. The temperature variations were now about seventy degrees from day to night. I shivered as the minutes seemed like hours. At one minute after midnight, we conducted the live anti-armor ambush, and my body began to warm up with the movement. We were shooting down into a pit, simulating enemy armor units moving up a wadi. The muzzle flashes were bright and gave me temporary night blindness. The training was a success and our platoon leader gave us an AAR (after action review). Upon completion of the ambush AAR, we began our movement back to our platoon location at Oasis. I was never so glad to road march as I was that night. The training was good, and I had just been enlightened as to how harsh this desert warfare could be.

On 10 December 1990, it was our turn to do MOUT (military occupation of urban terrain) training in the abandoned village nearby. It had been a while since I had trained in an urban environment, so I welcomed the exercise. During my first tour in the Army at Ft. Meade, Maryland as a Military Policeman, we had extensive MOUT training. I also had the best shooting skills in the unit and was the 519th MP Battalion's counter sniper, honing those MOUT skills to a very high level. With the unit's primary mission being the Washington, D.C. area in case of civil disturbance, I trained a lot in urban warfare. Being a counter sniper, I also spent days on the range with my national match M-14 rifle. Many soldiers hated spending time at the range. Not me. I loved shooting government ammo and testing myself on those tight shot groups.

The day at the village was productive as we led the platoon through exercises on clearing operations from streets to rooms to buildings. We broke the platoon down by squads and even smaller three man elements, teaching the techniques of observation, interlocking fields of fire, booby traps, and over-watch. We taught the platoon how to communicate with and cover other elements as they proceeded to objectives using concealment in an urban environment and the occupation of larger areas with a small force. Once occupation had been secured, the lessons of choke points and channeling opposing forces were taught. After each exercise, we would conduct an AAR with the platoon, talking about the good and bad points and lessons learned. It was a very good day at the village.

On the 11th of December 1990, we moved to PZ (pick up zone) posture on a makeshift runway at FOB Oasis for our ride back to KFIA. Everyone was looking forward to the cold showers, hot T-Rations, and luke-warm coffee waiting for us back at Camp Eagle II. I felt good about my training with 2nd platoon, and because of our work at FOB Bastogne and Oasis, I was made to feel more a part of the platoon. I was glad I had the opportunity to train with them and Marty before we had to fight. C-130 transports flew onto the dirt landing strip supported by steel grating, and without turning off their engines, troops climbed on board. After the crew chief secured the rearward door, the transports turned around, took off, and another would land. After we took off, the ride was a little bouncy, and I noticed one of the guys with his head in a trash sack. On hearing the soldier hurl into the bag, others would gag. I had a tendency to get car sick, but was lucky to have never gotten air sick. The soldier's reaction had little effect on me. It took us about forty-five minutes to make the trip back to KFIA where there were buses waiting to take us back to Camp Eagle II.

Sergeant Wiehe at the Oasis – December 1990

1/320th – FA Command Sergeant Major Kalub Duggins
Courtesy of Kalub Duggins

C Battery 1/320th – Gun Pose – From left to right:
Sgt. William Albritton, Sgt. Roger Smith, Cpl. Norman Sharp, SP4 Matthew Huff
Courtesy Matthew Huff

Sergeant Wiehe – Looking North
Courtesy of Ian Berkowitz

My desert hooch at FOB Oasis

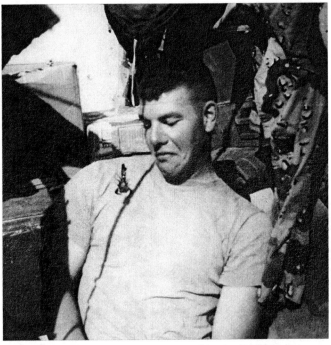

Martin McPherson – With a new friend – FOB Oasis

2nd Platoon after action review – MOUT training at the Oasis

2nd platoon MOUT training at the Oasis – December 10, 1990

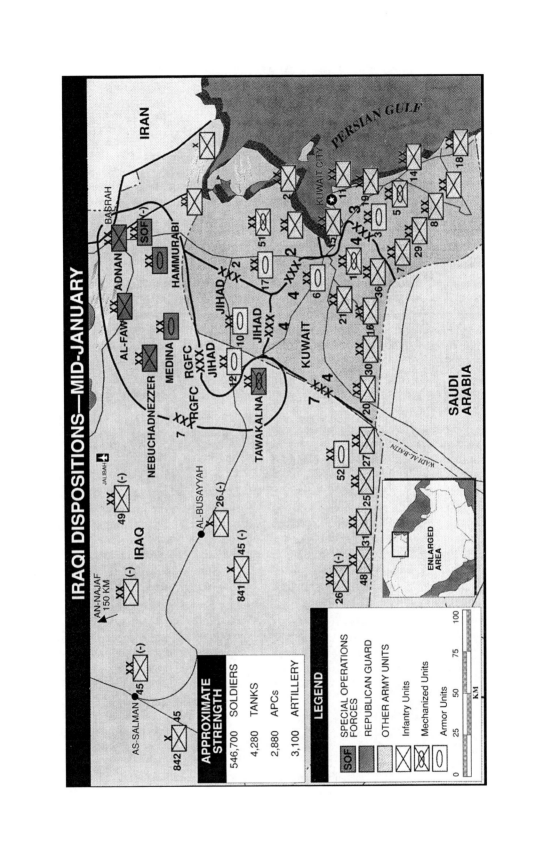

Chapter 5

Hafar al-Batin

At Camp Eagle II, sleep was more welcome than Christmas, and getting back to Tent City allowed me to catch up on my sleep. I enjoyed doing my job and bonding with my infantry brothers in the covering force mission at the FOBs, but sleep deprivation was tough. It's not hard for a few days or a week, but after a few weeks, it starts to wear on you. Marty (my RTO) and I were sharing guard responsibility as well as maintaining radio watch all night at Oasis, and there wasn't time to sleep during the day because of the brisk training schedule. It was part of living and working in a war zone for an FO. Marty and I got a maximum of three hours of sleep at night.

At Camp Eagle II, we were able to sleep on cots in Hajj (The Islamic pilgrimage to Mecca) tents instead of holes in the ground, enjoy hot chow (T-Rats) and luke-warm coffee served from the mess tent, write letters, and enjoy visiting with some Fire Support Team (FIST) friends from Ft. Lewis. On my recent trip to Bastogne and Oasis, SSG Ian Berkowitz (squad leader for 2nd platoon) and I became friends. Ian not only led troops, he also had the knack for making people laugh. If we were going through a stressful situation up at Oasis or Bastogne, Ian would find a way to lighten the mood. At Camp Eagle II, I also enjoyed catching up with Frank Giger and Ernie Swindle (Sandfill 27 Forward Observers from Ft. Lewis). During this time we also got to see the Bob Hope Show with Johnny Bench on Christmas Day. Before the show, Bob Hope and Johnny made their way through Camp Eagle II in a HUMMV with General Peay, shaking hands and wishing everyone a Merry Christmas. During the show I told my buddies, "We must be going to war; we are watching Bob Hope live."

Bob Hope entertaining the 101st at Camp Eagle II on Christmas Day
Courtesy of Ian Berkowitz

The time back at Camp Eagle II (The Saudi Country Club) was a break from the FOBs and the harsh desert climate, but oddly enough, with the exception of sleep deprivation, I felt better being in the desert doing my job. If I could take an occasional shower and maybe wash my desert BDUs every now and then,

I would have enjoyed just staying north along the border. Living conditions in the desert were harsh, but everyone had their space. At Camp Eagle II, the densely packed soldiers were sleeping six to eight per tent. With that many "Type-A" personalities living in the small area, heated arguments would erupt. At times, I was surprised the disagreements didn't escalate into fist fights. That's usually when I would grab my floppy desert hat and M-16 and walk over to the mess tent.

This rotation at the "Saudi Country Club" was different than when I checked in a couple months prior. The 15 January deadline for Iraq to pull out of Kuwait was approaching. We now knew the road back home was through Kuwait, and the defensive posture became an offensive one. There were rumors about troop rotations back to the states, but it became more apparent that there was no going home without expelling Saddam from Kuwait. On 29 December 1990, we received word we would not be going back to FOB Oasis. We didn't know where we would be going, but began training for offensive air assault missions. This meant we were going to war. Our fire support team began rehearsing "call for fire" missions, and the physical training in Charlie Company was stepped up. Even Special Forces came into our company to train us on the weapons of the enemy, including the AK-47 assault rifle and RPG (rocket propelled grenade).

While at Camp Eagle II, Ernie Swindle (one of the Sandfill NCOs) and I were able to interface with the crew of an Air Force AC-130 Spectre gunship at the adjacent KFIA. There were five AC-130Hs deployed to the KTO (Kuwaiti Theatre of Operation). Spectre was a Godsend to the infantry and special operations. It had a close air support mission and could orbit a battlefield for long periods of time in support of ground troops. It wasn't uncommon for Spectre to work four to five hours at a time. I remembered my friend Dave's stories back at Ft. Lewis describing the amazing firepower of Spectre in Operation Just Cause and the take-down of Rio Hato Airport in Panama. The commander of the 75th Rangers paid high compliments on the Spectre in Panama saying that their prepping the battlefield saved Ranger's lives.

71

Johnny Bench with David Ceurvels (left) and William Walter (right) on Christmas Day. Standing in front of "Spirit03" which would be shot down one month later. Courtesy of David Ceurvels.

The armament of the AC-130H Spectre was formidable. It had two 20mm M61 guns, one 40mm M2A1, and one 105mm M137 howitzer sticking out of its side. When the howitzer was fired, crewmembers could actually feel the airplane move sideways from the recoil. Actually, the whole airplane moved about 15 feet and put tremendous stress on the support structure underneath the 105mm howitzer. Ground crews spent a great deal of time working on minor damage that the howitzer created. Being an artillery FO, I was amazed that an airplane could withstand such stress. The AC-130 mission was a dangerous one for the crew, and susceptible to AAA (Anti-aircraft artillery) and SAM (surface-to-air missile) attacks. It took a special, brave person to fly in the gunship. We were told it was instilled in their training that they were there for the guys on the ground. The Spectre couldn't perform its job low and slow like the A-10. It flew high and slow as it circled targets and slugged it out with enemy units on the ground. As a result of their commitment to us, we felt a special kinship with the Spectre crews.

As we were being briefed by the gunship gunners, I was impressed with their knowledge of the aircraft's mission, its armaments and ordnance. I also was surprised that the crews spent many years together at Hurlburt Field, Florida unlike other military assignments where the maximum at any one place would be two or three years. This was a tight group of warriors who knew each other better than they did their own families. As we were being briefed on Spectre, the area was busy with activity as ground crews were busy working on the aircraft. If the planes weren't flying, they were being maintained. It was a never ending process. With it being Christmas, we talked about Bob Hope and Johnny Bench coming over to Saudi Arabia to entertain the troops. They didn't know who among them would be able to go see the USO Show as many of them were on alert status and couldn't leave the area. We never felt rushed as we visited with the gunners and pilots. They spent as much time as we wanted getting familiar with the gunship and seemed sincerely proud to show off what they had. As we said our good-byes and good lucks, I left feeling fortunate we had them on our side.

KFIA (Camp Eagle II) was also the A-10 base for the Air Force. While at Camp Eagle II, we would hear the constant takeoffs and landings of the A-10s. As with Spectre, the A-10 was created for a close air support mission and could sustain tremendous damage and still make it back alive. The A-10 Thunderbolt ("Warthog") was built around the GAU-8 Avenger, a heavy automatic 30mm Gatling gun equipped with a variety of air-to-ground and air-to-air missiles. The Warthog was a tank buster and I took comfort in knowing they were there for us. If Iraqi armored formations crossed the border in pursuit of the Saudi industrial facilities, the A-10 could take them out in large numbers. The high pitched sound of the engines during take offs and landings no longer kept me up at night. It was music to my ears, although it did take days after my visits to Camp Eagle II to get rid of those high pitched sounds ringing in my ears and my dreams.

All seemed rather quiet at Camp Eagle II, almost too quiet as I went about recovering equipment, training for offensive operations, and studying for my E-6 (Staff Sergeant) promotion board which was scheduled for 11 January, 1991. I was pleased that leadership was taking the time to consider my promotion while deployed as we were preparing for air assault operations. Having completed my Associates Degree from Pierce College back at Ft. Lewis, completing numerous U.S. Army correspondence courses, having the required time in service, time in grade requirements, as well as the BNCOC School, the board was the only step remaining for promotion. Looking at the cutoff scores in The Army Times, making staff sergeant looked like a shoe in. Once reaching staff sergeant, I would then be eligible for a Company FSNCO (Fire Support Non-Commissioned Officer) slot. Between the board preparation and working on air assault missions, there wasn't a lot of time for checking on my buddies. I was sure that if I was busy, they were busy.

I liked the air assault concept of flying over the enemy armored lines of defense. In my mind, the 101st was made for the offensive maneuvers, especially in a battle-field scenario like this. It reminded me of the paratroopers during WWII that dropped behind enemy lines at Normandy to secure key objectives. At Bastogne and Oasis we were waiting for the battle to come to us, and our light infantry would only be effective if the Apache helicopters, the A-10, and Spectre came to the rescue, or if we had enough tank on tank units to delay an approach. We did have TOW (wire guided anti-tank missile) mounted HUMMVs at our disposal, but I didn't like the idea of running a foot race against an armored opposing force. The desert offered limited areas of cover and the passage of lines between friendly units seemed difficult. It all seemed like we would be decisively engaged using soldier held anti-tank weapons at close range if air assets couldn't slow them down. We had my 1/320th Field Artillery in the area, but I questioned how effective 105mm guns would be against an armored onslaught. On the offense side however, we could quickly deploy an air assault behind enemy lines, establishing strongholds where there were no tanks thus disrupting supply routes and cutting lines of communication. I liked that idea much more than waiting for the war to come to me.

The 502nd (our unit) and the 1-320th received a warning order from Division on 8 January 1991 that they were needed by VII Corps and should prepare to move. VII Corps was having trouble getting their tanks and heavy equipment up to their area of operation from the coast due to delays in getting out of the German ports. There was a longshoreman's strike in Germany and inadequate sealift for General Frank's Corp, thus, they were having trouble closing into theatre. At this point we had no idea this was anything more than Bastogne and Oasis.

The 502nd was chosen by General Peay for this job because we were rested and refitted. 1st brigade had received orders for the air assault into FOB Cobra, and was in the middle of rehearsals for it. 3rd brigade had just returned from the covering force mission at Oasis and Bastogne. When we received the word, we immediately started going through our equipment checks and briefings. Bastogne and Oasis was serious business and a concerning defense, but this one was quickly developing into something greater. We made map recons of the area and it appeared we would be vulnerable to a large Iraqi attack. Oh great, I thought. My worst fears came upon me. We were going to be that Iraqi speed bump for a T-72 on the Kuwaiti border that I was worried about. Would I get an opportunity to call for fire or would I be reduced to just another infantryman using a LAW or AT-4 (light anti-tank weapon).

The plan was that our unit would initially move to the Al Qaysumah airfield just southeast of Hafar al-Batin. Now, for the second time, I sensed concern in our company as we meticulously went through our checklists. After our briefings, we were one hundred percent sure there would be an enemy engagement. Once we made our preparations, some sat near their rucks, and some knocked out what might be final letters home. There wasn't the normal joking around and coffee meetings at the mess tent.

We all stayed close to the company for further updates. I felt a little more at ease when I found out our tank busting Apaches and A-10s would be on station. But, then there was the next FO thought: how much would CAS (close air support) be able to slow down five Iraqi divisions before they got to me.

On 9 January 1991, we received the "prepare to move" order, and on the morning of 10 January, the 502ⁿᵈ along with our 1/320ᵗʰ artillery battalion, an Apache battalion, and the 9/101 lift battalion, we made the move to Hafar al-Batin. We traveled from Camp Eagle II three hundred miles northwest to the Al Qaysumah Airfield at Hafar al-Batin. The brigade made the trip by buses, tractor trailers, and C-130s. According to Colonel Purdom, Commander of the 502ⁿᵈ, 3800 soldiers, 700 vehicles, and 79 aircraft were moved in about 43 hours. Upon arrival, we were tactically controlled by the 1ˢᵗ Cavalry Division under VII Corps. On the long trip up to the AO, I was praying that when I had to "call for fire" I would get it right. There would be a lot of lives at stake. I also thought about the E-6 promotion board tomorrow that was not to be. Wow, that's timing, missing the board by one day. Oh well, if it is meant to be, it's meant to be. Shoot, after this ordeal, there might not be anyone to promote.

The air war was just one week away and with the UN deadline getting near, the war planners were concerned about a pre-emptive strike by the Iraqis down the Wadi al-Batin. Being west of the high concentration of Coalition forces, this appeared to be the spot Saddam had chosen for the strike. Hafar al-Batin was adjacent to the Wadi al-Batin, a wide dry river bed that ran north-south from the Iraqi-Kuwait border into Saudi Arabia. Forty miles south was King Khalid Military City (KKMC). We were told that the Iraqi attack across the border and the fall of KKMC would be a moral victory for Saddam. He might not win the war, but he would make a showing by invading Saudi Arabia and taking this key objective.

Just as Saddam did when building up along the Iraqi-Kuwait border before he invaded Kuwait, he was amassing his armor along the Iraqi-Saudi Arabia border. We received word from Special Forces that the Iraqis had breached their own obstacles, established command and control along the border, and were concentrating armored, mechanized, and infantry divisions along the border just north of us. Hafar al-Batin was an oil town with many Iraqi sympathizers and a large population of Jordanians. When Saudi Arabia turned the pipeline off between Iraq and Saudi Arabia due to the embargo, many people became unemployed and disgruntled. A tip-off for an impending attack was that locals were vacating the town, only to be re-occupied by Iraqis, therefore increasing the risk of terrorist attacks.

When we arrived at Al Qaysumah Airfield, the area to our immediate north was defended by Egyptians and Syrians. Saddam probably knew they wouldn't offer too much resistance. Also, the MSR (main supply route) Tapline Road ran southeast to northwest, and had a steady stream of coalition vehicles. If severed, it would have cut off the coalition's main supply route.

At Al Qaysumah Airfield fifteen miles southeast of Hafar al-Batin, we immediately began digging fighting positions. This was much different than digging at FOB Bastogne or Oasis where the sand was soft. Here, we were digging down a few inches and running into rocky shale. It was a bad feeling to think we were going to defend this area from an onslaught of enemy tanks just a few inches under the ground, but we kept digging. It wasn't the casual shoot the bull while you dig, it was almost frantic. Heavy equipment and dozers came in, but their mission was not to dig fighting positions for us, but dig the TOC (tactical operations center) and a long berm for TOW missile sites.

On 12 January 1991, our battalion moved northwest to a new defense position (into a quarry near Hafar al-Batin), and we left the 2nd and 3rd battalions breaking their entrenching tools at the Al Qaysumah Airfield. After our move, we were now closer to the town and the border, but I felt better there. Now, we were at least able to set up more defendable positions, and the ground was easier to dig. And dig we did. We set up hunter killer areas or bottle-necks with limited avenues of approach where we could engage the Iraqi tanks. SSG Berkowitz and his squad set up a fifty-five gallon drum obstacle at the entrance to the quarry. B Company, 1-502nd forward observers just to our north found an abandoned front-end loader and moved dirt to further limit avenues of approach. We set up kill zones where our AT-4s (anti-tank weapons) and claymore mines could be used. When I wasn't digging, I was preparing a target list to be used by my 1/320th Field Artillery and air support. It was a lonely feeling for our platoon at the quarry. There was no plan B. If we were over-run by the Iraqi tanks, then that was it. The mission was retain or "die in place." There was no delay and fall back and there would be no vehicles to get us out. If the Iraqis came, we would be decisively engaged. The 1st Cavalry Division would be prepared for a counter-attack, but the immediate prospect of our infantry versus their tanks was not a winning one.

The mass of Iraqi divisions north of Hafar al-Batin near the wadi was large. The Iraqis plan had the Tawalkana Republican Guard division coming down the wadi behind the 52nd Armored Division, and three other Iraqi divisions poised near the border. According to intelligence sources, the attack was for no later than 14 January 1991. Knowing history, I couldn't help but feel this could be another "Bastogne" for the 101st (not FOB Bastogne in Saudi Arabia, but Bastogne, Belgium during WWII). I am sure our commanders were sensing the same. During World War II, the 101st was cut off from Allied forces for days as they held their positions in defense of Bastogne. They were approached by the Germans to surrender and General Anthony C. McAuliffe sent the message back to the German commander, "NUTS." The quarry could easily be surrounded as the Iraqis made their way to KKMC.

On 13 January 1991, the rain and temperature made it miserable at the quarry. We dug all day and night to prepare for the inevitable attack. Our platoon NCOs were barking out orders all night. I assisted any way I could. We received truck loads of ammo, anti-tank weapons, claymore mines, and grenades. We were cold and wet, and the work helped to keep our body temperatures up. The temperature was probably in the high 40s, but soaked it felt like 30 degrees. I recalled some of our training at Ft. Lewis, and this felt as cold or colder after hours of being wet. I thought, "Could it be possible to get hypothermia in the desert?" I was asking God why it was going to be such a miserable night to die. I was praying and working at the same time. I think a lot of the guys were praying. I felt it would be the last night I would spend on earth. I'll bet there were thousands of Screaming Eagle prayers that went up that night from Hafar al-Batin and the Al Qaysumah Airfield.

SSG Ernie Swindle tired and dirty at Hafar al-Batin

With the bad weather came the thought, "How are we going to defend this area against tanks with 105s and limited air support?" The M102 howitzer was widely used in Vietnam and was intended for light infantry operations, not against armor. The 1-320th was mobile and fit nicely with the air assault concept, but our howitzer was only effective against soft skinned targets and other infantry. The 105's fuze could literally skip off of tanks and would have been like throwing darts against the armored formations.

There was an asset that we had that would work against the tanks, the AH-64 Apache Attack Helicopter. The Apache could strike and kill in any weather or light condition. The AH-64 was the right weapon for this war. The heat that comes off of the tank marks them for death by the Hellfire missile. The missile weighed 20 pounds, carrying its high explosive ordnance at supersonic speed, programmed to hit the tank at a perfect angle. The AGM-114 Hellfire could pierce anything and could easily take the turret off of a tank. The Apache could hold as many as 16 of them along with flechette rockets, and twelve hundred 30 millimeter rounds. If I could take any solace in the situation, it was having the Apache as one of our assets.

With the 502nd in a forward, "die-in-place" position, it became apparent to me that at best we would delay, but not stop the Iraqi attack. We were under control of the 1st Cavalry Division and they would have their hands full trying to defend and possibly counter attack the Iraqi flank. All in all, this was a bad place and a bad time for a light infantry unit.

CSM Kalub Duggins:

"Egyptian forces were in front of us and 1st Cav was way behind us so they could see the avenue of attack, thus allowing them to properly engage. Our mission was to hold and delay at all costs. The weather sucked and C Battery almost floated away. We were OPCON to 1st Cav and one of my big frustrations was that no one wanted to provide us with support, beans, bullets, fuel, etc. Colonel Purdom and Colonel Lawson were finally able to get support from the 101st even though the 1st Cav should have provided."

On the morning and day of 14 January 1991, we kept digging and working. Foxholes were full of water and everyone was wet. Some of the empty ammo boxes were used with ponchos to make hooches, but did little to keep us dry and warm. Later that day, we received what I thought was an answer to prayer.

Higher HQ learned from Special Forces that some of the Iraqi tank formations had bogged down in their approach into the wadi. The same weather that made us so miserable was the same weather that actually impeded the Iraqi plan of attack. Could it be that the rains caused enough water runoff into the wadi to stop them? There was a sense of relief in our platoon. I didn't know what actually stopped them, but I attributed it to God, the rain, and the prayers that went up from the 101st.

We kept digging and improving our fighting positions for the next two days and received word late on the 16th that the air war was going to begin in the early hours of 17 January 1991. As the time approached, I walked over to Marty's position to give him a heads up. Hey Marty. "What's up Sarge?" he replied. "The war is about to start." "Do I need to get up?" he said. "No, you don't need to get up. I just wanted to let you know." Obviously, Marty was more interested in catching some sleep. The fact was, none of us had slept more than a few hours since our move from Camp Eagle II and we would catch a nap whenever possible. I watched from my observation post as flashes and the subsequent rumbles signaled the beginning of Operation Desert Storm. It looked like a storm, with lightning and the rumbling of thunder. I was thankful the war had started. We were all excited to see the beginning of the end for Saddam and the defensive mission of Operation Desert Shield turn to a Operation Desert Storm offense. Maybe the Air Force will keep these Iraqi divisions off of us, I thought. Then on the other hand, maybe all of this will start an Iraqi counter-attack. I knew we had to remain vigilant and not let our guard down.

If our Air Force were to achieve the element of surprise, there were two Iraqi radar sites that had to go silent before attacking deep into Iraq. After eliminated, they could go deep and destroy key targets. The first shots of the war were from 101st Apache helicopters fifty miles inside Iraq. At precisely 0238 hrs on the morning of 17 January 1991, two radar sites seventy miles apart were destroyed by two teams of four Apaches escorted by two Air Force helicopters. The Red Team departed the staging area at

0100 and, The White Team followed seven minutes later. Guided by two U.S. Air Force MH-53 Pave Lows, Task Force Normandy crossed the Iraqi border at two different points at 0200. Using night vision goggles and forward looking infrared radars (FLIR), the two teams made their way to the sites flying nap of the earth using low-lying areas and wadis as cover. The teams only encountered small arms fire from border posts as they proceeded to their objectives.

Once at the radar sites, both teams had to wait until the predetermined engagement time to unleash their Hellfire missiles, 2.75" rockets and 30mm bullets. Within thirty seconds, the radars were out of commission, and within four minutes both sites were completely destroyed. After a brief reconnaissance by the team leaders to determine if the mission was successful, the teams turned back to Saudi Arabia.

With the twenty mile wide corridor open, Coalition aircraft could make their way to their objectives undetected. On the way back, Task Force Normandy again took small arms fire and was the target of one surface-to-air missile. None of the helicopters were hit except LTC Cody's. He experienced some unusual vibration coming out of Iraq, and it looked like one of his rotor blades took a hit from small arms fire. The damage was not significant enough to force him to land or keep him from making it back to base. On their way to Saudi Arabia, the task force experienced buffeting from the low flying attack aircraft flying north. Task Force Normandy could see the attack aircraft lights south of the border. The lights turned off as the jets streaked into Iraq toward their targets. The only evidence they were there was from radar and the buffeting above them.

After their return to Camp Eagle II, they found out with 2,388 Coalition Air Force sorties flown on 17 January, there was one Navy pilot lost on the first day. Expecting many losses on the first night, the TF Normandy mission was an overwhelming success.

On the night of 17 January 1991, my RTO and I accompanied a squad from our platoon on the first combat patrol in and around the quarry and Hafar al- Batin. The patrol began at 2330 hrs, and we were to patrol from our perimeter at the quarry to the outskirts southeast of the town. We were under orders not to enter the town. Our patrol was to gather information of possible targets in the area and observe any Iraqi locations. It was dark and eerie as we made our way through the quarry. All of us had an uneasy feeling as we moved. To add to the uneasiness, we heard the "call to prayer" beaming over the loud speakers from the mosques. I know it was just a call to prayer, but it almost felt like a warning to the occupants of the town of our approach. It made the hair on the back of my neck stand up. The area had very steep drop-offs, which at night seemed bottomless. Even with night vision equipment, walking up to one of those was disconcerting. As we moved around those cliffs, I was praying we wouldn't lose one of our guys over the edge. Sergeant Charlesworth from 2nd platoon was on point. Scott was a very capable, competent squad leader. He moved through the area like he had been there before and knew how to conduct the patrol.

Our instructions were not to enter the town, but to observe and report any movements southeast of Hafar al-Batin. For the patrol, I was given a GPS (Slugger). I used the slugger for navigation and to store coordinates of our patrol locations and possible preplanned target locations. As we approached the outskirts of Hafar al-Batin, we moved directly behind what appeared to be a junkyard. There were lights on a building and it appeared to be occupied. Since the only occupants in the area were suspected terrorists and Iraqis, I marked the location with my slugger. There are times when patrols give you a sense of vulnerability. You are away from your platoon and company if a firefight were to erupt. It's just a few of you against the enemy of unknown size. However, the intelligence that patrols brought back to the unit commanders was valuable; it was used to determine what their units were up against in their area of operation and to plan objectives.

We continued to move and observe. At times we would just stop and listen while conducting a security halt. After an hour or so into the patrol, I felt like we owned the night, like we were the ones observing rather than being observed. Our nocturnal movements would be extremely hard for the Iraqis to detect. During the Iran-Iraq war, both sides would generally drive to the battlefield during the day and go home at night. They would pound each other with artillery during the day and then get a good night's sleep and start over the next day. What a way to fight a war! It seemed neither side wanted to win. With that in mind, I could picture our enemy slumbering as we moved around them.

After a few hours on patrol, we made our way back to our company's location. It seemed like it took forever to get back as we traversed the steep walls of the quarry. Once we arrived, we were debriefed by our platoon leader and SSG Sizemore, C Company's Fire Support NCO. The patrol was mentally and physically exhausting. Perhaps because of the adrenalin, I didn't feel it until I got back. I know it didn't take very long to fall asleep that night. I don't even remember my head hitting the body armor I used as a pillow.

The next day was spent revising my pre-planned target list in case of an Iraqi counter attack. I planned my targets with "triggers." Those triggers were easy-to-see terrain features such as buildings and roads. If the enemy armor crossed that feature, I would fire the target number, and if I became a casualty, the targets would be easy for my RTO, Marty McPherson to execute under pressure. Pre-planning targets saves critical time in case of attack, and the call for fire would be immediate. There would be no time for corrections if the tanks started rolling towards us. All in all, I felt like we would be overrun, but we would sure give them their money's worth if they tried it.

I received a visit from LTC Harlan Lawson, the 1/320th Field Artillery commander. We went over my proposed target list and the triggers to fire the pre-planned targets in detail. He approved, and I was thankful I had my stuff together so he could go on to other observation posts. That was my first meeting with LTC Lawson because I was one of the fill-ins from Ft. Lewis. Lawson was very business-like and professional. I left our meeting feeling the leadership of the 1-320th was in good hands.

I had spent a little time with CSM Kalub Duggins back at Camp Eagle II, and was immediately impressed with him. I sized him up as a "soldiers' soldier" and recognized he had our welfare at heart. Normally, command sergeant majors are thrust into a more political environment as they are in command positions, but occasionally units are lucky enough to have someone like Duggins. He was a Vietnam vet and brought to the unit his combat experience which was a valuable commodity for us.

While at Hafar al-Batin, we began taking PB tablets. Pyridostigmine Bromide was issued to us in blister packs of 21 tablets. We took one every eight hours, three times a day. Each sleeve of PBs would last one week. We would literally watch each other take the tab. Those were the orders. With the Scud missile threat and Iraq's known production of chemical weapons, the PBs would give us a chance to survive a nerve agent attack. Given enough time for the drug to build up in the system, the PBs would not allow the nerve agent intended for paralysis and death to make a connection to the blood cell.

On the night of 18 January 1991, all of our M8A1 alarms went off. The alarm was the Army's main detection unit for chemical defense and had been used extensively since 1987. The M8A1 did have some false alarm tendencies as they would go off for a variety of reasons other than chemical detection. As a result of these "tendencies", some units would not take heed. However, we didn't take the alarm sound lightly. When ours went off that night, we quickly got into MOPP 4 (Mission Oriented Protective Posture). After securing our protection, we quickly made sure the other guys in the platoon did the same. The following morning, we received word that the M8A1 alarms had false alarmed due to fog in the area.

The days that followed at Hafar al-Batin were more relaxed than with our initial days. When the air war began, we were concerned with the counter-attack, but as days passed, the Air

Force began to take its toll on the Iraqis and had them going underground. It looked like the 502nd would not have to decisively engage the Iraqi armored formations. We did, however, have serious concerns about the Iraqi scud missiles and their capability for chemical weapon delivery.

With the more relaxed atmosphere came the humor. One morning we were notified we would be having a meeting with First Sergeant Batie of Charlie Company. SSG Ian Berkowitz, being the cut up that he was, brought a stray donkey up to our position just before the meeting. As he walked up the path he announced he was bringing the First Sergeant a "little ass." Berk had become a great friend and had the gift of making people laugh. Even in the most stressful situations, he would always have a joke or a funny story to tell. It was a blessing to have him among us, and it boosted our platoon's morale. He also had the rank to pull it off. If a private said and did some of that stuff, he would have quickly been put in his place.

SSG Ian Berkowitz with the 1st Sergeant's little donkey – Hafar al-Batin
Courtesy of Ian Berkowitz

My short-wave radio was the only link to the outside world and "news." I had the only short-wave, and guys would hover close by when they could. I felt like a news anchorman. The United States was sending Patriot missile defense systems to Israel, Iraqis were destroying oil-fields in Kuwait, scuds had attacked Riyadh, and a scud was hit by a Patriot missile north of Hafar al-Batin. I wondered if that scud was aimed at us or was intended to go further into Saudi Arabia. Even though there were a lot of reporting errors, that radio link to the outside world also improved morale.

The commanders in Riyadh had to be convinced that the enemy was sufficiently blind before we made our move northwest. As a result, Coalition Air Forces attacked the centralized command and control, communication facilities, and air defense systems, as well as the large enemy formations to our north. With the task force needing to move northwest toward Rafha, the Iraqis had to be pinned down so they couldn't see the movement from such a large force. Or, if they did, they would have limited communications to report it. Our movement was just a small piece of a giant task force staging for the attack into Iraq. The big stage could now be set for G-Day (Ground Operations Day) operations.

On 25 January 1991, after two weeks at Hafar al-Batin, the 502nd and 1-320th FA were released from the 1st Cavalry Division's tactical control. Our unit loaded up into buses and moved in a task force convoy a couple hundred miles northwest to task force assembly area (TAA) Campbell near Rafha. As the division was repositioning north, the blistering air bombardment of Iraq continued. Eight days into Operation Desert Storm and the air war, Coalition Air Forces had secured the air space and flown almost 20,000 sorties.

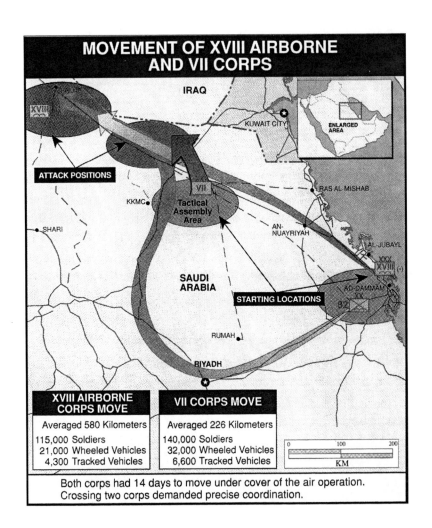

MOVEMENT OF XVIII AIRBORNE AND VII CORPS

IRAQ

KUWAIT CITY

ENLARGED AREA

ATTACK POSITIONS

XVIII

VII

RAS AL-MISHAB

KKMC

Tactical Assembly Area

AN-NUAYRIYAH

AL-JUBAYL

SHARI

XXX XVIII (-)

SAUDI ARABIA

AD-DAMMAM

STARTING LOCATIONS

XX 82

RUMAH

RIYADH

XVIII AIRBORNE CORPS MOVE	VII CORPS MOVE
Averaged 580 Kilometers	Averaged 226 Kilometers
115,000 Soldiers	140,000 Soldiers
21,000 Wheeled Vehicles	32,000 Wheeled Vehicles
4,300 Tracked Vehicles	6,600 Tracked Vehicles

0   100   200

KM

Both corps had 14 days to move under cover of the air operation.
Crossing two corps demanded precise coordination.

Chapter 6

TAA Campbell

Until the air war started, General Schwarzkopf, his division Generals, and their command staff were the only ones briefed on the move far to the west and G-Day (Ground Operations Day) operations. Company commanders and lower level leaders, (as well as Saddam), incorrectly perceived that the tri-border area of Iraq, Kuwait, and Saudi Arabia would be as far west as the Coalition forces would go before attacking. Saddam couldn't see our movement to the west because his eyes on the battlefield were blinded by relentless Coalition air attacks. Saddam was preparing for a pre-WWI style frontal assault, but General Schwarzkopf had something much greater in mind. On G-Day, his vision was to execute the "Hail Mary" plan to outflank and destroy the Iraqi forces. "The strategy was aimed as much at the enemy's mind and morale as weapons and troops." The plan would use the strengths of the 101st Airborne Division to attack deep, behind enemy lines, all the way to the Euphrates Valley and interdicting Highway 8. To prepare for this massive flanking movement, coalition forces would have to accomplish a risky, long range logistical move to the west. If successful, the division's attack would be far greater and deeper than previously envisioned. General Schwarzkopf's overall plan had his troop's welfare at heart. He wanted to accomplish a quick, strong attack that would minimize losses. He continually told his war planners, "Don't give me a meat-grinder."

Tapline Road is a major artery that runs beside an oil pipeline from the industrial ports of Saudi Arabia along the Persian Gulf and along the borders of Kuwait and Iraq to the northwest. The road had become a major Main Supply Route (MSR) for the movement of coalition troops and supplies, especially when commanders started building up corps level troops and armor divisions to the west. Tapline Road had bumper to bumper traffic with long convoys making their way west. The road earned the nickname "Suicide Alley" as local drivers weaved violently through the slow moving convoys.

For the 101st, the relocation from Camp Eagle II involved some 4,000 vehicles traveling six hundred fifteen miles with five hundred fifty C-130 Hercules sorties and three hundred fifty helicopters flying some three hundred air miles. The 101st moved over 17,000 soldiers by ground and air from Camp Eagle II to TAA Campbell, part of an even greater move by the XVIII Airborne Corps' which moved its three full combat divisions. General Luck's XVIII Airborne Corps total active, reserve combat support, and combat service support units brought his corps' total strength to over 115,000 soldiers, 21,000 vehicles, and 980 aircraft. The VII Corps combined strength would be over 140,000 soldiers, 32,000 vehicles and 600 aircraft. This great build-up of ground forces was in preparation for G-Day, when the two corps and Coalition forces south of Kuwait would unleash their massive force against Saddam Hussein's forces.

TAA Campbell was immense, and its 3,200 square kilometers took up an area equivalent to four times the land mass of New York City or two times the size of sprawling Houston, Texas. It was located approximately seventy-five kilometers southeast of Rafha, and five miles southwest of the disputed border between Iraq and Saudi Arabia. Once into position, the threat to the 101st would come from Iraqi artillery units and terrorists from Tapline Road.

It was cold and wet on 25 January when we arrived at TAA Campbell, and the annual rainy season was upon us. Reeling from the hypothermic conditions at Hafar al-Batin, I wasn't feeling great about another cold and wet location. We nicknamed it the "rock garden." It looked like another planet as rocks sprouted up out of a very flat, firm desert floor. We had all of our equipment, including shelter halves and sleeping bags which made the cold more bearable at night. Upon arrival, the platoon found a suitable place to dig fighting positions. After setting up our positions and security, we settled into our sleeping bags for the night. In the middle of the night it started raining, and water started flowing into our fighting positions. As we fought a losing battle with the rain, I was reminded of the quarry, and I knew we were facing another miserable night.

Although it was futile, I tried to dig a barrier around the tent but the water streamed in. My mind raced back to my youth. Mom and Dad were both school teachers, and during the summer break they would pack up our Volkswagon van with camping supplies, my brother, sister and me, and set out on wonderful scenic journeys and camping trips. During one of these excursions in New Mexico, we had just set up camp and settled into our warm sleeping bags for the night when the rains came.

In the mountains at night it got cold, yet our family was happy and snug in the tent hearing the rains come down. Everything was good until water started trickling into the tent. We weren't in a low lying area. We were just in the way of water coming into the campsite from the higher mountain above. Dad grabbed his entrenching tool, rushed out in the storm, and began digging a trench to divert the water around the tent. The trickle of water turned into a stream of water through the tent. After a half hour of futile digging, he made the command decision for the family to get into the car. We went to a local hotel while leaving the tent behind. The next day we drove back to the campsite and dried everything out. As all of this water was coming into the tent at TAA Campbell, I was outside the tent trying to dig a trench around it to divert the water. It was like digging around a bathtub full of water. The digging was to no avail as the quickly rising water overtook my position. I think I needed a pail instead of an e-tool. I was wishing I had a vehicle I could throw all of this crap into and go to a hotel to get warm and dry. It was just another day in paradise.

On Monday, it was all about drying our gear out and finding a more suitable position for the platoon. It was a clear, nice day, and it had *only* dipped down to twenty-nine degrees the night before. I turned on the shortwave to get a little news. The previous day, the New York Giants narrowly defeated the Buffalo Bills in the Super Bowl by a score of 20-19. Wow, close game. Wish I could have watched it. I was sure glad I had the radio. At least I got the score. The update from a taped report described the red, white, and blue hung at Tampa Stadium and the stirring rendition of the "Star Spangled Banner" sung by Whitney Houston. The reporter described the extreme patriotism shown at the game and that many became emotional at the sight. From a foxhole in the desert, it was reassuring to know people back home were supporting our mission and sharing the cause.

On 30 January 1991, we got word of a ground war clash between Marines and the Iraqis, and that eleven Marines had been killed in an engagement near Khafji. The first ground war operations were now underway, and we were far to the west of where the action was taking place. The first ground war now wasn't of our own making but that of Saddam. Receiving further word on 1 February 1990, we learned that Iraq was massing six divisions for an attack along the southern border of Kuwait and Saudi Arabia, stretching from the city of Umm Hujul to the city of Khafji which was fifty or so miles to the east. An artillery duel was going on between Marines and the Iraqis near Khafji. After massing along the border, the Iraqis began testing Coalition defenses while allied planes were bombing armored brigades and supply columns moving south into Saudi Arabia. It looked like the Iraqis had occupied Khafji for a time but had been run out by Coalition air and U.S. Marines. Then I got some real bad news; the previous day we lost a Spectre Gunship in the KTO (Kuwaiti

Theater of Operation) from a SAM (surface-to-air missile). There were no survivors. My mind raced. I thought about the gunship gunners back at KFIA that had given me the Spectre brief just the month before. Were any of my new friends lost? I wanted more news rather than the bits and pieces I was receiving. It felt as devastating as losing family members in a plane crash. It was my first real sense of loss in the war and it was excruciating not knowing the details.

On 4 February 1991, after ten days at TAA Campbell, we received our Company's Warning Order for FOB Cobra. The plan for the massive air assault was revealed. The 1st Battalion of the 502nd would join the 327th Infantry Regiment in the initial air assault into Iraq on G-Day morning. As the maps were unfolded, we saw that FOB Cobra was southeast of the city of As-Salman, and were told that after our landing to expect enemy armor moving from that direction. The early G-Day morning concept for the 101st was to seize Cobra ninety-three miles into Iraq, establishing a base for Apache attack helicopters to go even further into Iraq. The base would also be used for follow-on missions in and around Highway 8 and the Euphrates River Valley. Furthermore, the deep air assault into Iraq by the 101st would put the division in position to threaten Baghdad itself. After the warning order, we were briefed on Close Air Support (CAS) and artillery that would be at our disposal. Even as the plans for G-Day were being laid out, there was a flurry of activity from other nations to find a peaceful solution.

The world was seeing the destruction of Saddam's forces before its eyes. Now, after almost 45,000 Coalition Air Force sorties, we were told that 20 percent of the Iraqi tanks and artillery had been destroyed. As a result of the pounding, Iraq no longer had the fourth largest military. It was very good news to us as we went about our preparation for the largest air assault in history. During the briefing, I looked into the sky thinking about what we had just been told. I managed to catch a glimpse of a KC-135 Stratotanker flying high from the west to its southeast along the border. On a clear day, it was fun to see the refueler through my binoculars with a couple fighters positioning themselves behind to take on more fuel.

At TAA Campbell, the 502nd area of responsibility was the division rear as we were the last to arrive from Hafar al-Batin. We conducted patrols that would last most of the night. The area was so large, we marked the corners of our AO during the day with chem-lights so we would have a reference point at night. During the night-time patrols we would navigate from one illuminated checkpoint to another. I was concerned with our ability to navigate over long stretches and more concerned about overlapping other 101st patrols in the area and ending up in a friendly fire incident. We were looking for insurgent activity and protecting the division rear. A mis-oriented patrol could easily end up in a firefight with friendlies, not knowing either it or the other patrol is out of its area of responsibility. I was diligent in counting my paces, looking up to the sky for stars, using them and referring to my compass for direction. It was always a relief when a chem-light came into view.

The daily rehearsals for G-Day (the air assault into FOB Cobra), and night-time patrols kept us busy. To add to the G-Day preparations, we started rehearsing for the follow-on missions, "Strike" and "Gold." Objective Strike was a difficult airfield take-down northeast of Cobra at Tallil Airbase. Objective Gold was a known ASP (Ammo Supply Point) southeast of Tallil along Highway 8. The ASP was a known storage site for chemical weapons. Both objectives made me nervous because both were well defended, both required chemical protection, and we were told to expect casualties at both. It was always a tip-off about the objective when they said we could expect casualties.

G-Day was getting close as we were told the clock was set at G-7 (G-Day minus 7 days) on 14 February 1991. All of our preparations and rehearsals were starting to come together for this great invasion. With load plans and all objectives rehearsed, it was now time for the division and its commanders to determine what was ahead of us. On 17 February, the 101st was allowed by higher HQ to start feeling out what was ahead. Elements from our company were tasked with going across the border. As a result of this initial incursion into Iraqi territory, an Iraqi bunker complex was discovered. It didn't take long for our Apache helicopters to convince the small group to surrender by blasting them out of their cover. Twenty-six EPWs (enemy prisoners of war) were taken with no casualties in our unit. The prisoners from the 45th Division were in well-prepared positions and adequately supplied, but didn't show any will to fight, especially against the Apache helicopters. The following day our Company had the same mission. An Iraqi element of one hundred was discovered along MSR New Market, the supply route that was to be used by the 101st vehicle convoys to Cobra on G-Day. The Iraqi troops on our MSR were believed to be with the 45th Division, and were determined to be too large for our platoon to engage. I was thankful because at the end of the day our Blackhawk pilots ran into some mechanical difficulties when one of the helicopter's turbines and didn't have the power to get us in the air. We had to be left across the Iraqi border until another bird came to pick us up. It was a lonely feeling being left behind as the helicopters disappeared over the horizon. While waiting for a back-up, we set up perimeter security hoping the sun wouldn't go down before being extracted.

Over the next couple days we received further word about the Iraqi element of one hundred that was discovered on MSR New Market during our watch. It turned out these guys weren't so easy to defeat. They had to be blasted out of their positions by A-10s and attack helicopters; the force of one hundred turned out to be over four hundred. This Iraqi element from the 45th Division in the middle of our main supply route was labeled as an objective by division headquarters and given the name "Objective Toad." It was named for a toad in the road that had to be cleared if our convoys were to arrive at FOB Cobra on time. 1-187 was sent in to extract the prisoners, but it wasn't easy. Part of the force wanted to surrender while others wanted to resist and fight. It was basic infantry work: their unit had to shoot until no one shot back. The report came back that the Iraqis had good fighting positions.

I was upset about our helicopter's mechanical problems when these guys were initially discovered. And now, I was thankful our platoon didn't have to engage over four hundred. It would have been a bad day for 2nd platoon if we had flown into that hornet's nest.

On 19 February 1991, the G-Day clock was reset to G-5. We assumed the reset was due to Tariq Azziz, the Iraqi Foreign Minister working on a plan for peace crafted by the Russians. We didn't know or care. The extra couple days would give us more rehearsal time and perhaps more of the bad guys would be un-bunkered across the border.

It was great that some of the mail was now catching up with us. Letters and packages from home were always a morale booster. All of the letters from home were filled with words of encouragement and support as we were preparing for G-Day. As I leaned back on my ruck sack reading letters from home and eating stale cookies, I turned on the radio. Iraq was saying they were responding favorably to the Russian's 11th-hour negotiations to head off a ground war. Soviet leader, Mikhail Gorbachev had told President Bush that Saddam Hussein was no longer insisting that other Middle Eastern issues be tied to them pulling out of Kuwait and that Gorbachev insisted they be out of Kuwait in three weeks.

President Bush argued that Gorbachev's solution did not provide for reparations to Kuwait and compensation for environmental damage. It also did not deal with the Iraqi chemical, biological, and nuclear program. President Bush said their response fell short.

Bush stuck to his demand for the unconditional withdrawal of Iraqi forces from Kuwait which would begin no later than "12:00 U.N. time" on 23 February or the ground assault would proceed. On 22 February 1991, we got word that Iraq had said no to President Bush's seven day withdrawal ultimatum. In less than forty eight hours, G-Day would begin.

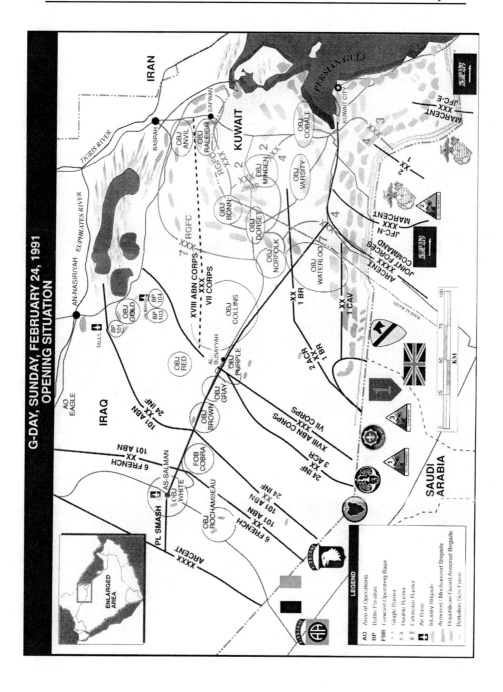

G-DAY, SUNDAY, FEBRUARY 24, 1991
OPENING SITUATION

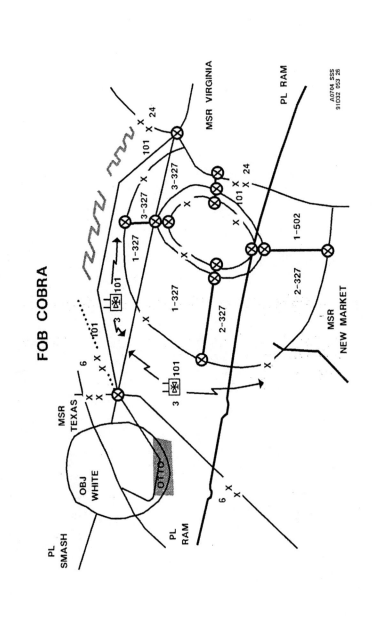

FOB COBRA

MSR VIRGINIA

PL RAM

MSR TEXAS

PL SMASH

OBJ WHITE

OTTO

PL RAM

MSR NEW MARKET

3-327

1-327

1-327

2-327

2-327

1-502

101

3

A0704 SSS
91D32 053 26

Chapter 7

G-Day
Forward Operating Base Cobra

The day of reckoning had arrived. President Bush gave the Iraqi dictator Saddam Hussein until 1700 hours Greenwich Mean Time on 23 February, 1991 to start pulling his forces out of Kuwait. By the end of one week, the Iraqi troops had to be completely out of the country. Saddam's regime said "no" to the demands.

Since mid-January, the Iraqis were blinded by the constant bombardment of the coalition's air campaign and, as a result, had limited knowledge of the XVIII Airborne Corps' mass movement to the northwest. Even if the Iraqis were aware of the movement, they could have done very little to prepare themselves and their defenses for what was to come. Even in our final preparations for G-Day, we were still wondering if Saddam would back down before the ground war began. There were many attempts, even by the Russians, to convince Saddam to accept a peaceful solution.

On Day G-2 (2 days until Ground Operations Day), at 0700 Zulu Hours, we received the following message from General Peay, the Commander of the 101st Airborne Division (Air Assault):

"SUBJECT: MESSAGE TO ALL SCREAMING EAGLES.

1. DIVISION OPORD 91-1 IS EFFECTIVE FOR EXECUTION UPON RECEIPT OF THIS MESSAGE. G-DAY H-HOUR IS 240600C FEB 91.

2. THE DIVISION'S NEXT RENDEZVOUS WITH DESTINY IS NORTH TO THE EUPHRATES RIVER. GOD SPEED AND GOOD LUCK!

3. AIR ASSAULT.

SIGNED MG PEAY"

After receipt of the message, we staged north of Pipeline Road with the 1st and 3rd Brigades. The move put all three brigades of the 101st in close proximity to each other. All three battalions of the 1st Brigade (327th Infantry) and our 1-502 would be part of the initial air assault: 93 miles into Iraq, code-named FOB Cobra. Securing the FOB fifty-six miles southeast of As Salman was critical to the 101st mission. Cobra would establish a necessary rapid refueling point (RRP) and provide a launching pad for the Screaming Eagles' follow-on missions in the Euphrates River Valley.

Our mission had been rehearsed for months. Our battalion would secure and occupy the southeast quadrant of the egg shaped FOB; the 2-327 would secure the southwest quadrant to our west; the 3-327 would secure the northeast quadrant to our north; and the 1-327 would secure the FOBs northwest side. The FOB was huge by any standards. Colonel Tom Hill's 1st Brigade plus our battalion (1-502) had the mission of securing an area encompassing two hundred square kilometers. The 101st Airborne Division's objective of severing the MSR along Highway 8, objectives "Strike" and "Gold", the "Baghdad Sequel", and any other follow-on missions would be hanging in the balance until FOB Cobra was secure. Without this objective, there would be no FARP (forward air refueling point) for our helicopters, and all of the division's air assault plans would stall.

We were prepared but anxious for what lay ahead of us. Our guys were charged up and ready to go as we made our move north of Pipeline in deuce and a half trucks. Some were talkative and laughing, while others were reflective and quiet. As for myself, I was a little of both, trying to exude that old Army NCO confidence outwardly and saying a prayer inwardly at the same time. Out of the blue, one of our infantry privates asked me, "Are you a religious man Sarge?" Startled by his question, and thinking my mental inward prayer had been out loud, I replied, "Yes I am." He said, "What does it take to be a religious man?" I thought for a second (or ten) and said, "Private, you don't have to go to church or see the chaplain to connect with God. Just pray, and Jesus will hear your prayer." The private asked if I would pray for him and I did. I was never a guy who wore my faith on my sleeve, but when asked, I would never shy away from a question about my beliefs. I always thought, rightly or wrongly, that people would be led in your direction if you had something they needed.

On 23 February 1991, G-1 (eve of Ground Operations Day), we co-located with our Blackhawk helicopters and with the rest of the brigade. As we moved closer to the pick-up zone (PZ), the only thing I could see in the desert were UH-60 Blackhawks, and to my right, CH-47 Chinooks. It was the first time since I had been in country that I had really seen the size and scope of the 101st Airborne Division and its helicopter assets in one place. At Camp Eagle II, we saw the rows and rows of tents, but I had never seen this many soldiers and helicopters together in my life. It sent chills up my spine as I thought, "There will never be a photograph that could capture this scene."

Shortly after our arrival at the PZ, LTC Donald, the 1-502nd Commander, gathered Charlie Company together and briefed us on "Sand Table Cobra" and what was about to take place. Donald said we were going to be placed next to the Blackhawk that would take us to FOB Cobra the next morning, and we were going to be a part of the "largest and longest air assault in history." He said if we were to become a casualty, we would not be left behind in Iraq. It was then that reality set in, envisioning the pivotal event that lay before us. While he was speaking, CH-47s were flying in and his voice could barely be heard over the roar of the engines.

After LTC Donald spoke, the 101st Chaplain came over and spoke to us and prayed. After sharing some scripture and words of encouragement, the Chaplain said, "None of us would be lost the next day." My mind raced as I heard those words and thought... no one will be lost in the largest and longest air assault in history? Wow! Those are powerful words there, chaplain. I hope you are right!

As we moved to our assigned Blackhawks, I couldn't help but notice there was nose art on all of the helicopters, like "Yosemite Sam" nearby and our helicopter had "White Lightning" drawn on her nose. I felt that the name on ours was "right on" and appreciated the crew chief's artistry. Upon introductions to the crew members, CW2 E. Joyce Strait, CW2 Alan Owenby, and crew chief, Sgt. Phil Barbera, I made the mental connection that one of the two pilots would be female. I didn't care either way. I just didn't know we had female pilots in the division. The crew was professional, upbeat, and accommodating as we surveyed the Blackhawk that would take us to our "Rendezvous with Destiny."

We rehearsed our load plan which involved fitting three crew members and sixteen soldiers plus ruck sacks onto a bird that should hold twelve soldiers and three crewmembers max (See appendix. White Lightning soldier and crew list). In the main cabin, there would be the crew chief and sixteen of us sitting on our ruck sacks. The first thing we did was to position all rucks upright on the floor of the helicopter, and then climbed on top of the rucks. It took us a while to figure it out. My comment was very inappropriate for the time, "This will look like a can of Spam if we go down tomorrow." No one laughed, not even me.

That evening we received our last mail call. It was bad, but yet good timing for packages from home. I am sure we looked like a pack of dogs as we tore into the packages hoping for something to eat. Here it was, 23 February 1991, and we haven't even seen a T-Ration since 9 January at Camp Eagle II, the night before we went to Hafar al-Batin. The only food we had since was MREs and a package from home I had received just a couple days before.

As we made our way through the boxes and packing material, there they were – the cookies and cakes that had been lovingly baked and sent three weeks before. Yeah, they may have been old, but at that time they tasted "freshly baked." Everyone at "White Lightning" shared in the feast from the States that G-Day eve, as though it were our "last supper." After we gorged ourselves on baked goods from home, we packed a roll of toilet paper from home along with the AA batteries I would use for the short wave radio, razor, and mini mag-lite and threw away the remainder. We then stripped and broke down our MREs into the bare necessities, allowing one meal a day for the next three days. Our rucks were over-weight, and with our canteens full of water and ammo, we would be carrying one hundred pounds or more. Very little extra stuff was taken in the "home on our backs."

As the sun set on G-Day eve, all of our final preparations were complete. Several of us had U.S. Flags we passed around for signing by all of the "White Lightning" crew and fellow soldiers: nineteen printed signatures on small flags. After signing the flags, we placed them back in the web-liners of our Kevlar helmets. In the dim light on 23 February 1991, the only thing I could see were the silhouettes of Blackhawk helicopters and the movement of soldiers around them. The reality of war was upon us. The enormity of the event was before us. For a while that evening, I reflected on the eve of the D-Day Invasion in 1944 and the 101st Airborne Division soldiers milling around their C-47 transports, the same as we were doing some forty-seven years later by our Blackhawks.

As night-time settled in, we dug out the MRE instant coffee packs. The crew chief of "White Lightning" showed us how to heat water using Jet-A fuel in an ammo can, half-filled with sand. We were impressed. We were used to heating water by burning some broken dry brush or some sterno in a hole about a foot deep during daylight, and we never would burn anything at night for fear of being spotted. The division planners stretched Cobra to the Blackhawk's operational limit. With every drop of fuel needed for our mission the following morning, I was in hopes we weren't using the last drops needed by our Blackhawk making coffee. As we enjoyed our aromatic "Jet-A" coffee, we talked about family and friends back home and wondered what they would be talking about tomorrow after the kick-off of the Ground War. We tried to relax, but it felt like we were on the eve of the Super Bowl and we were the players. The weather at TAA Campbell had been pleasant during the day, but turned cold at night. It was also a little windy as we huddled around "White Lightning" wrapped in our ponchos. There was very little sleep, but some tried.

While we were attempting to get a little shut-eye, division was putting the final touches on our air assault into Iraq. The air assault mission is a fluid one, capable of making last minute changes to get the upper hand on the opponent. It is very much like a quarterback making an audible or change in the play at the line of scrimmage after observing an unsatisfactory defensive alignment. At the last minute, Division Main Headquarters (DMAIN) found through other intelligence sources that the planned LZ (landing zone) for 1-327 was right on top of the Iraqis. Without constant diligence that involved checking and cross checking plans, the original LZ could result in substantial casualties. In addition to last minute re-checks by the DMAIN, long range recon patrols ("Lurps") or Long Range Surveillance Detachment (LRSD) teams were being inserted into Iraq. Their job was to observe and report any enemy activity back to DMAIN without being observed themselves. To avoid detection, Lurps teams blended into their environment and had the discipline to remain silent and motionless for hours on end. Lurps teams had nothing to report at FOB Cobra except clear weather. This sealed the LZ locations and required no further changes in the division's plan.

In the first few hours of G-Day morning, the fog rolled in as predicted. At 0330 hrs, an OH58D (observer helicopter) from the 1-9th Cav Target Acquisition and Reconnaissance Platoon which was to screen the pathfinder mission crashed, resulting in injury to the occupants, but no deaths. The crew was lucky it happened just ahead of our Line of Departure (LD). They were recovered by our guys instead of the Iraqis. As a result of the fog and the crash, the pathfinder mission was set back, and the division chose to insert pathfinders with the 1-101 AATK's screening mission. We were delayed. In perfect conditions, our Blackhawks would be stretching their fuel to get into Cobra, and the limited visibility would slow the helicopters down resulting in higher fuel consumption. Once we lifted off, it would be 90mph all the way to Cobra.

The original plan was for us to go into Cobra at 0500, but the fog would delay our departure time a couple of hours. While we were waiting, we stuffed White Lightning with our ruck sacks. Everyone was ready and eager to do our business, and the day of days had finally come for Saddam and his ruthless regime. As we waited, I turned on my short-wave radio to catch the news from around the world. Most of the report was about us and the impending ground attack. As we huddled around the radio, we heard the reporter from The White House stop what he was saying to announce that the President was about to speak. We heard the following:

President George H.W. Bush from The White House:

"Good evening. Yesterday, after conferring with my senior national security advisers, and following extensive consultations with our coalition partners, Saddam Hussein was given one last chance -- set forth in very explicit terms -- to do what he should have done more than 6 months ago: withdraw from Kuwait without condition or further delay, and comply fully with the resolutions passed by the United Nations Security Council.

Regrettably, the noon deadline passed without the agreement of the Government of Iraq to meet demands of United Nations Security Council Resolution 660, as set forth in the specific terms spelled out by the coalition to withdraw unconditionally from Kuwait. To the contrary, what we have seen is a redoubling of Saddam Hussein's efforts to destroy completely Kuwait and its people.

I have therefore directed General Norman Schwarzkopf, in conjunction with coalition forces, to use all forces available including ground forces to eject the Iraqi army from Kuwait. Once again, this was a decision made only after extensive consultations within our coalition partnership.

105

The liberation of Kuwait has now entered a final phase. I have complete confidence in the ability of the coalition forces swiftly and decisively to accomplish their mission.

Tonight, as this coalition of countries seeks to do that which is right and just, I ask only that all of you stop what you are doing and say a prayer for all the coalition forces, and especially for our men and women in uniform who this very moment are risking their lives for their country and for all of us.

May God bless and protect each and every one of them. And may God bless the United States of America. Thank you very much."

Within a few minutes after the President's announcement, four battalions of the 101ˢᵗ Airborne Division began loading their sixty-six Blackhawk helicopters. We crammed inside one at a time, taking our seats on the ruck sacks. Once all aboard, we closed the door and the engines began to warm up.

Along with our sixty-six UH-60 Blackhawks, there were thirty CH47 Chinooks accompanied by Cobra and Apache gunships as escorts. The Air Force was above the Screaming Eagle Armada to ensure the 101ˢᵗ package was delivered safely to Cobra. At 0730 hrs, as if choreographed by a symphony conductor, the flock of eagles lifted gracefully in the air, causing a near brown-out condition at the PZ. Once airborne, we all turned gently to the north and picked up speed until we reached ninety mph at fifty feet off the ground. Looking out of the windows of the tightly packed Blackhawk, the only thing I could see were birds in the air which caused my heart to race. As we reached cruising speed, the ground began rushing by us as we crossed the line of departure leaving TAA Campbell.

"Cry Havoc. Let loose the dogs of war," was First Brigade TF Commander Colonel Hill's quote as we thundered toward Cobra in the largest air assault attack ever mounted. The mood on White Lightning was solemn as we made the noisy, bumpy ride toward FOB Cobra. We were cramped and could barely move, but the speed that we were traveling as well as time felt like "fast forward." It took us about an hour to make the ninety-three mile trip. As we approached FOB Cobra, "Hot LZ" was yelled by the pilot. There was enemy contact. Our pilots came into our LZ quickly with Blackhawks in front and on our tail. The helicopter began to flare out as the pilots picked their spot, dropping the tail way below the nose and using the large rotors as a brake to reduce speed. About thirty feet off the ground, we popped the door.

G-Day Morning at FOB Cobra. February 24, 1991
Courtesy of the Don F. Pratt Museum

I could feel the tail wheel hit the ground and almost immediately the front wheels made contact. Once all wheels were on the ground, we flung the door open and jumped off the bird, belly flopping on rocks that were around the helicopter. Marty, my RTO was off-loading ruck sacks when one got hung up. He pulled until the jammed ruck released, throwing him to the ground. When he fell, I heard him say he was hurt and I was praying he hadn't been shot. As soon as all the rucks were unloaded, the Blackhawk leapt back in the air. When Marty fell down, he hit a sharp rock with his knee. One thing we were not accustomed to in the desert was rocks. It made for a firm landing pad for our Blackhawk, but a painful landing for our bodies. Marty had trouble getting up, and as 2nd platoon was rallying to proceed to the objective, I told the platoon sergeant to move on and we would catch up. After a few minutes, which seemed like a day, Marty and I started to make our way toward a hill on the southeast side of Cobra which was our Company's objective. Marty was limping badly, and the one hundred pound ruck sacks we were carrying didn't help him at all.

Thankfully, the hot LZ wasn't hot at our location or we would have had a bad day. Marty would not have been able to move. The hot LZ was northwest of us in the 1-327 AO. Had it not been for the last minute change back at TAA Campbell the night before, 1-327 would have landed right on top of an enemy bunker complex at the escarpment. Also, just north of us, 3-327 made contact with a small force of Iraqi soldiers. The Iraqis were quickly captured. Just to their west, A Company, 1-327 made contact with a much larger Iraqi force. The 1st Battalion, 82nd Brigade of Iraq's 45th Division was dug in well just north of MSR Virginia. A sharp firefight ensued.

The 3-327 called for fire support, and attack helicopters along with two A-10s strafed the Iraqi bunkers. One battery of six guns from the 2-320th also hit the Iraqi position with artillery, and marked the objective for the infantry. After the target was prepped, the 1-327 moved three miles toward the Iraqi bunker complex. When the 1-327 closed on the Iraqi position, the Iraqi battalion commander surrendered. After his surrender, the Iraqi commander was persuaded to use a bullhorn to convince his three hundred thirty-nine soldiers to lay down their arms.

While we were clearing Cobra, 101st Attack helicopters engaging in a screening mission to the north came under fire. One Apache was hit by anti-aircraft artillery (AAA) fire. Though damaged, the helicopter made it back to Cobra.

Marty and I made our way to our objective a little late, but better than never, and immediately began digging our fighting positions. Our guys seemed relieved to see we had made it back.

After checking Marty out, we moved to the edge of the hill and surveyed the desert floor below us. It appeared that there were some vehicles moving in our direction about three miles away with a Cobra gunship on their tail. Although they appeared a long way from us, we did not want to give away our position.

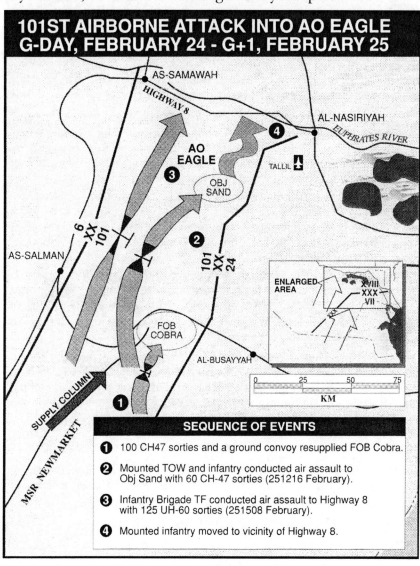

101ST AIRBORNE ATTACK INTO AO EAGLE
G-DAY, FEBRUARY 24 - G+1, FEBRUARY 25

AS-SAMAWAH

HIGHWAY 8

AL-NASIRIYAH

EUPHRATES RIVER

AO EAGLE

❹

TALLIL

❸

OBJ SAND

6 XX 101

AS-SALMAN

❷

101 XX 24

ENLARGED AREA

XVIII
XXX
VII

FOB COBRA

AL-BUSAYYAH

0   25   50   75
KM

SUPPLY COLUMN

❶

MSR NEWMARKET

SEQUENCE OF EVENTS

❶ 100 CH47 sorties and a ground convoy resupplied FOB Cobra.

❷ Mounted TOW and infantry conducted air assault to Obj Sand with 60 CH-47 sorties (251216 February).

❸ Infantry Brigade TF conducted air assault to Highway 8 with 125 UH-60 sorties (251508 February).

❹ Mounted infantry moved to vicinity of Highway 8.

Called a "bold and bodacious action" by the 101st public affairs officer, Cobra was now secure. The ninety-six aircraft completed the second lift from TAA Campbell by noon and had inserted over two thousand soldiers, fifty TOWs, and two artillery battalions. From my OP (observation post), Cobra looked like a very busy airport as CH47s and their sling loads made their way into Cobra from the south. What Command Sergeant Major Duggins called "The convoy from Hell": six hundred thirty-two vehicles carrying almost two thousand soldiers departed TAA Campbell making their slow journey north along MSR Newmarket to Cobra. I was grateful my cramped flight to Cobra only took an hour. It took the soldiers in vehicles half a day for the trip, and the final elements of the convoy arrived in the early morning hours of 25 February.

Vehicles moving up MSR New Market on G-Day
Courtesy of the Don F. Pratt Museum

FOB Cobra with its 750,000 gallon aviation refueling point was now a base of "critical tactical and operational importance." It could now serve as a base from which the division could launch its follow-on missions into the Euphrates River Valley, cutting the enemy's lines of communication and blocking the Iraqi escape route along Highway 8. If called upon, the base could also be used to launch an air assault on Baghdad itself. As Cobra was being established, final preparations were being made for Third Brigade's air assault into the Euphrates River on the 25th.

On G+1, the convoys from TAA Campbell had closed on Cobra, and we began staging for further operations. The shortwave news from the BBC said the 101st was deep in Iraq. It had established a refuel point, and there had been over 20,000 enemy prisoners of war taken by coalition forces. I wasn't real pleased with that news because it was also telling Baghdad where we were. As Third Brigade's task was to cut supply and communications along the Euphrates, "Strike" brigade had been given the task of taking down Tallil (Objective Strike). Tallil Airfield was a formidable objective and near the ancient city of Ur, the home of Abraham from which the three great religions of Judaism, Christianity, and Islam arose. The Air Force B-52s would be included, as well as every weapon in the sky, plus a massive artillery barrage from the 1-320th. The 101st thirty-eight Apaches with a concentration of Hellfire missiles unequalled in any one mission would help prep the objective.

Tallil Airfield was a vast complex of concrete and bunkers, with radar, AAA (anti-aircraft artillery), and surface-to-air missile sites. The perimeter of Tallil was secured by dug-in tanks and barbed wire fences. One day into the ground war, there had been no 101st deaths, but our leaders were prepping us for hundreds or more to be lost. This operation wasn't one of going where the enemy was not. It was going headfirst into a well defended, republican guard-held complex with the possibility of chemical weapons. There was apprehension. The take-down of Tallil would be massive in scope, and the hottest of LZs. What made Tallil even more difficult was that our attack would be within easy reach of the Iraqi radar.

During the Iran-Iraq war, Iraqi aircraft flying from Tallil attacked Iran with chemical weapons. There was an "S-shaped" bunker at Tallil that analysts associated with chemical weapons storage. Six kilometers northeast of Tallil was an ammunition storage point (ASP) made up of about one hundred ammunition storage buildings and bunkers. Before the Gulf War, U.S. Forces believed this to be a chemical weapons storage facility. The Tallil airfield take-down had all of us nervous. When sand table rehearsals included the possibility of chemical protection, it could not be a good thing. Fighting a war in chemical protection would be cumbersome, and none of us knew what chemicals were there or how they would be delivered. Shoot, the massive air prep on the objective may release the chemical agents, and the Iraqis wouldn't have to shoot a thing. We might kill ourselves!

Another known chemical storage site on the division radar was an objective to the southeast of Tallil, code-named Gold. Objective Gold was an ammo supply point that warehoused chemical weapons thirty-five kilometers southeast of An Nasiriyah near Khamisiyah. Objective Gold was just five kilometers south of the large ammunition supply point (ASP), covering forty square kilometers with approximately one hundred ammunition storage bunkers and eighty-eight ammunition storage buildings. Gold was south of a canal and Highway 8, and offered a direct route between Kuwait and Baghdad. The objective would not only be to secure the ASP, but block Iraq's forces attempting to escape Kuwait.

After the morning fog lifted, Third Brigade took off from TAA Campbell to make their way north of Cobra to the Euphrates. We heard them coming from the south, and watched as they made their way past Cobra. Flying by our perimeter, we could see the Blackhawks of TF Rakkasan as they raced toward AO Eagle and their Euphrates, Highway 8 objectives. I later found out that my forward observer buddies with the Rakkasans were sloshing around in the mud when they reached the Euphrates. With the 45th Iraqi Division's and world news report to Baghdad regarding the helicopter soldiers' occupation of the Euphrates and Cobra, Saddam was concerned about the 101st threat to Baghdad. Tariq Aziz, Saddam Hussein's foreign minister protested to the United Nations that our division's occupation in Iraq was outside the Security Council mandate, and Saddam started moving Republican Guard back up Highway 8 from Basrah.

On 26 February (G+2), we were stuck inside our desert hooches because of a sand storm. It was hard to see fifty yards, and no one strayed very far from our platoon AO for fear of getting lost. To my surprise, Vern Sizemore and his driver, PFC Farwell made their way to our location by HUMMV to share mapping information and radio frequencies on Tallil (Objective Strike) and the ASP at Objective Gold. Vern shared with us his all night ride on "The Highway from Hell" from TAA Campbell up MSR New Market to Cobra. After hearing about the "Convoy from Hell" once again, I was pleased I had made the ride by Blackhawk.

On the night of 26 February 1991, we received a change in mission, one that we had not rehearsed or planned. The war was moving quickly, and our Coalition's advance was moving faster than planned. VII Corps was carving their way through Iraqi armored divisions to the east nearing Kuwait, and Iraqi troops were attempting to move up Highway 8 to Baghdad. Because of the fast moving war, 24th Infantry Division got the nod for the Tallil take-down, and we received the new FOB Viper mission.

Viper would help tie the noose around Saddam and his Republican Guard forces now trapped in Kuwait and desperately trying to move back to Baghdad to defend Saddam himself. I didn't know what lay ahead at Viper, but felt like I had received another answer to prayer. As with Hafar al-Batin, when Iraqi armor bogged down in their approach to the wadi, we had somehow dodged two more bullets at Objectives Strike and Gold. The sand storm that had caused the delay in Third Brigade's move to the Euphrates and delayed Second Brigade's reconnection at Cobra was actually a blessing. Sometimes there is a bigger plan that can override the objectives of even the most lethal armies of the world. The bigger plan used rain and sand to force those battle plans to change. I am convinced that it saved lives on both sides.

One of the optional plans for the 101st at Cobra and the Euphrates was to perch the Screaming Eagles on the outskirts of Baghdad. Had we done so, the message to Saddam and the Iraqi people would have been clear. With his division only an hour and a half away, General Peay had that play in his playbook. I suspect had we done so, the Coalition would have splintered and perhaps agreed with Tariq Aziz that we were overstepping our UN mandate of just expelling Iraq from Kuwait.

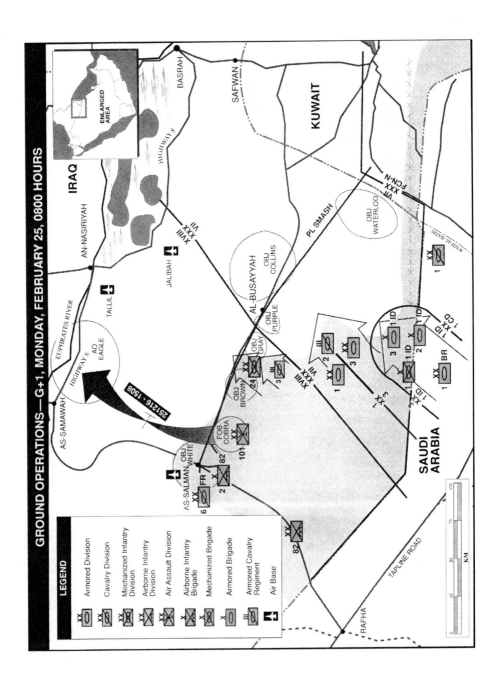

GROUND OPERATIONS—G+1, MONDAY, FEBRUARY 25, 0800 HOURS

LEGEND

Armored Division	
Cavalry Division	
Mechanized Infantry Division	
Airborne Infantry Division	
Air Assault Division	
Airborne Infantry Brigade	
Mechanized Brigade	
Armored Brigade	
Armored Cavalry Regiment	
Air Base	

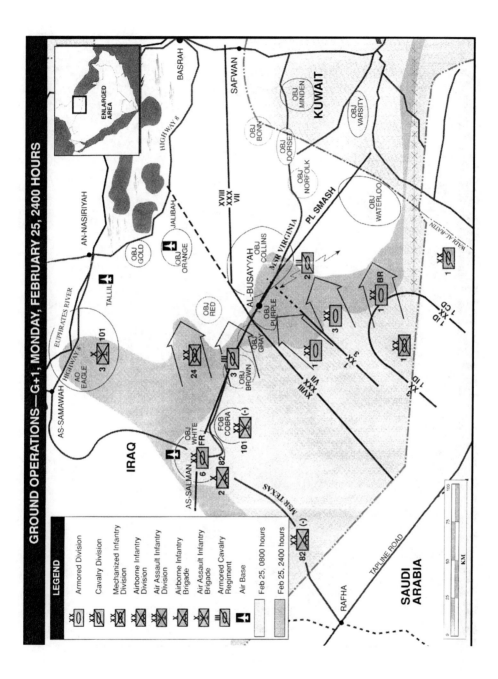

GROUND OPERATIONS—G+1, MONDAY, FEBRUARY 25, 2400 HOURS

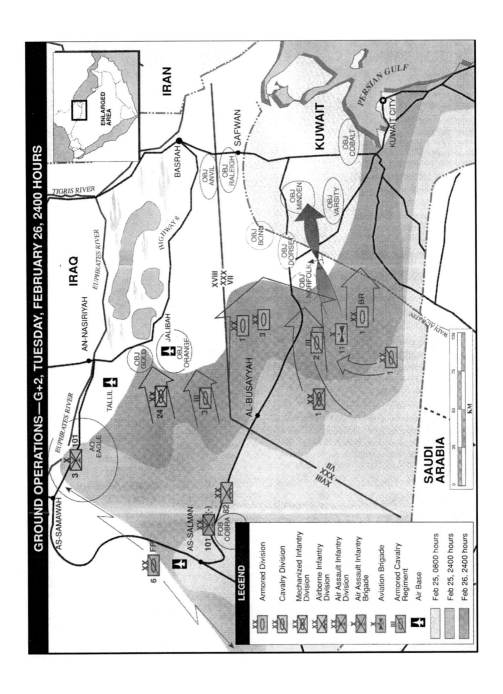

GROUND OPERATIONS—G+2, TUESDAY, FEBRUARY 26, 2400 HOURS

Cobra attack helicopters moving up Main Supply Route
New Market on G Day. Courtesy of the Don F. Pratt Museum

Chinook CH – 47 coming into FOB Cobra on G Day morning
Courtesy of the Don F. Pratt Museum

Helicopters at FOB Cobra on G Day
Courtesy of the Don F. Pratt Museum

Chinook CH – 47 coming into FOB Cobra with fuel blivots
Courtesy of the Don F. Pratt museum

Division scouts guiding vehicles to their unit locations on G Day
Courtesy of the Don F. Pratt Museum

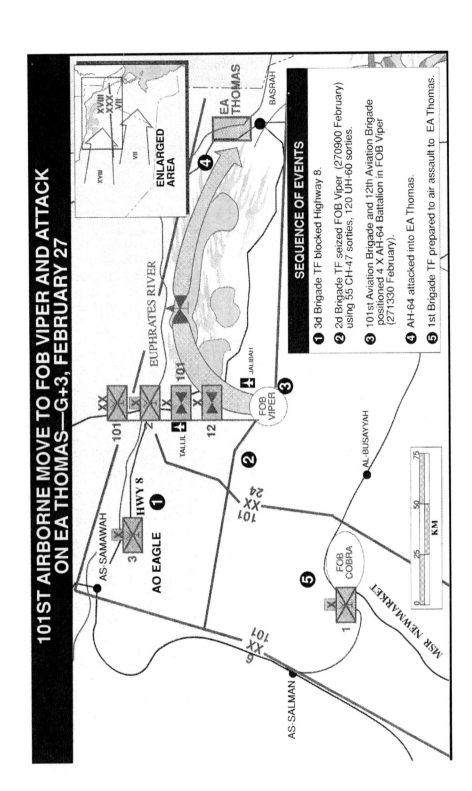

101ST AIRBORNE MOVE TO FOB VIPER AND ATTACK ON EA THOMAS—G+3, FEBRUARY 27

SEQUENCE OF EVENTS

1. 3d Brigade TF blocked Highway 8.
2. 2d Brigade TF seized FOB Viper (270900 February) using 55 CH-47 sorties, 120 UH-60 sorties.
3. 101st Aviation Brigade and 12th Aviation Brigade positioned 4 X AH-64 Battalion in FOB Viper (271330 February).
4. AH-64 attacked into EA Thomas.
5. 1st Brigade TF prepared to air assault to EA Thomas.

Chapter 8

FOB Viper
Lost in the Storm

Our battalion was located on the southeast quadrant of Cobra and had a long road march to reach the Blackhawks positioned for the early morning lift to Viper. As we made our way through the cool night air to the PZ, the extreme weight of my ruck tore into my shoulders. There was no comfortable position as I tried to ignore the agony of carrying the one hundred pound weight. Every couple minutes, we all would make feeble attempts to adjust our shoulder straps to relieve the pressure, but nothing would reduce the load. After a mile of that, I felt like a pack mule. As uncomfortable as it was, no one was talking or complaining as we made our slow move to the north. I was thankful that the ground was firm and that we weren't making this tortuous journey in loose sand. That night I also caught a glimpse of how immense this FOB was.

After what seemed to be days, we made it to our PZ, and Lt. Rysewyk quickly found the bird that would be transporting us to Viper. We shed the extra weight on our backs, and the relief came instantly. I tuned my shortwave radio to the BBC, and used my ear plugs to block any distracting ambient noise. The BBC reported that there were now over 50,000 EPWs (enemy prisoners of war) and that coalition forces were closing in on Kuwait City. Those that could sleep got a little shut eye leaning on their ruck sacks, and those of us that couldn't just talked about our new objective: Viper. I knew the area was covered in Blackhawks, but I couldn't see them in the dark. My mind shifted back to what seemed like weeks ago as we staged for our lift to Cobra, envisioning the massive sight of Blackhawks, as far as the eye could see. I would also catch myself as my thoughts drifted to home and what homecoming was going to be like, but then I forced myself to quickly refocus on the task and mission at hand.

FOB Viper was a 502nd, (2nd Brigade) mission. Colonel Ted Purdom regained control of us from 1st Brigade, and borrowed one of their battalions (3-327) for the air assault into Viper. Due to weather delays, 2nd Battalion of the 502nd (2nd Brigade) was still at TAA Campbell. Artillery support for the brigade would be provided by the 1-320th Field Artillery (FA) Battalion with their eighteen 105mm howitzers along with eight 155mm howitzers from C Battery of the 5-8th FA Battalion.

SSG Vern Sizemore shortly before lift to FOB Viper, 27 February
Courtesy Ernie Swindle

After a couple hours of waiting, we received the word to load up. As with our load plan at TAA Campbell on G-Day morning, we stuffed the Blackhawk with our ruck sacks and climbed aboard, sitting on top of them. After all of the anticipation and excitement of G-Day morning, this lift seemed routine as we positioned ourselves as comfortably as we could for the ride to Viper. As we took off, the Blackhawks gently turned to the east and stormed ninety miles to our new LZ.

FOB Viper would be a critical objective in the fast-paced ground war. The division would use the FOB for 101st attack helicopter assets to launch further northeast and to interdict Saddam's forces leaving Kuwait. It was important that as much of Iraq's war machine be destroyed as possible so it couldn't be used against coalition forces in a counter-attack or opposing the Iraqi resistance. When Iraqi armor defenses caved to the overwhelming approach of the Coalition forces, Saddam read the handwriting on the wall. He knew his days were limited in Kuwait. He was cut off from a substantial number of his elite forces and their equipment, so he gave the order for them to escape from Kuwait or risk annihilation. FOB Viper would be shutting the back door of a burning building full of snakes, with our attack helicopters waiting for them as they slithered out.

After the one hour chopper ride east, we landed at FOB Viper. We exited the Blackhawk as we had done at Cobra, and once the birds lifted we rallied together and set up a temporary perimeter. The Lt checked his map and made radio contact with the rest of the company. Shortly after this radio contact, the color left his face. I knew by his reaction something was very wrong. He got us together and made a most improbable statement. We had been dropped off in a minefield, and were several kilometers from our intended objective. My first thought and statement to him was that they had to come back, pick us up, and take us to the correct LZ. He made the call, but we were turned down. We now had to make a hasty map recon verifying our exact location and somehow make it to the objective on time.

General Peay and Colonel Purdom were unaware that there were large areas around Viper (auxiliary airbase, Jalibah Southeast) that had been used by the Iraqi Air Force as a bombing range, and those areas were littered with unexploded bomblets. Colonel Purdom's 502nd was sitting on top of a minefield filled with sensitive-to-the-touch un-activated mines. General Peay's assault CP (command post) was actually in the minefield. The division's hasty change of plans left some advanced planning out of the mix. As a result, there were stones left unturned that would have been discovered with adequate time and intelligence. Also that morning, a squadron from the 3d Armored Cavalry Regiment was still in the area because of a friendly fire incident with 1st Armored Division. Any time unit lines crossed on the battlefield, the possibility of friendly fire incidents went up.

We couldn't believe the situation we were in. We all felt abandoned and stranded out in the middle of nowhere. How would we make the desert march to our objective without stepping on a mine hidden under the loose sand? After doing a map recon, we put on our rucks and set out to our company objective which was seven to ten kilometers from us, but because of the situation, seemed a million miles away. As we proceeded, the ground we were walking on was not like what we were walking on hours earlier at Cobra. This was loose, desert sand that felt like we were taking two steps forward and one step back. The rolling mounds of sand took all the energy we could muster just to take a step with the hundred pounds we were carrying. We looked like we were trying to walk through quick sand.

We were in a wide formation so if one of us stepped on a mine, it wouldn't create more than one or two casualties. We were looking down for wires protruding out of the sand or the Christmas ornament-looking bomblets, all the while looking up for signs of enemy activity. The process was agonizing, and was quickly zapping all of our mental and physical energy. With the straps on our ruck sacks tearing into our shoulders, trying to see this invisible enemy lurking under the sand, and taking small steps that seemed to take us nowhere, I felt like we were on the road march through hell. I also felt while I was going through this hellish experience, the only way I could survive was to pray. I prayed that no one would step on a mine, prayed that we could all keep putting one foot in front of the other, prayed that we would not have to engage the enemy in this place, and prayed that everyone would hold up emotionally.

Each man had to be thinking that their next step may be their last, and while we wanted to halt, we also wanted to get as far away from that minefield as we could, and the sooner the better. The lieutenant was driven by higher headquarters to get out of the area ASAP and get the platoon to the intended AO (area of operation). Even with the misfortune of being dropped off in the wrong place, the FOB had to be secured for the FARP (forward air refueling point). He barked in threatening tones for us to keep up that blistering pace. After a couple kilometers, as we approached the brink of our physical and emotional limits, he finally relented when he saw the blinding flash of exhaustion and anger on many of the soldier's faces. He was forced to halt.

We stopped for a few minutes to check our maps, drop the rucks, drink some water, and take a breather. While at the halt, we set up a hasty security perimeter. It appeared we had made it through the minefield without incident, but were uneasy about the march ahead, wondering if in fact we had cleared the area with the unseen enemy. After what seemed like thirty seconds, we rucked up (which involved helping your buddy). The weight was so great, it took two and sometimes three to get loaded back up. Between the ruck sack which had quart canteens full of water in them, web gear that had ammunition pouches and smaller canteens on it, the bullet proof vest, and the M-16, it was quite a load. In addition to my basic load, I had binoculars and a heavy, outdated range finder. Marty, my RTO, had the radio in addition to his basic load. Once loaded up, one of the infantryman made the announcement that he couldn't carry the AT-4 (anti-tank weapon) he was assigned to carry. None of his infantry buddies stepped up to carry his load. Marty piped up, "I'll carry it." I couldn't believe what I was hearing. Marty was probably carrying the heaviest weight of all and just volunteered to carry even more. I was pretty proud of my guy for being a stud and stepping up, but I was concerned about his ability to carry the additional weight several more miles.

Marty was a great RTO and a competent Fire Support Specialist (13F – Forward Observer). Even though he was an FO and not an infantryman, he was a team player and was always willing to help other soldiers. Volunteering was great, but I was concerned because of the injury to his knee back at Cobra. The last thing I needed out here was to lose my RTO.

After another kilometer of trudging through the sand, relief came when I saw an American flag lying on the ground. I was thinking the American flag should never touch the ground! One of our tanks or trailing vehicles must have lost it the previous night or early that morning. It was an indication that we had made it through the minefield. I immediately picked up and dusted off the flag, putting it in the web liner of my helmet with the other flags I was carrying. It also gave me some peace of mind that there were friendlies in the area and we weren't alone.

Even though we had made it out of the minefield, the march was hard. We continued to take periodic halts to check maps, take a breather, and drink some water. During the march we found an abandoned trailer stuck in the sand. We checked the trailer for equipment and sensitive material, and finding the trailer empty, we continued. After a couple more kilometers, the hair on the back of my neck stood up. It was one of those eerie feelings like we have when we're being watched. I told the lieutenant and we stopped. I got my binoculars and started scanning the desert. After a minute or so I spotted the very top of a turret on an M1 Abrams tank. The barrel on the tank was pointing straight at us. I told the lieutenant what I had spotted, and I stood up so the friendly tank could see my uniform. The sand berms would offer us little defense against an M1 projectile if the gunner thought we were the enemy. Their projectiles could easily penetrate a berm. After this road march through hell, I sure didn't want to be killed by our own guys. After a few seconds, which seemed like eternity, the tank identified us as friendly and moved on. I suspected it was one of the 3d ACR or 24th Infantry Division (Mechanized) tanks.

After another hour or so of difficult march, the sand became firmer as we moved up in elevation. With the firmer conditions, we began to pick up some speed and closed on our objective. After arriving at the 'correct location', we verified our position with our company headquarters and immediately set up a security perimeter and began digging in. After we shed the load off of our backs we quickly got to work. Even though digging a hole in the ground was not what we really wanted to do, it meant we were going to stay for a while. While setting up our perimeter and fighting positions, we were startled by a tank firing his weapon right over the hill behind us. The ground shook with a head rattling blast. The report of the tank meant there were Iraqis still in the area. The same tank we saw earlier was protecting us as we established our AO. It was a relief having big brother taking up for us on the playground. The Abrams tank continued moving to the east, clearing suspected enemy positions and enemy vehicles. It was a very comforting sight seeing his barrel pointing east rather than at me.

After Viper was secure, the 7-101 lifts began bringing in fuel for the Apache FARP (Forward Air Refueling Point). The pace picked up and the Viper mission of getting Apaches in the air was launched. The FOB was now a viable springboard for our attack helicopters to go into action. The 1-101 and 2-229 were about to have an attack helicopter feeding frenzy with the Republican Guard. Air observers had seen Iraqi forces along the causeway southwest of Basrah, and without being stopped they could make it to 3d Brigade's position along Highway 8. The Air Force was having trouble seeing the route because of the dense smoke from the oil well fires, so it was our attack helicopters' time to do some damage.

The 101st Aviation Brigade began screening the XVIII Airborne Corps' northern flank. Joining the attack was 2-229th, 1-101st and two battalions of the 12th Combat Aviation Brigade.

127

Small arms fire and near black out conditions from the oil fires along the causeway kept us from making it a shooting gallery, but almost four hours of attacks produced some results. Our aviation brothers destroyed fourteen Iraqi armored personnel carriers, eight BM21 multiple rocket launchers, four M16 helicopters, fifty-six trucks, and two SA6 radars. In addition to the destruction of enemy equipment, the brigade damaged a major bridge across the Euphrates that was being used as an escape route.

That evening, our aviation brigade was called to the rescue of a downed F-16 in our AO. The 2-229th sent a Blackhawk with a crew of seven and a flight surgeon to retrieve the downed pilot. The helicopter was hit with small arms fire and was shot down, killing five of our soldiers. An escorting Apache barely managed to escape being shot down in the barrage of gunfire. Another search and rescue mission had to recover the five bodies and the three that survived were taken as POWs by the Iraqis. One of the survivors was the 2-229's flight surgeon.

On the night of 27 February 1991, I was exhausted and hungry. At TAA Campbell before Cobra, we stripped our MREs down to just three meals, or one a day. We kept the main courses and threw away the rest. We weren't carrying anything that wasn't just absolutely necessary because of the weight. We sat down that evening on the edge of our holes and had the last of our one course meals which would take about two minutes to eat. After this desert feast, we prepared some cold coffee with a hot chocolate pack and "shared the cup." This had become a regular thing among a few of us. We called it "the coffee club." After heating the water (sometimes cold), adding the instant coffee, cream, and hot chocolate, three or four of us would share the nasty, filthy canteen cup.

After our evening 'coffee', we made our way back to our holes in the desert. Marty and I made radio checks and decided how we were going to alternate the radio watch throughout the night. Usually, Marty would stay up a couple hours, and then I would do radio watch for a couple hours. I realized that this would be a tough radio watch night as neither one of us had much sleep for the previous five days, and the days had been exhausting. Marty wanted the first watch so I crawled in my hole with the pancho stretched over the top and went to sleep. After what seemed to be five minutes, Marty was waking me up for my shift. I would usually listen to the shortwave to keep me up or walk around looking at the stars. After about three hours, I woke Marty up for his shift. Again, I don't remember falling asleep, but I did. After about five minutes, I was startled and awakened by an Iraqi soldier with an AK-47 standing at the foot of my hole. I jumped up pushing my way through the poncho over my hole and at the same time woke up. It was a dream. There was no Iraqi soldier. My dreams had become so vivid that I thought I was being attacked. Wow, I thought. This has got to end.

V-Day

On the morning of 28 February 1991, we got word from the lieutenant that the war would be over soon. I hurriedly turned on my shortwave and tuned into the Voice of America. The news was that Kuwait had been liberated. Emotions were running high as we received the word early in the morning. Everyone was excited that the end of the war had come as we heard the President's speech to the world.

President George H.W. Bush:

1991-02-27 United States 9:02 PM, (0602 hrs 28 Feb, Local Time)

"Kuwait is liberated. Iraq's army is defeated. Our military objectives are met. Kuwait is once more in the hands of Kuwaitis, in control of their own destiny. We share in their joy, a joy tempered only by our compassion for their ordeal.

Tonight the Kuwaiti flag once again flies above the capital of a free and sovereign nation. And the American flag flies above our Embassy.

Seven months ago, America and the world drew a line in the sand. We declared that the aggression against Kuwait would not stand. And tonight, America and the world have kept their word.

This is not a time of euphoria, certainly not a time to gloat. But it is a time of pride: pride in our troops; pride in the friends who stood with us in the crisis; pride in our nation and the people whose strength and resolve made victory quick, decisive, and just. And soon we will open wide our arms to welcome back home to America our magnificent fighting forces.

No one country can claim this victory as its own. It was not only a victory for Kuwait but a victory for all the coalition partners. This is a victory for the United Nations, for all mankind, for the rule of law, and for what is right.

After consulting with Secretary of Defense Cheney, the Chairman of the Joint Chiefs of Staff, General Powell, and our coalition partners, I am pleased to announce that at midnight tonight eastern standard time, exactly 100 hours since ground operations commenced and 6 weeks since the start of Desert Storm, all United States and coalition forces will suspend offensive combat operations. It is up to Iraq whether this suspension on the part of the coalition becomes a permanent cease-fire.

Coalition political and military terms for a formal cease-fire include the following requirements:

Iraq must release immediately all coalition prisoners of war, third country nationals, and the remains of all who have fallen. Iraq must release all Kuwaiti detainees. Iraq also must inform Kuwaiti authorities of the location and nature of all land and sea mines. Iraq must comply fully with all relevant United Nations Security Council resolutions. This includes a rescinding of Iraq's August decision to annex Kuwait and acceptance in principle of Iraq's responsibility to pay compensation for the loss, damage, and injury its aggression has caused.

The coalition calls upon the Iraqi Government to designate military commanders to meet within 48 hours with their coalition counterparts at a place in the theater of operations to be specified to arrange for military aspects of the cease-fire. Further, I have asked Secretary of State Baker to request that the United Nations Security Council meet to formulate the necessary arrangements for this war to be ended.

This suspension of offensive combat operations is contingent upon Iraq's not firing upon any coalition forces and not launching Scud missiles against any other country. If Iraq violates these terms, coalition forces will be free to resume military operations.

At every opportunity, I have said to the people of Iraq that our quarrel was not with them but instead with their leadership and, above all, with Saddam Hussein. This remains the case. You, the people of Iraq, are not our enemy. We do not seek your destruction. We have treated your POW's with kindness. Coalition forces fought this war only as a last resort and look forward to the day when Iraq is led by people prepared to live in peace with their neighbors.

We must now begin to look beyond victory and war. We must meet the challenge of securing the peace. In the future, as before, we will consult with our coalition partners. We've already done a good deal of thinking and planning for the postwar period, and Secretary Baker has already begun to consult with our coalition partners on the region's challenges. There can be, and will be, no solely American answer to all these challenges. But we can assist and support the countries of the region and be a catalyst for peace. In this spirit, Secretary Baker will go to the region next week to begin a new round of consultations.

This war is now behind us. Ahead of us is the difficult task of securing a potentially historic peace. Tonight though, let us be proud of what we have accomplished. Let us give thanks to those who risked their lives. Let us never forget those who gave their lives. May God bless our valiant military forces and their families, and let us all remember them in our prayers.

Good night, and may God bless the United States of America."

Note: The address was broadcast from the Oval Office at the White House live on nationwide radio and television.

We had many questions, but very few answers. What we did find out on the radio and through headquarters was out of forty-two Iraqi Divisions, forty of them were now ineffective. We knew that almost 100,000 enemy prisoners of war had been taken, and there were many ground skirmishes still happening with pockets of uninformed Iraqi resistance. Our questions at that point were what follow-on missions we would be involved with and how long it would take us to leave.

We were warned that these skirmishes could happen at any time, and not to let our guard down. At any moment, Iraqi soldiers could appear, not thinking the war is over, resulting in casualties. Later that morning, we heard the sound of a vehicle approaching from our east, which in our minds meant from Kuwait. We locked and loaded and Marty picked up the AT-4 (Anti-Tank Weapon). As the vehicle topped the hill we saw that it was a small pickup truck moving pretty quick for the desert conditions. When the occupants of the pickup saw us they started waving their hands as if to indicate they were un-armed. From the short distance, we could see their eyes were wide opened like they had just seen a ghost. My RTO was at the ready to send the anti-tank's armament streaking toward the small vehicle. I called off the attack. If it had been a few hours earlier, the small truck and its occupants might not have been so lucky if they hadn't stopped. I suspected the guys in the truck, both wearing civilian clothes, were Iraqi officers.

Later in the day, a sandstorm hit us, and visibility reduced to less than one hundred yards. Through the howling winds, we heard the sound of tracks moving in our direction from the west. Marty secured the radio for a possible fire mission with the AT-4 by his side. As the sound of tracks moved closer and closer, tensions rose. We were in no position to call in artillery due to the lack of visibility and the close proximity of the unidentified tracked vehicle. As the vehicle emerged out of the cloud of dust, luckily it was one of ours: a tank recovery vehicle was lost in the storm. I walked up to the vehicle and was surprised to see a CSM in the passenger seat. I greeted the Sergeant Major and jokingly told him how close he was to getting lit up. He thanked me for showing restraint and asked where he was. After showing him on the map, he proceeded east toward his unit. Though the war was over, we were not convinced that everyone knew it.

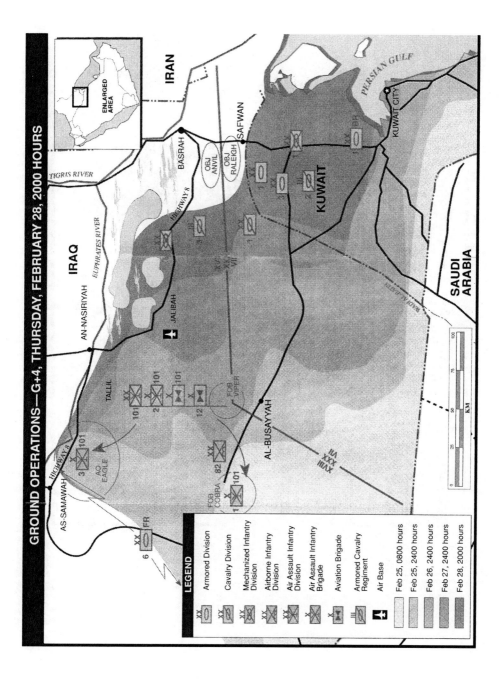

اوقف القتال الان، حافظ على حياتك

من الملجأ، يجب على حامله التقيد بالخطوات التالية:
للبحث بالسلام

١. اسحب مخزن الذخيرة من سلاحك.
سلاحك على كتفك الايسر مع توجيه الماسورة الى الاسفل

٢. احمل

٣. ارفع يديك فوق رأسك.
من مواقع القوات المتعددة الجنسيات ببطء، وي فرد في

٤. اقترب
المقدمة يرفع هذه الوثيقة فوق رأس.

٥. اذا عملت هذا تنجو من الموت.

CEASE RESISTANCE - BE SAFE

To seek refuge safely, the bearer must strictly adhere to the following procedures:

1. Remove the magazine from your weapon.

2. Sling your weapon over your left shoulder, muzzle down.

3. Have both arms raised above your head.

4. Approach the Multi - National Forces' positions slowly, with the lead soldier holding this document above his head.

5. If you do this, you will not die.

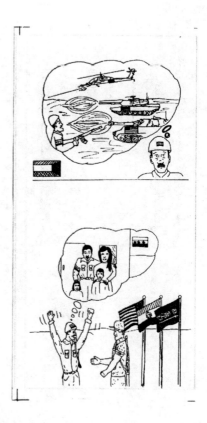

C-130s loading soldiers at Rafha Airport, March 1991
Courtesy of the U.S. Army

Chapter 9

Cease Fire
Where's The Champagne?

One might think we would be celebrating, jumping up and down, shaking hands, and having celebratory hugs, but that was far from our minds. We knew senior military leaders were trying to sort out the cease-fire, and we were aware that United Nations diplomats were putting the post-war sanctions and resolutions in place. However, we were in no position to take our eye off the ball and crack open a bottle of champagne to celebrate. In this theatre, for American soldiers under General Order Number One, there wasn't a drop of alcohol anyway. We had not eaten in a day, and our war rations were gone with no hope of being re-supplied. We were also "danger close" on our water supply. The thought of an uninformed Iraqi soldier wandering into our unit's AO was possible, and so our security was still at risk. We remained on alert and maintained a tight security perimeter.

Living in the sand and desert for months had taken its toll. The long term exposure to the harsh conditions left our bodies severely dehydrated, deteriorating and screaming for fluid replenishment. Due to the lack of sufficient drinking water during our ordeal, upper respiratory ailments began to manifest themselves. After talking about these problems to Doc Slater, our Company medic, we began encouraging each other to drink as much as we could; starting early every morning and continuing until the close of day. If Doc could have had his way, he would have made drinking water mandatory. The insidious effects from constant exposure to the punishing sun-drenched Iraqi-desert conditions left the skin on our arms and hands dried, cracked, and easily bleeding.

One of the less than appealing conditions of grunt life was the lack of any opportunity to maintain any sort of personal hygiene. Here it was the month of March, and we had the benefit of just one shower since January. Thankfully we had that one shower back at TAA Campbell in February where the National Guard had set up a shower tent. Other than that, it had been almost three months since we had our last shower back at Camp Eagle II.

Our first real opportunity to celebrate came on the morning of March 1st when a Blackhawk helicopter appeared with a water blivot for C Company. Finally, our champagne arrived in the form of precious life-sustaining water. A couple hours later, we saw a train of U.S. Army heavy rough terrain tankers (HEMITs) and supply vehicles making their way east from Cobra. A cloud of dust followed them as they made their way along the desert floor, and it eventually appeared they were moving in our direction. As the HEMITs got closer, and to our surprise, soldiers in the back of the HEMITs started waving and throwing cases of MREs to us. Looking closely, we could see these HEMITs were not from our division, and since every MRE box had to be accounted for, this special delivery was even more surprising. After the HEMIT train passed through, we hurriedly picked up the boxes and dispersed them through C Company. You would have thought that these were steaks that had just been dropped on us by the way we reacted. After receiving water and food, things started to look up.

On the 2 March 1991, we got the word from the Company Commander that the United Nations had agreed on the terms of the ceasefire and there were mass demonstrations taking place against Saddam Hussein throughout Iraq. The war had created a leadership vacuum and there were factions seeking an opportunity to overthrow the regime.

The CO also started laying the groundwork for C Company's re-deployment to TAA Campbell. All of us had waited for those words because it meant we would be going home. It also meant we were now turning the corner where we could finally allow ourselves the luxury of thinking about family and friends.

On 3 March 1991, we got word that the generals were meeting on the conditions of the ceasefire and the release of POWs. General Schwarzkopf said there had been some progress made in the talks. Even as these negotiations were taking place, elements of our platoon were being tasked with a search of an Iraqi Bedouin camp in our AO. These camps frequently had weapons and ammunition stored there by the Iraqi army.

After the camp was secure, we began venturing out a few hundred meters from our perimeter, picking up coalition leaflets that had been dropped days earlier. Realizing the historical nature of these leaflets, we picked up as many as we could. The leaflets showed graphic images of Iraqi troops being blown up by coalition aircraft and tanks. They also showed coalition troops greeting the Iraqi troops with smiles, providing them food, and showing pictures of them back with their families. Our Psychological Operations (PSYOPS) teams prepared these leaflets, and they had been well thought out, including explicit Arabic language surrender instructions with added translations into English for our soldiers.

CEASE RESISTANCE – BE SAFE

To seek refuge safely, the bearer must strictly adhere to the following procedures:

1. Remove the magazine from your weapon.

2. Sling your weapon over your left shoulder, muzzle down.

3. Have both arms raised above your head.

4. Approach the Multi-National Forces positions slowly, with the lead soldier holding this document above his head.

5. If you do this, you will not die.

As a result of our leaflet and PSYOPS campaign, tens of thousands of Iraqi troops were able to surrender and survive. In my mind, thousands of our soldiers also survived because we gave the enemy a way out. If cornered, with no hope of survival, Iraqis would have felt they had to fight to have any chance to live. The bottom line was that the leaflets saved lives on both sides.

As we settled back in at our base camp at Viper, we began reminiscing about where our unit had come and where we had gone. It was like a family talking about days gone by. It was at that time that I received some of the best compliments of my life. Our platoon sergeant and others thought I should try to switch MOSs from 13F (FO-Fire Support Specialist) to 11B (Infantryman). We had established such a bond that they wanted me as one of their own, and wanted me to make the change once we got back to Campbell. I can't think of a better compliment, and I seriously considered it because of the relationship I had established with them. Some of the conversation was about how our unit had somehow been spared the losses and wrath of war. I was grateful God had led us through great danger and, miraculously, been spared.

On 4 March 1991, we moved to PZ Posture (Pick up Zone) which was several kilometers north to be picked up by Blackhawks and taken back to TAA Campbell. The long road-march was bitter-sweet: bitter in that we were road marching several kilometers with the heavy rucks, and sweet because it was our first steps towards home.

Shortly after our arrival at the PZ, the Blackhawks that would carry us back to Saudi Arabia landed. Our scheduled departure time was the following morning. I turned on my shortwave radio, which for months had been our primary source for outside news, and learned that the Iraqis were going to release our POWs. In turn, we would release up to 5,000 of their POWs daily.

The following morning, the weather was overcast, rainy, and windy; not exactly the ideal forecast for our scheduled flight to TAA Campbell. After a morning of weather delays, the overcast lifted enough to reach the Blackhawk pilot's minimum required conditions for flight. The minimum acceptable flight weather conditions did nothing to soothe our nerves about the first flight leg of our trip home. We were told before we left Viper that Charlie Company should be ready to move once they got to TAA Campbell, as they were one of the chosen units of the 101st to go back home early. Upon hearing that I was struck by how fast they would be rotating home, and wondered if things were going to be as expeditious for me. After all, I had been with them all this time.

After a few minutes of pilots running preflight checklists, starting engines, receiving flight clearance, and warming up the Blackhawks, we were finally in the air. In the high winds, the choppers seem to struggle to get airborne, and once aloft, visibility seemed obscured. As we proceeded southwest to TAA Campbell, I replayed the events of the past five months in my mind. It had been an exhilarating, butt-puckering rendezvous with the Screaming Eagles.

Once we landed at TAA Campbell, it soon became apparent that I would not be accompanying my infantry brethren home. They told me I would reunite with the 1-320th at TAA Campbell and return home with the artillery at a later date. My RTO and I had an hour or so to say our goodbyes, and off we went to the artillery side of the task force assembly area (TAA). Once on the ground at the TAA, I truly felt the war might be over, but they did say we would be there until they had determined we would not have to go back in. The absence of war in Iraq left chaos, and with that chaos, uncertainty about follow on missions. What I did know was that if we were called to do any of those missions, it would not be with Charlie Company.

On the morning of 6 March 1991, Charlie Company was transported to Rafha Airport to be transported back to KFIA and Camp Eagle II by C-130s and would be back at Fort

Campbell, Kentucky the following day. Charlie Company left us at TAA Campbell (in a sandstorm). We weren't sure how long it would be before we would leave, but it sure felt good to be back on Saudi ground and out of Iraq. Now that we were not at war, the rumor mill was alive and well. One day we were going back with 2nd Brigade, and the next we were going back home with DIVARTY which could delay our departure by months. It became an emotional yo-yo for the guys because everyone wanted to go home.

While at the TAA, we were able to take a ride by HUMMV into Rafha. Supposedly there was some chicken and pita bread in the town which sounded too good to pass up. It took a while to make it to Rafha, and when we did, it looked like a town from long ago. As we drove into the town, everyone was staring at us. No smiles, no emotion, just stares, as we probably looked as strange to them as they did to us. The fact that we were carrying M16s and the town was located on the border between Iraq and Saudi Arabia probably had something to do with the cool reception. Once we arrived at the town market, we loaded up on fresh roasted chicken and freshly baked pita bread. Truthfully, nothing ever tasted and smelled so good. We hadn't had a hot meal since January. Once we had our fill, we bought some chicken and pita for the guys and headed back to the desert camp.

The next few days were filled with sandstorms and intermittent nice weather as we waited for our turn to fly to Camp Eagle II. On the 12 March 1991, we were moved to the Rafha Airport which was located along Pipeline Road. We got there in the late afternoon and the small airport was filled with soldiers waiting for their flights. When I got to the airport, I ran into Sergeant Snead, a Sandfill 27 forward observer from Ft. Lewis. We compared notes and did some catching up on our unit movements. Once at the airport, they informed us we would be the last flight out for the day, departing Rafha at 2230, and arriving back at KFIA at 0030 hrs on the 13th.

All evening we watched C-130s come and go. They would come in, load up the troops, and take off. By the time it was our turn, the small busy airport had become empty and desolate. It was almost a two hour flight back to KFIA and I was ready to get back to Camp Eagle II. I dreamed of a shower, hot food, and warm coffee, thinking it will be great to reconnect with my old buddies, Frank Giger and Ernie Swindle. When we arrived at KFIA, we were bused from the airport to Camp Eagle II. Once we unloaded the buses and made our way to the tents, I immediately headed for the showers. They were freezing cold at night, but I didn't care as I lathered up. A shower had never felt oh so good and oh so bad, all at the same time.

Waking up the first day at Camp Eagle II was a great feeling. With the pressure of war lifted off my shoulders, I began hunting down my buddies. When talking with Ernie, I got bad news about Frank. He was involved in a friendly fire incident back at TAA Campbell. Information was sketchy, but we were told a saw-gunner (squad automatic weapon) had shot him in the knee and he was taken back to the states. After hearing the news, I was thinking how pissed off he would have been to be taken away from the war. He was a hard-charging young sergeant and I knew he would never have stopped wanting to finish off Saddam. If allowed, Frank would have fought on one leg or until his last breath. That's just the way he was.

We spent a lot of our time breaking down equipment for the agriculture inspectors (a little surprise we didn't know about until we got back). The agriculture department was now requiring all units that were deployed to theatre to undergo a tortuous inspection of all equipment before being allowed to come back to the U.S. The days of cleaning and re-cleaning seemed like harassment after what we had gone through, and our leadership felt the same way. After a day of cleaning, we had time to sit down and compare notes about the war and what it would be like to get home. Later that day, the convoy arrived from TAA Campbell.

On the 15 March 1991, we got some unsettling news that Iraq had already violated the ceasefire agreement by illegally moving aircraft. We also got word that the 101st would be moving back to their old defensive positions. That turned out to be untrue, at least the part about us moving back. Another rumor mill note was from our brigade FSO. He was telling us that we will not have a movement window back to Ft. Campbell until May 4 and yet another rumor was a return on or about 3 April. We got to where we didn't trust any information we received. What we did know for sure was that the equipment had to be inspected, cleaned, and re-inspected again and again. Loss reports had to be filled out and battle damage reported. We began doing physical training. Standards were set high with the 101st, and even though we were just back from war, those standards needed to be assessed. I began to get some insight into how this division would function in garrison back at Ft. Campbell. The 101st Airborne Division (Air Assault) would be ready to go at any time and at any place.

It was encouraging to see the 1st Brigade and the remaining elements arrive back at Camp Eagle II between 21 and 25 March. The closing of the brigades meant we really might be going home and not sent back to the desert to police the Iraqis. On 26 March, I received a surprise visit from a dear friend of mine's son, Marc Skeen. I had heard that he was in the Army, but had no idea he was in the 101st. Marc was trained as a Chinook mechanic and assigned to the 7/101. It was amazing that he found me in Tent City. Marc had made trips to both Cobra and Viper during his short tour to Saudi Arabia and Iraq. Shortly after his graduation from AIT (Advanced Individual Training), he was sent to Saudi Arabia. The air war had already started and Marc arrived in country during a scud alert. Having only been issued an aviator's gas mask with no straps included, his battle buddy, another private, duct taped the mask to his head during the alert. If chemicals had been delivered, Marc would have survived due to the heroic actions of his battle buddy. I would have given top dollar for a photograph of that.

Things were changing rapidly within the division. Instead of the appearance of a battle weary and desert worn division, the 101st was cleaning up pretty nice. Everyone was showered, shaved, and the uniforms were clean. Rather than ninety percent of the division wearing their web gear unlocked at the waist which was our custom in war, everyone was standing tall and looking good. Then there were the "fashion police." Their job was to spot the rag tag soldiers and shape them up. I'm sure the order came down from higher, but many of us thought it was kind of a joke since there were few outsiders in Tent City. Then to our surprise, U.S. citizens working for the oil company, Saudi Aramco, were allowed to come into Camp Eagle II and throw us a large picnic. Now we figured out what the fashion police were all about. The oil industry workers brought into Tent City thousands of pounds of fresh food and soft-drinks, cranked up their grills and cooked for us all day. It was the first taste we had of home in months. We were all very grateful for their generosity and efforts. As grateful as we were, they were even more so. "Thank you" poured out of their mouths as they prepared the picnic feast. It was touching to all of us to visit with such an appreciative crowd.

I had no idea how many civilian workers there were in Saudi Arabia and the multitude of people's lives that hung in the balance during this war. If Iraqi armored formations had crossed the border into Saudi Arabia, there would have been thousands of civilians of all nationalities who would have lost their lives. Iraqi troops had tortured and killed thousands of Kuwaitis in August during their invasion, and had it not been for the United States' rapid deployment of troops, Saudi Arabia itself could have been lost. Given only a few more days, the fourth largest army in the world might have been given the toe hold it needed to hold the world hostage.

We received good news at Camp Eagle II on 28 March 1991. We would be leaving Saudi Arabia on Easter Sunday. Time began to go into fast forward, and the final customs inspections and shakedowns were of little inconvenience, with just one exception. The Jimmy Lile knives I was carrying got some attention from a Customs MP. We were not allowed to take anything back that was not "issued." The customs soldier asked me where the knives came from. I told him that I had bought them prior to deployment, and who made them. At that point I had probably

145

said too much. I saw the wheels turning in his head as he was frothing at the mouth trying to figure out how he could separate me from the blades. After a minute or so, he said that they were "unauthorized" but he would let them go. I felt like a smuggler but it didn't matter. "Gray Ghost" was going back home with me. Whew!

On Saturday, 30 March at 2100 hrs, we all said our goodbyes to Camp Eagle II as we loaded up buses that would take us over to King Fahd International Airport. I was glad we were going home, but also knew I was leaving some of me behind.

As we boarded the Pan Am 747, there were red, white, blue, and yellow ribbons in the cabin of the aircraft. It was reported that the Assistant Division Commander General Shelton was on board. The flight back was long, but we were going home. We stopped in Rome for a refuel, and as with our trip to Saudi Arabia, we weren't allowed off the plane. After the short refueling stop, we were back in the air. Next stop: the United States of America.

On our flight back, we visited with friends, ate and slept. Some of the guys were still playing their Gameboys passing the time. After crossing the Atlantic, we began making our descent into JFK Airport when we heard the announcement from the captain. "We have just entered United States airspace and will be landing at New York's JFK Airport shortly." A jubilant roar erupted from the soldiers, with all shedding a tear or two of joy and relief.

After landing and pulling up to our designated spot at the terminal, I couldn't help but notice a Russian Aeroflot commercial jet parked next to us. I knew we were in New York, but it was strange seeing the jet next to us. After hours in the air, we were now able to depart the aircraft and stretch our legs while our bird was being refueled. As I made my way up the ramp, I heard some applause and noticed a number of people waiting to see and greet us. I had the pleasure of a gentleman in his late 60s walk up to me, grab my hand, and welcome me home. The man had a distinct European accent. He wouldn't let me go. He wanted to be a part of the greeting party and told me he was from Russia.

He said, "You did a great job and welcome home." It turned out that he was a scientist from the Ukraine. He gave me one Russian ruble as a memento of our meeting and then departed for his gate. It was ironic that I had made it all this way and had just taken this unbelievable journey, only to be welcomed back to America by a Russian.

It sure felt good to be on American soil and to be welcomed back home, rather than being spit on like my Vietnam brothers were. Being a Vietnam era vet and seeing first hand what many of our citizens thought of us back then made me want this homecoming for all veterans. It made a huge difference to be wanted back home and be told that we did a good job.

Freedom Bird PAN AM 747 upon arrival at Fort Campbell, Kentucky, Easter Sunday, 1991. Courtesy of Ernie Swindle

After our brief layover, we re-boarded the 747 for our final leg back to Ft. Campbell. The trip from JFK to Ft. Campbell was a flash. No sooner than achieving cruising altitude, we were beginning our descent. As we approached Campbell Army Airfield from the northeast, the captain made another announcement. "Soldiers of the 101st Airborne Division, this is your captain. It has been a pleasure to bring you home. As you look over the left

147

wing, you can see a lot of flags waving. Those are your family and friends. Thank you for your service to our country, and the whole crew wishes you a job well done." I was sitting on the left side of the 747 and the only thing I could see on the ground were rows and rows of people waving the American flag. I broke down and cried. There probably wasn't a dry eye on the plane. We arrived at Ft. Campbell at 1750 hrs local time on Easter Sunday, 31 March. It was a Resurrection Sunday I will never forget.

As we exited the plane, we thanked the captain and flight attendants, and made our way down the steps into a hanger used as a reception area for family and soldiers. The only thing I remember were hugs and tears as soldiers reunited with their parents, wives, children, and friends. I still had one more leg to go in my homecoming. It would be the following day when I would fly from Nashville to Seattle. After the reunions, we were bused to the 1/320th where we turned in our weapons and received a safety briefing. The barracks were opened, and those having family members waiting, signed out on leave. Others went to their rooms, changed into civilian clothes and then went out on the town. I didn't have a room assignment and it would be the next day before I could sign out of the unit, so Vern Sizemore and his wife had me over to their house to spend the night. The bed never felt so good. It was great to be back in the United States.

The next day I signed out of the 1/320th and made my way by ground transportation to the Nashville Airport. My flight left late that night and didn't arrive in Seattle till 0130 hrs on the 2nd. Homecoming at SeaTac Airport was a surprising one. Not only was my wife and four year old daughter Kristen there, but also a group from the 3/11th Field Artillery, my other Army family. It was great to see everyone, especially with it being late Monday night into early Tuesday morning. I was shocked that my Army buddies had made such an effort to greet me. It was good to be home.

The majority of the 101st left Saudi Arabia the first two weeks of April, with the Division colors returning with General Peay on

12 April. A small contingent under General Adams, the division's Assistant Division Commander for Support, remained at Camp Eagle II to move the division's equipment to port. The last 101st soldier to leave Saudi Arabia departed on 1 May 1991.

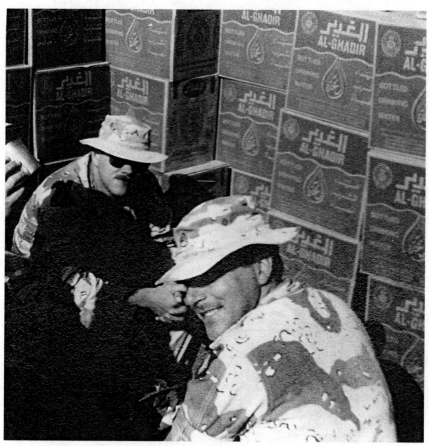

Doc Slater and Vern Sizemore at Camp Eagle II
Courtesy of Ian Berkowitz

149

Sergeant Steve Wiehe at the mess tent, March 1991

2nd Platoon, Charlie Company Coffee Club, March 1991
Courtesy of Ian Berkowitz

Sergeant Wiehe – Camp Eagle II

Camp Eagle II – One Happy Camper

Kristen and I visiting with Marguerite Naiser's class, April 1991

Chapter 10

After The Storm

Once I returned to Ft. Lewis, it felt like I had never left. After a couple days, I dropped in on the guys at the 3/11th and it was like a reunion. Everyone was happy to see me, and I them. The guys wanted to hear all about Desert Shield and Desert Storm. On this trip to the unit however, I had the Screaming Eagle patch on my left and right sleeve instead of the 9th Infantry Division Octofoil patch. All of my buddies were Army green with envy and I was very proud to show off the eagles. I was on three week block leave and thought I wouldn't be going back to Ft. Campbell. Our unit was told we were on loan to the 101st when we left Ft. Lewis, and would be returning to our old unit after the war. Shoot, even the Commanding General of the 9th felt like we would be coming back to Lewis. That wasn't the truth. We actually were assigned to the 101st "as per our orders," so we would not be returning to our old units. There was another set of orders re-assigning me back to Ft. Lewis that had been rescinded. The 3/11th CSM called personnel and The Department of the Army, and both confirmed the PCS orders. I would be returning to Ft. Campbell. They went on to say that I had made the cut-off score for promotion to E-6 and, upon my return, I would be promoted. I had just received some bitter-sweet news.

I had no real issues with going back to Ft. Campbell other than having to move my family. However, we had on-post housing at Ft. Lewis and my wife was settled into a good job in the Seattle area. It was going to be a juggling act trying to figure out a timeline for the unexpected PCS (permanent change of station). We decided that I would request additional leave upon my return to the 1-320th, and then fly back to Seattle to move the family to Clarksville, Tennessee. This would give my wife time to manage the move. She had to give notice at her job, spend a week cleaning our Ft. Lewis house for inspection and pack. After she packed and cleaned, I would fly back to Ft. Lewis, load the U-Haul and spend a couple days driving from Ft. Lewis to Ft. Campbell. After getting to Ft. Campbell, we would have to search for housing. My homecoming had just become a stressful one for the family. I wished I had known about those re-assignment orders being rescinded.

Desert Storm Parade, Midland, Texas
Courtesy of my Grandmother

We flew to Texas on a whirlwind four day visit with our families. I made a point to visit the two schools that had adopted me as well as my brother's church in Baytown, Texas. The family set up the three speaking engagements for me and the short time in Texas was on a set time schedule. My first visit was to Bess Brannen Elementary School in Lake Jackson, Texas. My Mom, an elementary music teacher, is an energetic go-getter. While I was in Desert Shield/Desert Storm she had orchestrated many letter writing campaigns with the school kids as well as submitting my letters home to the local newspaper. Without my knowledge, my letters home were actually to the whole community. The whole area knew what I had written. I was thankful that I had the sense not to write about any operational movements, etc.

Student Assembly, Bess Brannen Elementary School, April 1991

On the day of the assembly, I thought I would be talking to a classroom of kids at Bess Brannen, but it turned out to be the whole school. Mom had organized an assembly with every kid and teacher in the school. I was glad I didn't mind public speaking; otherwise, the situation would have been very intimidating.

When all the kids were settled and the principal had given her introduction, I spent a few minutes telling the kids what it was like to spend nights in the desert under the stars and living with the scorpions, dung beetles and snakes. I tried to keep it light and on their level. After my talk, I opened it up for questions. I don't think I should have done that because the young students were only interested in how many Iraqis I had killed. After the assembly, the principal presented me with flags, banners, posters, drawings and notes from the kids. It was a great time for me and the children. They were now able to put a real soldiers' face with the letters of support they had written.

The next day, we drove to Wild Peach Elementary School, which is a short distance from Lake Jackson between West Columbia and Brazoria, to meet with the second school that had adopted me. Chuck and Marguerite Naiser were very close friends and Marguerite was a 3rd grade teacher at the school. She and her class sent me countless letters and well wishes. Upon arrival to her class, I immediately received hugs from everyone. I couldn't help but notice an American flag hung proudly in her room along with a map of the Middle East. I spent time with the kids, explaining on the map where I had been and what I had done with the Army. Their eyes were glued on me as I talked. Just as I had done at Bess Brannen, I opened it up for questioning, only this time it was in a small, intimate setting. The polite 3rd graders asked their questions one at a time. It was a family time, as my daughter Kristen was sitting on the lap of Marguerite as I told them my story. Whatever pain and discomfort I endured as a soldier seemed to disappear and wash away as I sat with the kids. It was good for me to tell my story.

I felt it was necessary to visit the kids and for them to see face to face the Army sergeant they had been writing all these months. They had developed a real concern for me and wanted all of us to come back home safely. The teachers were sincerely concerned also, but took advantage of the opportunity to hone those writing, artistic and geography skills with their students as well. Visiting with the children was an experience I would not soon forget, and I thanked my Mom and Marguerite for making it happen at their schools.

Marguerite Naiser's class, April 1991

My next visit came on Sunday evening at my brother's church. He and his wife were associate ministers at a church in Baytown, Texas. Don's wife, Beth, had a brother who was with the 82nd Airborne Division in Desert Shield and Desert Storm, so they asked him to share his experiences in the desert also. Andrew was a young professional Airborne Lieutenant based out of Ft. Bragg, North Carolina and was the first to tell his story. The church was large and, for a Sunday evening service, there were many people in the pews. With Don and Beth both having brothers that served in Desert Storm, there was quite a bit of interest in our experiences.

With the 82nd and the 101st Airborne Divisions being in the XVIII Airborne Corps, our movements were similar. Andrew delivered a well thought out speech about his experiences in the desert and the division. I was impressed with his ability to speak to such a large group of people. As I was sitting behind Andrew as he spoke from the pulpit, I was thankful that I had public speaking experience and felt calm about what could have been an intimidating experience for many. After Andrew gave his talk, the church stood and applauded. Following the sustained applause, my brother introduced me.

I not only wanted to share my "how I lived" in the desert experiences, but felt compelled to share some operational ones as well. Once I began talking, I explained how I felt we had supernaturally avoided a decisive "die in place" contact with the Iraqis at Hafar al-Batin. I felt in my heart that there was a higher power that had kept that engagement from happening. I shared what I knew at the time and that there were several Iraqi divisions prepared to come down the wadi, blitzing toward King Khalid Military City to our southwest. The thrust into Saudi Arabia and the overthrow of the Saudi military town even temporarily would have been a moral victory for Saddam. I told them that I felt like the miserable rains that we had received the night before his planned attack played a part in them not being able to execute their plan. I sincerely felt that God had his hand in "The greatest battle that never was" at the Wadi al-Batin.

After sharing with the church G-Day and the end of the war, I thanked them for their support of the troops. The people began to applaud and I asked if there were any veterans in the group. Many WWII, Korean, and Vietnam era veterans stood up. After they stood, I asked that the applause be directed to them and to welcome them home as well. The tears welled up in my eyes several times before and after Andrew and I shared our stories, as the church shared without hesitation their gratitude. It was a very moving, patriotic experience for us all.

After the church service, Andrew and I were greeted by family and the church. It turned into a receiving line as they individually wanted to thank us and welcome us home. After the line broke down, I was cornered by a gentleman that identified himself as a reserve captain in the Army. He thanked me for my service and welcomed me home. He went on to tell me that my recollections about Hafar al-Batin seemed incorrect because "they" were never told about it in their Army Reserve unit. I was taken aback by his comments and interrupted him. I said, "Sir, the only thing I know is that I was there and the movements of the Iraqis were being observed by Special Forces units on the ground. Higher HQ saw a real threat and sent our unit there to assist 1st Cav in the defense. I shared what I knew to the best of my ability. The only thing I wasn't told at the time was that God had his hand in stopping the attack. That was my opinion."

Had this conversation taken place somewhere other than a church, I would have had more to say to this part-time captain, and my actions would have gotten me into hot water. The encounter could have escalated into yet another battle. And, as with The Wadi al-Batin, I thanked God that the confrontation never materialized. I did leave Don and Beth's church that night filled with honor and gratitude. The people in Baytown were down-home Texas Patriots.

After our short trip to Texas, I used the remainder of my time at Ft. Lewis to unwind, relax, and spend time with family and friends. I had missed my daughter Kristen and her flanking movements and counter-attacks as I lay on the floor. She was a smart, rough and tumble four year old that was lively and active. I think she had missed me as much as I her, so the reunion was sweet. My only regret was that we would have to say our goodbyes again when I went back to Ft. Campbell. Her words stuck in my head. "Dad, I don't want you to be a Screaming Eagle anymore." Out of the mouth of babes, my four year old had a real sense of loss when I was gone or about to leave. She knew the last time I said goodbye, it was for months. When reality set in, I realized I had been selfish, thinking I was the one who was making the sacrifice serving my country. Those thoughts couldn't have been further from the truth; all of our soldiers' families were making the "real sacrifice." They were the ones managing all of the household affairs while we were gone. They were the ones who had to manage the kids and finances by themselves. They were the ones having to wait by the phone or fear a knock on the door by casualty assistance officers. It was an enormous stress for families.

After returning to Ft. Campbell following block leave, the 1/320th was active. We were recovering from the war and the general mood around the battalion was a relaxed one. We were getting back into the swing of garrison life. The battery leadership "was not" pleased that I was requesting an additional one week leave to move the family from Ft. Lewis and were not sympathetic. Some felt like all of that moving stuff should have been accomplished in the previous two weeks after I found out the reassignment orders back to Ft. Lewis had been rescinded. Even after explaining the "impossible logistics" of a short move across the country, they weren't happy. I thought, "What a way to get introduced to my new unit." These guys didn't see my performance first hand in Desert Storm as I was with the infantry, and the last thing I wanted was to draw "this kind" of attention to myself. Not a good deal. This had turned into a "Ye Old Army Cluster ----" which seemed to happen in the Army when communication was lacking or non-existent. When the war started, the priority was to move tens of thousands of soldiers into Saudi Arabia, not how an Army sergeant is going to move his family from Ft. Lewis, Washington to Ft. Campbell, Kentucky. I didn't blame anyone because leaders at Lewis and Campbell were just doing the best they could in the situation they were in. Single personnel from Ft. Lewis had less trouble making the hasty transition after the war, just some families.

We received two reports of bad news after we came back to Campbell. One of our FOs from Ft. Lewis had been tragically killed in a vehicle accident on leave. We were told he was in his car when it left the road on a slick highway and hit a tree. To add to the bad news, we found out that Command Sergeant Major Dulin had passed away in his backyard, just three weeks after our return. CSM Dulin, the DIVARTY (Division Artillery) Command Sergeant Major was the first person to brief me when I got to Saudi Arabia. Our CSM Duggins escorted the body back to Florida for burial. Two of our own had made it through the war and died on leave. It didn't seem possible and was devastating to our close knit group.

Now that I was back, I couldn't wait to talk to Frank and get the story about the friendly fire incident back at TAA Campbell. Frank told me he was rehabbing his knee and held no remorse towards the PFC that mis-fired the SAW. He was a "take-life-how-it-dishes-it-out" type of guy. I think that is why I liked him so much. He was a lot like me.

Frank Giger: The Friendliest of Fire or The luckiest unlucky affair of my career.

"On the 12th of February I found myself somewhere in the Neutral Zone along with the whole of the 101st Airborne Division awaiting the time for the Ground War phase of Desert Storm. A not to mention his name PFC had just been moved from rifleman to SAW gunner, and a spot inspection of his weapon had gained him the ire of his team leader – it was substandard in every way. Apparently his ego had been bruised to the point that said team leader had asked that I assist him in tearing down his weapon and cleaning it, while making sure it gets done right and his head gets screwed on straight. Sometimes, when a team or squad leader rips one's head off in a certain way for infractions it really isn't a bad idea to have a disinterested party see that proper alignment is set on replacement.

Forgive the digression, but let me explain the nature of the M249 Squad Automatic Weapon (SAW). It is an automatic rifle of sorts, belt or magazine fed, that uses the same ammunition of the M16A2 rifles we had (5.56mm/.223) and fits immediately between the rifle and the next automatic weapon, the 7.62mm/.308 M60 machine gun. It is light, reliable, and puts out a "hel-luv-alot" of firepower. It works much like its larger counter-part with a top ammunition feed tray cover and fires from the open (rearwards) bolt.

So we spent the balance of the morning in the squad tent tearing apart the weapon and putting back together the PFC's self esteem. I gave the; "if they thought you were that bad they wouldn't have promoted you to SAW gunner" and the "why we are here" homilies in pretty good form, I thought. He certainly walked out standing up straighter than when he came in.

We were also to have visitors! The press was to descend on us. We had the same opinion of the press as we did the long feathered boa of a stripper - pretty much useless and ultimately in the way of doing or seeing anything productive; and we knew the stripper was far more honest and forthright in means and motives. However, it also meant we got a large box of "Honest-by-God-Bee-Steaks" which were being grilled by the senior NCO's of the Company. My job was to "escort" one of the photographers around the platoon and allow the squads to eat their steaks (I had wheedled one off of the grill early on, and it was my punishment for it). He took a load of photographs and didn't seem to be inherently evil; he was suitably impressed with the fighting position the PFC and I had literally chiseled out by hand (six picks gave their all) of three foot thick layers of solid rock.

Eventually, they left and the business of getting ready for the nightly patrol began. During the pre-patrol inspection, the PFC had a problem with loading the five round "starter belt" into the SAW. The idea was that a troop would load the first five rounds of an ammunition belt and, at the start of hostilities, quickly attach the other 195 rounds and get to serious shooting. This allowed the remainder of the belt to be hidden from sand, dust, water, cigarette ashes, tobacco spit, coffee, and all the other hazards of combat zone life. It's easy to load the rounds upside down with the links facing down instead of up, particularly in the dark with a SAW, owing to the small caliber of the rounds (and therefore the links). The starter belt is loaded on top of the closed (forward) bolt for safety. But as we know, this weapon had the bolt to the rear, and was set in the firing position.

It was 1900 hours, after dark, and as A. one could only make coffee, B. smoke, and C. generally hang out in the squad tent, there I was, even though this time I wasn't to be on the patrol, as the company radio watch guy had fallen asleep the night before and they wanted someone who they knew would stay awake on it this time – namely myself. Enemy contact was not expected but there were less than ten or fifteen kilometers from the Iraqi border, and we took these all-night patrols seriously.

Sergeant Waggle, one of the team leaders of the squad that was going out and I were bantering back and forth about how the "Real Men" were going out on foot into the desert night and the "Slack Wannabe" would be listening on the radio all about it when I realized I was out of cigarettes (or, more correctly, had no more on my person – I'd pantomime for the Bedouins and trade with them for smokes if I ran out, always had a pack or two available, much to the dismay and delight of my comrades). I turned to him to ask for one before they left out and three loud reports made our ears ring.

About three feet behind me, the PFC had been cheating and jumping the gun on loading the five round starter belt into his SAW. Normally, weapons are loaded at the appropriately named Weapons Load Line, which is marked by the perimeter of the company line, but he decided that the unreliable light of a whack-to-make-it-work issue angle flashlight was preferable. When he tried to close the feed tray cover gently to cover his break in protocol, it didn't want to, owing to the misaligned feed track, so he raised it and figured he'd just slap it down. When he did, the weapon slipped from his other hand and he caught it with his fingers – right through the trigger grip. Weapon on fire, bolt to the rear, trigger pulled. Bpap bpap bpap, three rounds went flying.

The first round went through my Kevlar helmet, which was on the ground. From three feet the bullet hit the front flat and went straight through, but it hit the inside at an angle and was stopped via a semi-circular path inside the layers of it. It is my best "war trophy" and I kept it. The second round struck the back of my left knee, slightly off center into the left of the femur's bulbous socket, went straight through and out of the front (just nicking the knee cap and putting a half moon in it) and over SGT Waggle's head (he was sitting on a cot). SGT Waggle later said it literally parted his hair. The third round went left and high, passing harmlessly through the tent wall and into the night sky.

There was immediate bedlam with troops emptying the tent in a nano-second. In the movies when someone is shot they fly through the air in a dramatic fashion and copious amounts of blood spatter everywhere, and the victim instantly falls to the ground either unconscious or screaming. In my experience, said shot person does none of that – he hops up and down on one leg saying the "F word" over and over again and resists the urge to grab the center pole that holds the tent up.

Sergeant Waggle took charge, standing up and commanded that "everyone get out, he's been shot!" while I looked at him and sincerely asked "who got shot?" while grabbing his shoulder with one hand to keep standing. I was thinking one of the rapidly exiting troops had kicked me.

"You have, you dumb-ass, lay down and shut up," he said calmly as he unceremoniously pushed me off of him and onto the dirt floor.

It's one of those things people say to you that burn themselves into hard memory, and still makes me chuckle.

So, I pulled myself up into a sitting position and we take a look. There's a hole the size of a number two pencil in the top of my pant leg, and as I twist the leg around, a match in the back.

"Huh, look at that," he said in a perfectly conversational tone.

"Weird, isn't it?" I asked, and bent my leg back and forth without effort.

"It doesn't look too bad."

"You probably shouldn't do that."

"I guess you're right."

"Hurt much?" he asked, as if we were talking about stubbing a toe.

"Naw, sort of like getting kicked. It smarts is all."

"Medic should be here in a minute."

"So do I get that cigarette or not?" I asked.

And so I did.

Our medic was a very green and inexperienced Private whom I had taken under my wing early on, and his eyes were as big as pancakes as he came in. He looked like he was about to cry from the shock of seeing me sitting on the floor with my legs out, propped up with my back to a cot smoking a cigarette.

Waggle and I both laughed despite ourselves as he just stood there with his mouth open.

"Jesus, Private," Waggle said, "where's your aid bag?"

He made a quick U-turn out of the tent to go get it, and we gave each other the standard "fricking Privates" look all NCOs keep on quick reserve.

The third platoon medic burst through the tent door, aid bag in hand with a much more action oriented demeanor. He was old — an ancient twenty five years of age — and had been an EMT before joining the Army.

"Wait for my guy," I advised, *"he'll need to watch."*

The wait was about ten seconds, but we took an additional thirty calming him down.

The scissors came out and the first fight with the medical establishment began. No way was I going to let him cut the laces of my boot to get it off. You could get replacement boots, but laces were nigh impossible to acquire in theatre. The trouser was a different story, though I insisted that he work along the seam if I had to repair them later.

Since the bullet hit skin-bone-skin, the amount of blood was very small, and so I instructed that we get a nice look at the wound, both entry and exit, so that my medic could see what one looked like (we were working under the premise that the Iraqis were going to put up a helluva fight, something that didn't bear out).

The obligatory IV was started, a bandage applied, and a tortuous plastic splint that went from foot to groin rolled up my leg and inflated. As soon as it filled and put pressure on my knee the real pain started, going from a sort of ache to actual ouch, ouch GD that hurts pain.

Outside came the sounds of a huge scuffle that included someone crying and the unmistakable thwack-thwack of punches landing. The PFC was being counseled on his lacking of professionalism by the balance of the patrol in a most rude manner; it went on until the arrival of the First Sergeant. It actually went a long way in the healing process for my inadvertent assailant; he felt like he needed an ass whooping for shooting me and got one.

Humvees arrived and brass began to fill the tent. Our very good Platoon Leader, Second Lieutenant Cartwright, peeked in early on, saw it was under control, gave me a thumbs up, and made sure the platoon kept to its duties, order was maintained, and that the Platoon Sergeant got the medivac wheels rolling.

The Battalion XO and Company Commander arrived with a flourish, announced themselves, and then sat on cots opposite me. The Captain looked like he was more worried that he was in some sort of trouble than he was concerned for my welfare.

Some guy came in wearing a night vision goggle head harness and seemed to see the humor of the situation – far from the reports of my leg having been

165

blown off (things had been exaggerated in transmission up the chain), he saw a buck sergeant sitting up more or less comfortably, smoking cigarettes and having a heated debate with a medic as to why he couldn't drink coffee, since it was a leg wound and had nothing to do with the digestive tract.

"Looking good," he said.

"Thanks, dude," I replied.

"That's the Battalion Commander!" The XO exclaimed.

"Oh, sorry," I amended, "Thanks, sir," and gave him a thumbs up. LTC Benjamin (who was on my Good Guy list before that evening) gave me one back.

About fifteen minutes later a runner came in and spoke into his ear, and he walked over to me.

"We're sending you to the Brigade Aid Station by ground, using the lowest, most tactical means available."

"Okay, sir."

"We don't want to advertise our position with a helicopter."

"Got it, sir."

"The Iraqis don't know we're here, and I want to keep it that way."

"Makes sense to me."

I was somewhat perplexed as to why he would go to such lengths to explain to me why I would go by Field Litter Ambulance (FLA) rather than by air; he was downright apologetic. But heck, this was the 101st, and we did everything in the most tactical manner. In the hospital I met a guy who got a Blackhawk ride over a broken thumb (an injury inflicted during a volleyball match) he sniffed at the idea of wasting resources like that.

However, in this case the apology was warranted. I knew it was going to be a long night when I heard the FLA crew asking if anyone had some night vision goggles they could borrow since they didn't have any and it was a moonless night after they arrived an hour later.

Nobody was willing to hand over five thousand dollars worth of equipment they had signed for and would never see again to some ambulance drivers. The driver looked competent, though, and they put me on a stretcher for placement into the FLA. Just for a laugh, I started singing the 101ˢᵗ Airborne Division song as they carried me out of the tent.

"Must be shock," the XO said too loudly.

"Naw, he does that," sighed Sergeant Waggle, who had hung around the whole time. Indeed, I made it a ritual to stand on top of my position right after the morning stand-to ended to lead the platoon in singing it. It was both funny (we liked to emulate the Battalion Commander, who was a big fan of opera and had a unique style in singing it) and morale boosting. We might not have vehicles, heat, food other than field rations (MREs), electricity, shade, clean clothes, or even water to spare for washing up, but as long as we had ammo and each other we were damned proud to be where we were and who we were with.

This little female medic was in the back with me as we set out cross country in search of the infamous Brigade Aid Station. The stupid plastic leg splint was really starting to bug me, so I stealthily pulled my bayonet and put a small hole in it, which made it slowly deflate. Every time she noticed it was flat she'd re-inflate it, which hurt like hell.

It soon became clear two things were going to describe this journey: One that we were lost and two that the means of finding the way involved driving over every large rock or into every deep hole that could be found in the dark. I began to swear with gusto every time the cot was raised into the air and slammed back down. "Slow this M-Fer down" was the nicest thing I said.

The poor girl stuck with my abuse became cowed by it, whimpering to the guy up front in a high pitched voice. "Bill," she'd plead as I went on another tirade in a small voice, "Bill..." It was hilarious! But I didn't cut her any slack – things were starting to really smart, and every big bump and jolt was like getting kicked by a mule. Hell, that ride hurt more than getting shot, and was the worst of the whole affair.

Finally, by luck, the driver found the one paved road in that part of the world, Tapline Road, and I told the girl medic that she was not to re-inflate the splint unless she wanted to get knocked on her ass and that I was going to try and get some sleep.

Sorry for yet another digression, but it needs to be explained that your average combat troop can sleep in almost any situation, but particularly when

167

in vehicles on the move. Infantrymen treat sleep as an invaluable commodity; since we never know when or for how long we will have to go without it, we train ourselves to knock out whenever we can. Transit in a vehicle is prime sleep time, since there is little one can do when in a moving vehicle anyway.

Eventually, we made it to the Brigade Aid Station, which was a pretty big deal – they had pavement! Arabia is a strange place. Here in the desert off of Tapline was what looked like a big parking lot, and on it a bunch of great big GP Large tents. I was ushered into a credible looking medical tent outfitted to a forward surgery, where the Brigade Command Sergeant Major, the senior Non-Commissioned officer of the show, received me, overhearing me lecture the fellows carrying me on my stretcher.

"The next guy that tries to put me in an FLA is going to find there is more than one gunshot wound being treated tonight," I warned.

One of the guys laughed, and the CSM interrupted him with a stern look.

"You need to listen to him," he advised, then turned to me, "you meant that, didn't you?"

"I still have my ammo and my rifle," I honestly answered. The medics jumped back from me like I was a rattlesnake.

While we waited on the surgeon, he appraised my wound and demeanor, which had soured considerably.

"That doesn't look too bad, Sergeant," he frowned at me.

"It isn't, Sergeant Major, but I just spent three hours bouncing around the desert because the M-F driver got lost."

"Aw, the morphine should have made it an easy ride."

"I didn't get any morphine."

"What?" he asked, as if I had arrived to the battlefield without a rifle, "You didn't get your morphine?"

"Um, no," I admitted, somewhat sheepishly.

"Hell, I got shot twice in Vietnam, and each time was high as a kite in minutes."

So when the surgeon arrived to cut the deflated splint off of me (he clucked that they put it on wrong, but the CSM correctly pointed out that it had clearly been cut by me) and express disappointment at the straight forward nature of my injury ("they got me out of bed for this?") the difference of medical opinion as to pain relief played out.

"Three grains of morphine," the doctor declared.

"Five," the Sergeant Major countered.

"He's awful small," the doctor admonished. Hell, I went 150 pounds of pure muscle, able to carry far more than that and fight!

"They f'd him earlier and cheated him out of it," the Sergeant Major advised, "Give the man a ride."

"When did you get shot?" he asked.

"1900 hours," I said.

"It's zero four hundred;" the Sergeant Major pointed out, "and they've been bouncing him around the desert in the back of an FLA since then."

Five it was. Ah, sweet morphine. If ever I were to use an illicit drug, this would be the one – but then again, I like it so much that I know I'd instantly become a hopeless addict. One can still feel the pain, but one just doesn't care about it. Three feet thick and just pleased as punch about everything. I was very complacent when one of the stretcher minions crept up to say that there had to be a very short ambulance ride to the Blackhawk helicopter. As I agreed it was okay I noticed that the CSM had stripped me of my rifle and placed it on the other side of the room."

It was good to see Frank was ok, and reconnecting with the other guys back at Campbell was a good thing. 1/320th Field Artillery Regiment had a professional group of NCOs and officers. I had just spent months in the desert with the infantry but had very little time with my artillery brothers. I was impressed with them and comfortable with their ability to get the battalion up to speed. Our lack of physical training during the past few weeks of time off was immediately addressed as physical training was stepped up and the battery runs got longer. When the equipment arrived from Saudi Arabia, the vast majority of our time during the day was spent in the motor pool accounting for and maintaining our equipment. The division was working hard,

169

and had to get back up to 101st Airborne Division standards in case we were called on to go to war again.

On 1 May, 1991 I was promoted to E-6 (Staff Sergeant). The 1-320th Field Artillery Battalion was in formation as CSM Kalub Duggins called me to the front. As I stood at attention in front of him, LTC Lawson read my promotion:

CERTIFICATE OF PROMOTION

Know Ye, that reposing special trust and confidence in the fidelity and abilities of

STEPHEN D. WIEHE

I do promote him to Staff Sergeant in the United States Army to rank as such from the First day of May nineteen hundred and ninety one.

You will discharge carefully and diligently the duties of the grade to which promoted and uphold the traditions and standards of the Army.

Soldiers of lesser rank are required to obey your lawful orders. Accordingly you accept responsibility for their actions. As a noncommissioned officer you are charged to observe and follow the orders and directions given by superiors acting according to the laws, articles and rules governing the discipline of the Army, and to correct conditions detriment to the readiness thereof. In so doing, you fulfill your greatest obligation as a leader and thereby confirm your status as a Noncommissioned Officer in the United States Army.

Signed: Harlan A. Lawson, LTC, FA

After reading my promotion he began telling the story about our meeting at the quarry in Hafar al-Batin and reviewing the target list that I had prepared for an Iraqi armor attack down the wadi. He recounted the event in detail. I was impressed with his recollection of specifics (not having to recap the story with me prior to the formation).

A few days later, I received the Army Commendation Medal

for my job in the desert. I was pleased with the comments on the orders by my superiors, including Sgt Wiehe's professionalism and expertise helped in distinguishing himself as "the best forward observer in the company." The short and sweet comment that meant more to me than any others was from LTC. Lawson: "One of the best FOs in the battalion."

With the promotion came additional responsibility. The 1-320th gave me the Fire Support NCO slot for C Company 3/502nd Infantry Regiment, 101st Airborne Division. The 3/502nd had a storied history, as do all of the Screaming Eagles, but the battalion did have the distinction of having the greatest loss. On 12 December 1985, the unit was coming back for Christmas from peace-keeping responsibilities in the Sinai when their Arrow Airlines flight 1285, a DC-8, crashed shortly after take-off from Gander International Airport, Gander Newfoundland, Canada. All 248 soldiers and a crew of 8 perished in the crash. The unit was a part of the MFO (Multi-National Force and Observers) which was made up of an international contingent of ten nations charged with enforcing a 1979 Peace Treaty between Egypt and Israel. The crash was the worst peace-time loss in military history. It was devastating not only to the 101st and the Army, but to our country as well. President Ronald Reagan and his wife, Nancy (among other dignitaries), attended the division's ceremony honoring the soldiers that were lost.

A week after my promotion, I was called into battalion HQ. I had a phone call on hold from Marilyn Lile, the wife of Jimmy Lile calling from Russellville, Arkansas. She said, "I have some bad news for you Steve; your friend passed away." I was devastated. Jimmy and I had been friends for years, and I had just talked to him on the phone from Ft. Lewis before I was deployed. Marilyn asked me if I had heard anything about Jimmy's death, and unfortunately I had not. She went on to say that Paul Harvey talked about the Arkansas Knife Maker and his history on one of his radio shows. I passed on my condolences to Marilyn and after we hung up I was in shock. After the shock came the guilt for not calling him the minute I got back. I had promised him that report on "Gray Ghost." He was one of kindest and most compassionate gentlemen I have ever met. He not only was the maker of the "Rambo Knife", but his knives were sought after by dignitaries. Presidents Nixon, Ford, and Reagan owned them.

On 21 June, General JH Binford Peay, III gave his farewell to the 101st. He was not just a general but he was "Our General." After being promoted to the rank of Lieutenant General, he would now be the Army's Deputy Chief of Staff for Operations and Plans, and Senior Army Member, United States Military Committee. It was like our dad was leaving. We were happy about his promotion, but sad he was leaving. He would be leaving shoes that would be hard to fill.

These are some of General Peay's comments upon his departure.

"In August 1990, the Eagle was in full flight. We were the first combat division to totally close in Saudi Arabia. We had two great missions: providing the covering force along the Kuwait border to ensure the defense of Saudi Arabia…and conducting an offensive attack deep into Iraq to destroy the Iraqi enemy and cut his lines of communication. Both were accomplished. We developed a splendid plan characterized by innovation, surprise and boldness representative of the Division's history. Contingency plans were also developed for flexibility. Screaming Eagles executed the plans to perfection. They were able to do so because of their demanding training at Fort Campbell and their hard work in the harsh environment of the desert before crossing the line of departure in February. They made history just like the great veterans and alumni of this division who marched before them. Just as impressive was their organization, special discipline and pride. It was unsurpassed, and this carried the day in the final analysis. Their morale was high because of their belief in the cause, and in their units, leaders and fellow soldiers. You are a special breed of soldier. When you wear the patch, you set the standards. It is as simple as that.

The support we received from home was tremendous. We simply can't thank you enough: for your care, for your prayers, and for your constancy of support. All America was helpful, but you patriots from these surrounding and contiguous communities, you civilian workers and military members that operated our post and rear detachments and you family support groups made a major difference. You were combat power...and I am convinced that the enemy knew it. It was genuine on your part and we felt it! Your resolve contributed in no small part to the enemy's lack of will to fight and directly influenced this stunning victory. We thank you a hundred times over.

As I leave command today, I am certain of the challenges that face this Division in the future. In two short weeks, you must be prepared to again march off to war if the nation calls. The stark reality is that "freedom is never free." Certainly the result of a well-trained and proud Army, outfitted with solid equipment and the latest technology, ably led, and with support at home are clear...and this is a continuing requirement to ensure our nation's and our children's destiny. Screaming Eagles returned to Fort Campbell desert-hardened, broader, wiser and more mature. The young officers and enlisted soldiers are our senior officers and noncommissioned officers of tomorrow. This experience has prepared them well for that mantle of leadership and the role they will play in the future security of our country. My very best to each of you in your next rendezvous with destiny."

AIR ASSAULT![1]

My final days with the 101st Airborne Division were filled with FTX (field training exercises) and training. Everyone seemed to go in different directions as soldiers do following a war. Some of my buddies stayed in the Army, and others like me made the decision to leave. My decision to leave the Army came with health concerns and family. It was the most difficult decision I had ever faced because of my love for the Army community, its soldiers, and the 101st Airborne Division. I separated from the Army in December, 1991 and moved back to Texas with my family. With separation from the Army as a staff sergeant, I received the "customary" Army Commendation Medal in the mail some three weeks after my Honorable Discharge.

The 9th Infantry Division "Old Reliables" from whence I came also cased its colors in December, 1991 and disbanded in 1992.

---

1   By special permission from General Peay, I was able to use his comments from the yearbook, 101st Airborne Division: North to the Euphrates. Since there were some dedications noted in his comments, they were omitted as I in no way wanted to imply that those dedications were for this book.

Parade in Midland, Texas - March 25, 1991.
Courtesy of my Grandmother

Chapter 11

The Military Family
For Meritorious Service from a Grateful Nation

There is not enough said about military families and the tremendous sacrifice they make for our country; their contribution to a war effort and the effect on troop morale cannot be overstated. Our comments like "holding down the fort" don't even scratch the surface about what they do while soldiers are deployed to a hostile environment. A medal should be awarded for the wife or husband that stays behind, managing the day to day while striving to provide a sense of normalcy. In fact, the medal should be for *"Meritorious Service from a Grateful Nation."*

General Peay not only acknowledged the families in his farewell to the 101st but paid tribute to the military family as a whole, made up of "patriots from surrounding and contiguous communities, civilian workers, and military members that operated post and rear detachments, and family support groups."

It wasn't just the soldiers that made us successful in the desert. During the Gulf War, we saw an unprecedented show of support, rivaled only by the war effort of World War II. The nation and the military families were joined together for a common cause and the soldiers knew it. Even in the harsh, desert conditions of Saudi Arabia and Iraq, we were keenly aware of this common cause.

The military family and concerned citizens would do anything to show those soldiers in harm's way that they were being thought of and supported. Letters and care packages from home, schools, and support groups reinforced the connection to home. Mail was sporadic at best while we were in the Gulf, but when we did get mail I always received something from my wife, Kristen, Mom and Dad, Don (my brother), Angela (my sister), grandparents, cousins, aunts, uncles, friends, and kids from the schools. As a result of all this mail, I never felt forgotten.

The 1-320th Field Artillery and the 1-502nd wives and families' efforts were simply amazing. With the entire 101st Airborne Division deployed to theatre, everyone in the Fort Campbell-Clarksville area was in some way touched by the deployment.

Alison Duggins, CSM Kalub Duggins' daughter, was nineteen years old at the time and Barbara Duggins' "right hand" during the war.

Alison Duggins:

"As a daughter of a soldier, I was used to my father being gone on training missions overseas while living in Germany but Desert Storm was totally new for my age group. My mother had been through this during Vietnam. Uncertainty was right there in your face. My father was the CSM of the 1-320th Field Artillery Battalion; mom and I were his support. She and the other wives had to keep things going during this war.

Mom and I made up boxes not only for my father but those soldiers who might not be getting anything from home. We did not have the luxury of email and cell phones at the time (both technologies were still in the early stages). Handling everyday situations such as bills, illnesses, and crisis amongst the women was just something that had to be done. No one questioned what we were doing; we just did what was deemed the right thing to do.

Communication was via letters and a few phone calls. Lots of cards and letters were exchanged. Any soldier mail had become popular during that time. Schools across the country would adopt soldiers. Soldiers were quoted as receiving as many as 60 letters from a school. It seems that is what kept the motivation for the men to get the job done in Desert Storm.

Each wife handled the war differently. Some worked and volunteered and there were others who went home as they just did not know what was going to happen. Connections were important for getting through the day. The wives had a phone roster. Everyone checked on everyone, especially those with small children. I was working and going to school and Mom was busy with the little things. She and the Colonel's wife would do a monthly newsletter. Those newsletters would have information about what to do about lost I.D. cards, hospital situations, and how to prepare in the event a soldier was killed in the war.

Mom told me it was rather easy compared to Vietnam, but there were moments of stress. Usually it was when you would hear about an accident or bombing. No one would know if their husband was hurt. Communication on that level was not as prominent as Desert Storm or even as the current war in Afghanistan. Mail was slower in 1968 versus 1990 and today. What would take three weeks some forty years ago, now often takes seven days. Comparing the two wars is difficult, but there were differences on how things were handled. Communication definitely did improve during Desert Storm.

Routine was key and the support amongst the wives. FRG (family readiness group) was just getting started during the time. We also came together when we knew they were coming home. We set up and cleaned Dad's and the Colonel's office. We did 'Welcome Home Greets' for the soldiers as they came home."

At Fort Lewis, the political climate and the opinion regarding the war were different than at Fort Campbell. The 9th Infantry Division was not deployed to Saudi Arabia, but there were quite a few from Lewis (like me) who were. Even though the vast majority of the citizens in the Seattle-Tacoma area were patriotic and supportive of the military, a few were not. The surrounding areas near Fort Campbell were there because of the military, and enjoyed popular support. In some ways it was just the opposite at Fort Lewis. The fort was in the community but not the reason for it, so there were diverse opinions regarding the war. During the Gulf War, protestors would line the entrance to the main gate at Fort Lewis, reminiscent of the Vietnam War protestors from twenty years earlier. My wife and daughter would have to go through that gate every day and there were times when news crews from Seattle would be covering the protestors.

The military family at Ft. Lewis was very supportive, and leading the way for the 3-11th FA Battalion was LTC Reitz' wife. There were only five from the battalion that were deployed, so her list was small. She would check in with my wife occasionally and would have been there for support, if necessary. Sherrie was independent and capable of managing the household affairs and maintaining a sense of normalcy for our four-year-old daughter, Kristen. She had a job in Federal Way, up the road from Fort Lewis, dropping our daughter off at day care (close by her job) on the way to work. Even though many wives from the Fort Lewis group went back to their homes for family support, mine stayed in "on-post" housing at Lewis.

Communication resources and FRG (family readiness group) structure has changed for the better in the past two decades, but some challenges remain the same. Twenty years later, issues that are usually manageable like car repair, finances, and the children still can become problematic for the "single parent" during long deployments. Rear detachment personnel can lend a sympathetic ear to a dependent's personal problems, but usually refers the spouse to a support group organized to handle every day affairs. The truth is that life goes on for spouses and dependents that are left behind. The bills still have to be paid, the kids still have to get to school and do their homework, and every day challenges still have to be addressed.

Even well balanced, level-headed couples recognize the stresses of saying, "Goodbye" and "Welcome Home." Unfortunately, when the soldier comes back, they come back with more than their TA-50. When a soldier steps off the plane, they are immersed into family and garrison life, but still needing time to decompress from combat. The dependent is worn out and needs help, but just because the soldier is home doesn't mean they are "capable." Switching gears can be complicated for the military family. Spouses that were accustomed to managing "everything" during a deployment now have to explain their decisions. Some soldiers coming back want to put their "two-cents-worth" into every family decision, and others don't want to hear anything about managing the household. For couples reuniting, it can be a challenge resetting house norms. This transition can take a few days, a few months, and for a few, never. Multiply these ups and downs times three or more deployments to a "war zone" and the sacrifices these families make for our country become enormous.

After eight years of war in Iraq and Afghanistan (with multiple deployments) the military has acknowledged the importance of taking care of the military dependent left behind. "Family Readiness Groups" are now Army sponsored organizations comprising family members, volunteers, and soldiers, which provide an avenue of mutual support and assistance. The leaders of these groups are now accountable for monitoring the unit's dependent needs. They now have the internet and unit websites at their disposal that can disseminate information quickly and efficiently to family members wherever they are in the world. As a result, group leaders are no longer solely dependent on call rosters to get the word out as was the case during the Gulf War.

Great organizations like the National Military Family Organization set up specifically for the military family is just one of many resources available today. They have a wonderful website that is easy to navigate and includes guidance on a variety of challenges that face the soldier and their dependents. Topics like preparing for the upcoming deployment, talking to kids, the reunion, back at home, reestablishing roles and reintegration are just a few of the topics they cover. Because of the internet, there are many more tools available at the fingertips of the military family than there were twenty years ago.

The military family comes together more quickly today than in past wars because of enhanced communication channels. Soldiers are now taking cell phones with them to combat zones enabling them to talk to loved ones and access social media. However, the technology of the internet, cell phones, and social media comes with a double-edged-sword. Dependents and family are starved for information regarding their soldier in harm's way, and

179

talk on the phone and communicate via email and social media whenever they can. When these communications are "blacked out", it's because there has been a casualty. Commanders don't want their soldiers in the field prematurely notifying loved ones about the details. Command authority wants time to personally send casualty assistance officers to the next of kin to make the notification and to offer immediate counseling. The black out time can be excruciating, as family and friends light up the phones trying to get some word on their soldier.

In the past, when a soldier came home injured or disabled, they were expeditiously discharged and sent home to be rehabilitated and counseled by the nearest Veteran's Administration Medical Center. The soldier is no longer forgotten as in wars past and there is no longer a stigma attached to coming back wounded. The VA has made noticeable improvements over the past ten years in taking care of our wounded soldiers' emotional and physical needs. Even with their enormous responsibilities, they are doing a much better job of identifying service connected disabilities, healing the physical and psychological impacts of war.

There are established organizations like the Wounded Warrior Project that are doing a tremendous job in assisting the warrior's transition back home. The motto, "The greatest casualty is being forgotten" forges the way for this non-profit organization to advocate for the wounded soldier and their families. The WWP has many initiatives, including family support, education on dealing with unique learning challenges, care-giver education and counseling, and even coordinating transportation. The WWP also offers rehabilitation through adaptive sports, health, nutrition and recreational activities as well as combat stress recovery programs and the tools to assist the soldier in finding employment and long term stability for themselves and their families.

When I talk about the military family, I'm not just talking about the active duty military and their immediate family. I am also talking about the military community as a whole; a brother and sisterhood of patriots that extend far beyond the post boundaries and communities that surround bases and installations. Citizen soldiers, veterans' groups and organizations, retirees, government employees, defense contractors, and even the adopted civilian patriots feel connected to this special close knit family. I have been out of the Army for almost twenty years and still consider myself part of the military family.

I still feel that gut wrenching pain when I find out there has been a casualty; thinking about the dependents, family, and friends that are left behind. Even though we have served and fought for the greatest nation on earth and the constitutional freedoms associated with it, I feel sick to my stomach when I see those freedoms abused. The First Amendment to The United States Constitution protects "Free Speech" but it nauseates me to see groups protest at military funerals. I can't even imagine the pain of losing a family member in service to our country. I cannot fathom a protest while families are paying tribute and honor to their fallen. It is incomprehensible how these actions can be justified.

In March 2011, the Supreme Court of the United States ruled in *Snyder v. Phelps*, that the fringe "Westboro" church's (small c intentional) demonstrations at fallen soldiers funerals are protected speech. The opinion upheld a jury's decision to throw out a lawsuit filed by a military family to prevent the church from picketing at their son's funeral. Marine Lance Cpl. Matthew Snyder's father sued this weird family church (almost solely made up of the family of "pastor" Fred Phelps), claiming that the protests amounted to harassment and infliction of emotional distress. But the Court held in an 8-1 decision in favor of the church. Justice Samuel Alito was the lone dissenter, saying: "Our profound national commitment to free and open debate is not a license for the vicious verbal assault that occurred in this case."

Chief Justice John Roberts wrote, "Speech is powerful. It can stir people to action, move them to tears of both joy and sorrow, and– as it did here– inflict great pain. On the facts before us, we cannot react to that pain by punishing the speaker." The majority of justices in this case felt the First Amendment rights must be upheld because the protests were directed at "public not private" matters and a ruling in favor of the father of the deceased soldier could become a slippery slope of restraining future political speech.

I agree that our First Amendment rights should be protected and fought for, but this hurtful exercise of it by these venomous groups is an assault on "My Family."

Anyone connected to the military family are concerned about the attacks on our military and national security by internet sites bent on publishing sensitive, classified material from anonymous sources. Our country remains at war with radical jihadists who ceaselessly plot to murder our citizens and those of other freedom loving nations. There are corners of the world where evil men plot to destroy us and our way of life. These leaks are not entertaining nor are they a voice performing an invaluable service to the world with a commitment to the protection of human rights and the rule of law. It is amazing that organizations focused on releasing such information have received world-wide recognition and support. In World War II, such activities would have been deemed treasonous, but today they receive commendations for transparency. These cyber-treason leaks are exposing our soldiers, citizens, and military family to extremists who are determined to retaliate. This crime is an assault on "My Family."

Chapter 12

G-Day Plus 20 Years

I called my good friend Roy Ayers, an Air Force veteran, to see if he would like to drive with me to Texas A&M University to see the twenty year Gulf War Commemoration hosted by President George H.W. Bush. He readily agreed. I heard just one day before about the notable gathering of decision makers from Operation Desert Storm from President Bush's office in Houston, but due to my job, felt like I couldn't go. On the morning of the event, after my wife Sue saw a news report on the commemoration, she told me it shouldn't even be a question. I needed to go. This historic commemoration was an opportunity of a lifetime for me to see most of the leaders that had impacted my life when I was with the 101st Airborne Division. I quickly juggled my schedule for the day, and off we went. The memories from the Gulf War flooded my mind on the trip from Austin to College Station as Roy and I shared memories of the events from two decades ago. On the way, I called my daughter Kristen, who was working on her masters at Texas A&M and asked her to go by and pick up tickets for us. I was thinking about how time flies. She was only four years old during the Gulf War, and now she is five years older than Marty, who was my RTO/FO during the war. My son, Clay, now as tall as I am, was not even born during the Gulf War. With him being a senior in high school, my only son is at that prime age. With at least three more years remaining in the "War on Terror" in Afghanistan, my prayer as a father is that he not be a participant.

As we walked into Reed Arena at Texas A&M University, a large crowd was gathering; most had already taken their seats with the Corps of Cadets filling the North end of the arena. The band played, and it didn't take long before I began to feel some of the pride that I felt years ago. The event was hosted by President George H.W. Bush, and there would be a panel discussion that included then-Defense Secretary Dick Cheney, former Secretary of State James Baker, former Chairman of the Joint Chiefs of Staff General Colin Powell, then-National Security Advisor Brent Scowcroft, and then-Marine General Walter Boomer. Also on the panel was Kuwaiti's ambassador to the United Nations during the Gulf War, H.E. Mohammad Abdullah Abulhasan.

After showing a short film about Operation Desert Shield and the buildup to Operation Desert Storm, President Bush gave a short introductory speech and was joined by former Vice President Dan Quayle. The President said that helping to liberate Kuwait as commander in chief of the U.S. – led coalition was one the greatest honors of his life. He said, "A few things I probably could have done better, but in the case of Desert Storm, history will say we got this one right." The President was someone I had never talked to personally (although I shook his hand once at an Astros game when he was Vice President some twenty-four years ago), yet he was like part of the family to me. I felt that way about very few presidents. Ok, maybe it was because he resided in Texas and liked baseball. Or, maybe it was because he was a veteran of WWII. I don't know, but even before the Gulf War, I had felt a special connection to him.

As a Desert Storm soldier, I have a great deal of respect and gratitude for the President and the leaders that surrounded him during the Gulf War. Twenty years ago, the President and his "decision makers" had a thorough knowledge of foreign policy, the world's geopolitical situation, and the military. Astounding to this day, this circle put together an historic coalition to defend the region and vacate Saddam Hussein from Kuwait, while defeating the fourth largest army in the world. Even if I had been on the outside looking in, the way the war and the coalition were so efficiently managed by our leaders would have amazed me. To have actually participated in this campaign was a tremendous honor.

After The President spoke, Sheikh Ahmad Humood Jaber Al-Sabah, representing Kuwait's emir, who was unable to attend due to an Arab Economic Summit, thanked the President, his former advisors, the United States, and its military forces. "Believe me, Kuwait and its people will never forget you," he said. "Each and every day we carry in our hearts what you did for us."

After the panel was introduced and took their seats, Colin Powell read a letter from General H. Norman Schwarzkopf who was ill and could not attend. In General Schwarzkopf's letter he said, "Our mission was victorious because we had the best-trained military in the world, a president that had the fortitude to make tough choices when they needed to be made, and the unwavering support of the American people. Our mission in Kuwait ended twenty years ago, but the impact will endure for generations to come."

As the panel began discussing the decisions they made, my mind automatically filled in where I was and what I was doing at that time. I was amazed at James Baker's dialogue regarding the possibility of Saddam using chemical weapons against us. Saddam had been ready, willing, and able to use them in the past, even on his own people and in the Iran-Iraq war. Chemical weapons were one of our great "fears" in the Gulf War. If Saddam had chosen to use them, thousands of coalition troops would have died. Baker talked about his conversation with Tariq Aziz, the Iraqi Foreign Minister, at the Geneva Peace Conference on January 9, 1991. We will never know if Saddam was planning to use chemical weapons, but I sincerely believe if he were considering it, Baker's warning would have echoed in his head. Baker told Aziz that if a conflict starts, God forbid, and chemical or biological weapons are used against our forces, the American people would demand revenge, and we have the means to implement this. The strong implication, though not said, was that we would use nuclear weapons to "exact" that revenge.

The President wanted to give Saddam ample time to conform to the United Nations resolutions and to give peace a chance. At the Geneva Peace Conference, Saddam wanted to tie other Middle East issues regarding Israel and Palestine to his withdrawal from Kuwait. The United Nations Security Council passed Resolution 678 on November 29, 1990, authorizing member states to use all necessary means to uphold and implement all previous resolutions demanding the immediate withdrawal of Iraq from Kuwait. The President's position was clear. The United States and its allies would not agree to anything less than an unconditional, full withdrawal of Kuwait. The meeting in Geneva was historic; however, both sides held firm to their positions.

Following the January 9th meeting in Geneva, the next hurdle the administration faced was a vote in Congress to use our forces to extract Saddam from Kuwait. The President had authority to act without Congressional approval in executing UN Security Council resolutions, but he still sought Congressional approval for the war. In January, the administration felt it had the necessary votes for authorization and after intense debate, the Senate (by a vote of 52 to 47) and the House (by a vote of 250 to 183), gave the president authority to use force. Rather than strand a half million soldiers in the gulf, all of the decision makers say they would have encouraged the President to proceed with war even without Congressional approval.

There had been numerous books written by Generals and notable writers about the Gulf War, giving me the impression that my story seemed miniscule in comparison. But, the more the panelists shared with the audience their decisions surrounding the event, the more I felt validation for telling my story. I wasn't a decorated war hero or one that made the decisions that impacted the lives of the participants. I was just "one" of 543,000. In talking to some of my comrades from the Gulf War twenty years later, I quickly found out how memories fade and our movements in the desert had been diminished to a long field training exercise (FTX) in their minds. These assertions couldn't be further from the truth, and without putting what really happened in print, our families and the generations to follow would have never known our history.

When Saddam invaded Kuwait, we were at a distinct disadvantage. Even with our President's "Line in the sand", we were extremely exposed in the desert for the first few months. It would take months, not days, to send enough troops and equipment to the region to adequately defend. It would take even more time to adequately build our forces to the level necessary to go on the offense to remove Iraqi forces from Kuwait. Had he invaded Saudi Arabia early, history would have played out much differently. Instead of evicting Saddam out of Kuwait, we would have had the monumental task of taking him out of the region. With no toe-hold as we had in Saudi Arabia, the mission would have been much more difficult with much more loss of life. Because we had the ability to set up bases expeditiously in Saudi Arabia, the coalition's strength and ability grew quickly. Because of President Bush's decisive action, history played out in our favor, and Saddam blinked.

At the conclusion of the 20th Gulf War Commemoration at Texas A&M, the moderator posed the question of mistakes made in the Gulf War. "I think it was probably a mistake for us to let him fly his helicopters," James Baker responded. Colin Powell said that the Shiite and Kurd uprisings were "unfortunate" and said, "There's a legitimate argument we have as to whether or not we stopped too soon." Dick Cheney said that the American military "had done a tremendous job" and the Iraqi Army was by then so weak that it was a question of whether the administration wanted to ask the military to continue to slaughter the enemy.

Twenty years after G-Day and the Gulf War, I still get questions from the ill-informed, asking, "Why we didn't do more?" After they find out I am a Desert Storm veteran, the debate begins with why we couldn't have gone all the way to Baghdad to finish Saddam off the first time? Or, why we didn't support the uprising of the Kurds and Shiites after our President encouraged them to do so? Never shying away from an argument, I always start by talking about the facts. The coalition would have splintered if we had done anything other than to get him out of Kuwait. We were bound by UN Resolutions to stop the aggression and nothing more. Our job was not to annihilate or exterminate his troops, but to remove him from Kuwait. Had we pursued and killed more retreating troops, the decisive, quick victory in the Gulf War could have easily turned into a black-eye for America.

In the last days of television coverage of the war, viewers saw Iraqi conscripts pouring from foxholes waiving their hands in surrender. What they failed to report fully were the atrocities committed by the Republican Guard thugs who had murdered and raped their way through Kuwait. They were our targets, not the citizen soldier who had been forced to serve or risk death.

As President Bush said in a 1995 interview with David Frost, "Our argument wasn't with the people of Iraq or with the military of Iraq. It was with Saddam Hussein himself. We could have killed another couple hundred tanks and thus further diminished the capability of the Republican Guard to project their horror, but I don't think you measure the totality of its success by whether you can shoot down another – kill another 50,000 fleeing soldiers, murderous though they had been in Kuwait."

In the same interview, The President said he was told by Secretary Cheney and General Powell that the objective to end the aggression was complete and said it is time to end the war. The President asked the question, "Do our commanders agree? Do Schwarzkopf and the men in the field agree?" And they said, "Yes." "They got Schwarzkopf on the phone from the Oval Office, and he confirmed to me that the time had come to end the war," said Bush. "I've always had this feeling that that kind of decision should be defined by the military. The military said, "The war is over; we've accomplished our objectives."

Some say we should have demanded Saddam show up personally at Safwan to surrender. I say, had we done so, and he said "No," then what? Do we send troops into Baghdad to apprehend him? The President felt if we had gone to Baghdad, "We're an occupying force in an Arab land. The coalition shatters." He went on to say, "I think history will say we did the right thing."

The President's words that the United States would be ready to better its relations with Iraq when Saddam was out of power was interpreted by the Shiites as the U.S. would support them militarily in their fight. That was not the case. The President as well as the Arab world felt Saddam could not maintain power after the Gulf War. Once he left power, the United States would look forward to establishing relations. The Kurds and Shiites were hungry for change and saw this statement from the President as a green light to overthrow the Hussein regime with United States' help and support. Of course our President and leadership wanted and anticipated the change in Iraq, but not at the expense of our troops' lives, and bogging down in a quagmire with no exit strategy.

If the war had continued, our 101st Airborne Division Commander General Peay had a follow on plan, which if called on to execute, would have "threatened a lethal strike against his capital, and shut off his escape." Schwarzkopf and Peay's audible at the line of scrimmage would have come with the risk of heavy fighting with Saddam's faithful Republican Guard and run the risk of now being seen as occupiers of an Arab land. Had our leadership been called upon to execute this plan, the presence of the 101st Airborne Division would have sent a strong message to Saddam, the people of Iraq, and the resistance that we had undeniably won the war. Saddam Hussein would have been separated from a large number of his Republican Guard that had been committed to Kuwait, giving the coalition an opportunity to temporarily disable his war machine and allowing an insurrection of Kurds and Shiites to take root.

If the play had been called, the follow-on mission would have cut Saddam's communication lines between him and the

Republican Guard, while coalition troops took prisoners and impounded Iraqi armor and weaponry. This limited action would have eliminated his immediate ability to retaliate against the insurgency without us having to "slaughter" the Iraqi troops or destroy their ability to defend from a future Iranian threat. By February 28, the Iraqis had a limited will to fight, so another few days or weeks of coalition troops policing up the area would have had minimal additional loss of life without us having to permanently occupy or rebuild the country.

True or not, my conjectures twenty years later are like arm-chair quarterbacking. In reality, I am pleased that our Generals were prepared to execute a plan which would have further tightened the noose around Saddam Hussein's neck. After hearing the decision-makers speak twenty years later, I am sure all options with the associated risks were debated at length, and I stand by and with their decisions. Of concern to the President and the Generals were "our lives." There had been minimal loss of life up to February 28th and if we had gone further, most certainly there would have been additional casualties. The coalition had succeeded in stopping the aggression, and Saddam's troops were retreating. With one wrong move on our part, the victorious defeat of Saddam could have turned into a muddy, downhill slide. I am thankful we had leaders that were concerned about us.

When we left Iraq, it did give Saddam the opportunity to regroup and brutally quell the resistance. Amazingly, he was more ruthless solidifying and defending his dictatorship than he was fighting the coalition. Also, in the years that followed the Gulf War, UNSCOM inspectors were suppressed and deceived by Saddam as they searched for WMDs (weapons of mass destruction). The inspectors did in fact locate chemical depots and proof of Iraq's pursuit of nuclear weapons, but the question was did they find them all? There is an assumption in the intelligence community that Iraq moved chemical weapons to Syria, which was working on its own chemical weapons programs prior to the invasion in 2003.

One of the sources of our intelligence was admittedly faulty in the days leading up to the 2003 invasion. The source was information German Intelligence received from Rafid Ahmed Alwan al-Janabi or "Curveball." Alwan was a trained Iraqi chemical engineer who just this year admitted he lied about Saddam Hussein's bio-weapons capability when he was seeking asylum in Germany years ago. His claim was "The BND (German Intelligence) knew in 2000 that I was lying after they talked to my former boss, Dr Bassil Latif, who told them there were no bio-weapons factories."

In making a case for war on 5 February 2003, Secretary of State Powell went before the UN Security Council using the faulty information in his speech. He referred to firsthand descriptions of biological weapons factories on wheels and on rails (that was provided by "Curveball"). The President also used this information in his state of the union address to the nation. After the admission from Alwan came out in 2011, Powell said the CIA and DIA should be forced to explain why "Curveball's" information was put into the key intelligence assessment (NIE).

Our troops never found the portable bio-weapons factories they were looking for in 2003, but we would be naïve to think that he did not have WMD or that he was not trying to produce them. In an unclassified U.S. House of Representatives report dated June 21, 2006 giving a summary of chemical weapons munitions found since 2004, Coalition forces had recovered approximately 500 weapons/munitions which contained degraded mustard or sarin nerve agent. The report also said that despite many efforts to locate and destroy Iraq's pre-Gulf War chemical munitions, pre-Gulf War chemical munitions are assessed to still exist. It did note that pre-Gulf War Iraqi chemicals could be sold on the black market and the use of these weapons by terrorists or insurgent groups was a possibility, and in addition, the use outside of Iraq could not be ruled out.

At the heart of the 2003 invasion was a ruthless dictator who had been and was in hot pursuit of WMD. After capture, Saddam was convicted of crimes against humanity by his own people and sentenced to death. What we are left with in the region is a government elected by the people with an infant democracy. As fractured and fragile as this new government of Iraq is, it is now a government that represents the diverse people living there. Only time will tell if the new government will succeed. Our prayer is that it will.

Notably, after the Gulf War, a large number of Desert Storm soldiers became ill for no apparent reason. The wide range of symptoms included fatigue, headaches, dizziness, memory issues, joint pain, digestive tract problems, skin problems, immune system disorders, and an increase in birth defects, collectively becoming known as Gulf War Syndrome. It still perplexes researchers. Soldiers in the Gulf War were exposed to a variety of chemicals including PB (Pyridostigmine Bromide) pills, chemical weapons destruction, depleted uranium, and the use of organophosphate pesticides. These chemicals are believed to be a few sources of the illnesses.

In one study, an estimated 125,000 U.S. soldiers were exposed to nerve gas and mustard gas when the Iraqi weapons depot in Khamisiyah (Objective Gold) was destroyed. A couple years after the war, I remember watching "Day One", a primetime ABC News documentary about chemicals in the Gulf War. During the report, they showed two purple triangles in the area of Hafar al-Batin at the time we were there. The report said it was confirmed after Desert Storm that two Czech chemical detection units picked up traces of chemicals in the area of Hafar al-Batin on January 19th, 1991. The chemical detection equipment used by the Czechs included the Russian-made GSP-11 and a portable CHP-71 used as a backup. Their equipment was determined to be reliable. The Czech units detected low levels of nerve agent at points approximately two kilometers apart while moving in a convoy northeast of Hafar al-Batin. About a half hour later, a second Czech unit detected low levels of nerve agent about twenty-five kilometers northeast. U.S. chemical response units were called in to verify the detection, but were unable to verify any agents at those locations. At that time, while we were at Hafar al-Batin, all of our M-8 alarms went off signaling us to get into MOPP-4. Could these low levels of chemicals that the Czechs detected have set off our alarms? Could chemicals have been released by our bombardment after the air war started? I doubt if we will ever know if a nerve agent or fog set off our alarms as we were told the following morning.

I, as well as most of my Desert Storm brothers, received a letter in the mail some six years after the Gulf War, encouraging us to receive a post war evaluation at our nearest Veterans Administration Medical facility. The letter stated we could have been in an area exposed to chemical weapons. Twenty years after the Gulf War, the syndrome is still being researched. To the VA's credit, they have recognized and are treating specific health problems associated with the Gulf War.

The Army changed after the September 11, 2001 terrorist attacks on the World Trade Center and the Pentagon. It became a "War on Terror." Instead of fighting an enemy that could be seen for miles in the desert, the attacks became much more sinister. Improvised explosive devices (IEDs) and suicide bombers, with no regard for their own safety, plague our military and transportation security personnel. It is no longer just our Army that fights another army. The enemies of the day are Islamic extremists, Al-Qaeda trained fighters and suicide bombers that are just as bent on killing our citizenry as they are our military. These extremists hate our Western ideals and all that we stand for in America. This "War on Terror" is many faceted, resulting in an enormous expense to our nation. It's not only the military fighting the Taliban in Afghanistan, but our police agencies who are on the front lines right here in America. My hat goes off to our intelligence community, FBI, Homeland Security, and local police departments fighting this war on the home-front.

I have a neighbor who served the U.S. Army as an interpreter during Iraqi Freedom. As a result of this job, he was labeled a traitor and targeted for death. His own brothers were killed by

193

militants, and he and his family had to flee Iraq seeking asylum as refugees in the United States. His wife and children are working hard to learn the English language and integrate into our schools and community. His statement to me about America is that he cannot believe how peaceful it is. I am thankful and appreciative of his service to our Army, and my thoughts and prayers are with him and his family as they make a new life in the United States.

Twenty years after Desert Storm, and with American combat forces withdrawing from Iraq, the United States Army continues to fight the war on terror in Afghanistan. The Taliban are relentlessly training their fighters in Pakistan, pouring them over the border to their deaths. In 2014, President Barack Obama wants to conclude our military involvement in the region. As a result, the Army and Special Operations Forces are working hard to gain the trust of village leaders, train a new Afghan military, defend Afghanistan from Taliban incursions, and build relationships (mostly shaky ones between the Afghan government and regions that have been susceptible to militant extremism). In addition to all of this, our military is working with the Afghan government and villages on infrastructure and economic issues.

Just because there is an end date to our troop commitment in Afghanistan does not mean there will be no more wars. There is a tremendous fire storm spreading through the Middle East, and no country in the region seems to be immune. Once these sparks of revolt ignite the kindling, the fire cannot be put out. These are uprisings from the masses: citizens wanting equality, freedom, and a voice. The people of Egypt, Libya, Iran, Saudi Arabia, Bahrain, Syria, Yemen, and Jordan are all seeking liberty and democracy.

As dictatorships fall under the weight of cries from its citizens, there are factions waiting to fill the leadership vacuum, without any guarantee that they won't be worse than the one they are trying to replace. We saw an example in 1979, when the Shah of Iran was deposed, only to be replaced by the Ayatollah Khomeini. With Khomeini in power, the United States wanted to create balance

194

in the region, which led to military support of Saddam Hussein. Today, we are facing an international crisis originating from Iran, with President Ahmadinejad of Iran's pursuit of nuclear weapons and his export of terrorism.

The poor living conditions for most of the people in the region sparked December 2010 demonstrations in Tunisia to oust longtime President Zine El Abidine Ben Ali. Food inflation, high unemployment, and a general lack of freedom and the dignity that goes with it spilled into protests and political unrest. After Tunisia's President fled to Saudi Arabia in January of 2011, the Tunisia revolt turned out to be not such an isolated event. In fact, it appears to have been a catalyst for revolution in the region. Neighboring Egypt was next.

The people of Egypt had the military on their side, so the ousting of Hosni Mubarak occurred without bloodshed after eighteen days of demonstrations. Mubarak turned control over to the military and left office with his final words being, "May God help everyone." Not wanting to put words in Mubarak's mouth, maybe his thought was his country will need God's help in the vacuum that had just been created.

The fire spread to Egypt's neighbor Libya. Starting as peaceful protests that Colonel Qaddafi attempted to repress, it soon became evident that the uprising had spread across the country and Qaddafi was losing control. When the Colonel responded with military force, blocking of communications and censorship, the situation then escalated into armed conflict and at the time of this writing, it appears the outcome in Libya is unclear. Libya's military fully supports Colonel Muammar el-Qaddafi, the author of the terrorist attack against Pan-Am Flight 103 just before Christmas 1988 that killed two hundred fifty-nine on board and eleven on the ground. Qaddafi, in power since 1969, is lashing out against anti-government rebels with military and mercenaries, prompting the United Nations to vote in favor of a no-fly zone using all necessary measures to protect civilians. On 19 March 2011, the United States along with the British and French

195

launched their attack against Qaddafi. By 24 March 2011, the administration said that preliminary objectives were met and the United States passed command of the operation to the United Nations. On the night of 30 April 2011, Libyan government and state media officials asserted that Saif, Qaddafi's youngest son, was killed by a NATO air strike. While Qaddafi was reported to have escaped harm in the bombing, the claims are that three of Qaddafi's grandchildren were killed during the strike. As of this writing, questions persist regarding the rebels and their ties to the Muslim Brotherhood and its affiliation with Al Qaeda. Similarly, just exactly who the United Nations No-Fly-Zone and NATO forces are supporting remains to be seen. On May 1, 2011, before the newsprint dried that announced Qaddafi's son's death, a colossal moment in history was about to, at least temporarily, overshadow events in Libya. Some 3,500 miles away in Abbattabad, Pakistan, Osama bin Laden, the leader of Al Qaeda and the architect of the attacks on September 11, 2001 met his just fate at the hands of an elite counter-terrorism unit known as "Seal Team Six." In spite of the irresistible urge to join in world-wide celebration of this monumental event, we cannot be lulled into a state of complacency with premature declarations of victory in the war on terror. As proud as we are of our military and intelligence professionals' ability to execute the daring plan to cut off the head of the snake, we cannot forget that there are autonomous Al Qaeda franchises throughout the world that are ready, willing, and able to fill the leadership vacuum, and take the reins of this insidious organization.

Years ago, bin Laden spawned a multi-headed snake that for years has had the ability to plan, move, and operate without his direct guidance and leadership. There will be some that will use the death of bin Laden to recommend the speedy withdrawal of troops from Afghanistan and declare the war on terror all but over. This is the time when we should be in a heightened state of vigilance both here and abroad. This is the time when we should go after the multi-headed snake and use our toe-hold in the region to pursue the Taliban and Al Qaeda. We can be certain that Al Qaeda will use this opportunity to reassert their influence, avenge their leader's death, and show the world that they are still a viable organization.

Presidents and soldiers hope and pray that their war will be the last, and that their sons and daughters will never have to shoulder and endure that horrible burden again. Most war veterans would wear the uniform again today so that our nation's young wouldn't have to see the horrors of war. Soldiers die and are injured both physically and mentally. Some that have somehow survived physically have to endure tremendous mental and physical challenges long after their war is over. The casualty of war doesn't stop with the participant. Their sacrifice touches families and friends for generations. A soldier that has gone to war can never forget. Families can never forget. Friends can never forget. The time is etched in their minds and memories forever. Some choose to not remember, but they never forget.

My thoughts and prayers go out to the soldiers and their families who are currently serving our Nation. I went into harm's way one time, but some of the Gulf War brothers that I ate desert sand with have gone back into hostile territory many times since. If you are one of those who have made multiple deployments, I salute you. If you are a family member of one of those soldiers, I salute you. You are true patriots.

If you are a Vietnam veteran, thank you for your service and Welcome Home!

I would be honored for you to join me in this simple prayer:

God, as you did for me, please be with our Soldiers, Sailors, Airmen, Marines and Coast Guard who are in harm's way, and with those who are standing in the gap for us throughout the world. Dear Lord, please be with our policemen, firemen, and all of those protecting us on the home-front. God, please be with the families and friends of those who are serving. Lord, I ask that you would provide quick emotional and physical healing for those who were wounded while serving. God, please give our leaders great wisdom and courage so they may see through your eyes the battles that are waging about us. Dear Lord, be with the chaplains, pastors, counselors, and medical personnel who are giving assistance to our soldiers and families in their time of need. And God, be with those who have made the ultimate sacrifice while serving. Wrap your arms around them and give them eternal peace.

God Bless Our Troops!

President George H. W. and Barbara Bush
Courtesy of President Bush's Office, Houston, Texas

AFTERWARDS

While doing research for this book, I knew I wanted to recognize and pay tribute to our Air Force brothers whenever I could. Having been a forward observer and not to recognize them would be like ignoring the 800 pound gorilla in the room. Without the Air Force in Desert Storm, we would not have enjoyed a 50% degraded enemy that our armored divisions steamrolled on G-Day and the three days following. Had it not been for the Air Force, we would have lost thousands of lives instead of the one hundred forty-eight hostile deaths incurred during the war. The Air Force flew over 65,000 sorties during the war, and destroyed over four hundred Iraqi aircraft without a single loss in air-to-air combat. Our Air Force quickly took control of the airspace thereby opening the door to the most lethal and accurate air attacks in history.[2]

What some call the "100 Hour War" is not accurate. It may have taken us four days to finish the job, but the offense (Desert Storm) took forty-two days, not "100 hours." To subscribe to that statement overlooks the critical role of the Air Force. The Gulf War encompassed Desert Shield _and_ Desert Storm. History shows that major conflicts have never been fought using just

---

2   There was a Navy pilot lost on the first night of the air war. His name is Lieutenant Commander Michael Scott Speicher, of VFA-81.

offensive operations alone. Some revisionists wanted to change the history of this war to one hundred hours. This inaccurate depiction diminished the Coalitions' actions from August 1990 through March 1991, and overlooked months of defensive and thirty-eight days of offensive preparatory operations.

During Desert Storm, Coalition aircraft averaged 2,500 sorties per day. Allied air forces destroyed or disabled most of the Iraqi air force, command and control, communications facilities, and air defense systems. Due to the Coalition's relentless air attacks, the Iraqi army suffered severe attrition. Before the first Allied boots stepped on Iraqi ground, they no longer had the fourth largest army in the world. The Desert Storm air campaign established air supremacy and kept it. Also, heavy bombing of Iraqi bunker systems psychologically diminished the enemy's will to fight, allowing unprecedented freedom of maneuver for the ground war.

Most air campaign planners of the time would cringe at the sound of some airpower zealots proclaiming a new era was born and airpower alone could win future wars. Smart airmen knew what ground warriors knew and paid for in blood: the loss of ninety-eight Army, twenty-four Marines, and six Navy killed in action from a total loss of human life numbering one hundred forty-eight was the price we paid for taking and holding territory, the only true measure of victory in this war.

Senior Master Sergeant Patrick McGee, US Air Force (Retired), related to me that he and his two repair teams (located on opposite ends of KFIA) kept the A-10 "Warthog" in the air. Their ABDR (Aircraft Battle Damage Repair) teams worked tirelessly keeping our close air support brothers flying. One hundred forty-eight Warthogs flew almost 8,100 sorties (over 12 percent of the total), yet maintained an unheard of mission capable rate of 95.7 percent —five percent above its peacetime rates. Despite numerous hits and extensive damage, the Warthog proved it could do a variety of missions successfully. *One of the best stories I heard was one where the enemy tried to surrender to an A-10.* Even with the staggering amount of sorties flown,

202

there were only six lost in combat during Desert Storm, with two killed in action.

When visiting with Patrick about his aircraft battle damage repair teams, I thought about my Granddad Doyle Riddle, who was a shop foreman at a B-17 repair facility in England during World War II. Granddad shared stories with me about the bomber and its ability to survive tremendous battle damage. His shop would patch and repair the bombers and get them back in the air. The B-17's lethal strikes against the massive German industrial complex, along with its P-51 Mustang fighter escorts, were directly responsible for shortening that war.

In December 1990, while at King Fahd International Airport (Camp Eagle II), I made contact with Spectre (AC-130H) crews who proudly showed us their aircraft and its capabilities. After making the connection with them at KFIA, I remember the loss I felt when I learned one of the gunships was shot down on 31 January 1991. In the Battle of Khafji, fourteen of the twenty Air Force personnel killed in Desert Storm were from the Spirit 03 crew. One sortie out of 65,581 was responsible for 70 percent of the Air Force loss. It was a horrible tragedy that some say could have been avoided if they had turned back prior to going critical on fuel.

In the early days of this project, wanting to include the story and pay tribute to Spirit 03, I made contact with the Spectre Association requesting information. They forwarded my request to Bill Walter, a retired Chief Master Sergeant who was a Spectre gunner for the greater part of his career. Bill was so kind as to review with me information on Spectre and the gunship world. My initial request was for the capabilities of the gunship, and secondly, to research the story of Spirit 03 and the guys that were shot down in the early morning hours of 31 January 1991. This story was retold by Bill on the night of 30 January, 2011 during the 20th year remembrance dinner for the crew of Spirit 03.

"The story of "Spirit 03" takes us back to the Battle of Khafji, which was the first major ground engagement during Operation Desert Storm. On 29 January 1991, Saddam Hussein launched an assault from Kuwait into

203

Saudi Arabia. Despite a pounding from coalition forces, a large Iraqi Force, which included 40 tanks and 500 troops, occupied the town of Khafji near the Kuwait and Saudi border. While coalition ground forces pulled back from Khafji, two Marine reconnaissance teams were left behind. These recon teams found themselves completely surrounded by Iraqi forces.

Once coalition ground forces pulled back from Khafji, coalition airpower began to focus on targets near and around Khafji from 30-31 January. Among these aircraft were three AC-130H gunships assigned call signs Spirit 01, Spirit 02 and Spirit 03. During the evening of 30 January, Spirit 01 and Spirit 02 launched from their base, while Spirit 03 prepared to take off later that night.

Once Spirit 01 and Spirit 02 reached the battle area, they were assigned targets north of Khafji. While the two AC-130 gunships fired on their targets, Spirit 03 took off from its base and prepared for combat operations. Meanwhile, Spirit 01 had returned to base after exhausting its ammunition and shortly thereafter, Spirit 02 ran low on fuel and had to return to base. During their transition, Spirit 02 briefed Spirit 03 on the ground situation and enemy threats in the area. Following their hand-off briefing at 0500 hours, a Marine Forward Air Controller directed Spirit 03 to fire on targets directly on the border post.

By 0525 hours, Spirit 03 began to fire on the border post, a large concrete structure the Iraqis were using to shelter troops and Free Rocket Over Ground (also known as FROG) weapons. The crew of Spirit 03 continued their attack for one hour inflicting damage and casualties on the Iraqi force.

At 0625, low on fuel with daylight about to break over the horizon, the crew of Spirit 03 continued their attack. Within one half orbit of rolling out to return to base, an Iraqi surface to air missile hit the left wing directly between the engines. With their wing on fire and badly damaged, the crew of Spirit 03 fought desperately to control the fire. Tragedy struck quickly when the left wing broke off as they were running their emergency procedures checklist. As a result, the aircraft spiraled out of control and literally fell from the sky, trapping the crew of Spirit 03 inside. The aircraft crashed into the shallows of the Persian Gulf at high rate of speed, inverted and in a near vertical descent. There were no survivors.

Historians acknowledge this fact; the battle of Khafji was a turning point in the war. Spectre contributed a critical aspect to the Iraqi defeat, including Spirit 03s persistent and deadly fire. As a result of this combat loss, new tactics, procedures and aircraft systems were developed to counter missile threats. The true legacy of Spirit 03 is found today in everyone flying the AC-130. Whether modern day crews know it or not, the lessons learned from the Spirit 03 tragedy have contributed to Air Commandos successes in Bosnia, Somalia, Haiti, Kosovo, Afghanistan, and Iraq. For this, we owe the crew of Spirit 03 our utmost respect."

To this day I hold Spectre and their crews in high esteem for what they do for our ground forces.

I had the opportunity to share with Bill the story about Dave Gurley's first hand account of the gunship's capabilities in the battle for Rio Hato Airport in Panama, who was with 2/75th Rangers in December 1989 (Operation Just Cause). After telling him the story, Bill told me he was one of the Spectre gunners on station at Rio Hato that night. I was in shock. Twenty-one years later just by chance when I requested information, I had made contact with a gunship gunner that may have saved the life of a friend.

Between January 17, 1991 and February 28, 1991, Desert Storm coalition aircraft flew more sorties in the history of warfare than had ever been seen in such a short span of time. A total of 100,876 sorties were flown, including: 23,455 attack sorties against strategic targets; 43,735 against fielded forces in Kuwait; 15,434 tanker air refueling sorties. These sorties set the conditions for victory. It was an awesome six week air campaign that paved the way for the four day ground blitz that followed.

General H. Norman Schwarzkopf decided early in Desert Shield that it would take more Allied forces to evict Saddam from Kuwait. With the addition of VII Corps' heavy armor divisions from Germany, Schwarzkopf planned an offensive attack that would expel Iraq from Kuwait. Saddam had a formidable Army. Even with the attrition, he still had a large number of the original twenty-six divisions (over 545,000 soldiers) in the KTO (Kuwaiti Theatre of Operations) that were willing to fight.

When General Schwarzkopf delivered his concept of offensive operations to his division generals, he wanted them to "attack Iraqi command and control, gain and maintain air superiority, cut supply lines, and destroy his chemical, biological, and nuclear capability." His intent for General Luck's XVIII Airborne Corps was to go deep to the Euphrates and then turn east, and for Frank's VII Corps (Armored Divisions) to come into Iraq west of Kuwait. They were to turn east attacking the Republican Guard, pinning their backs to the sea, wiping them out. His instructions to Franks' VII Corps and its division generals were to "destroy the Republican Guard." He said, "When you are finished, I don't want them to be an effective fighting force anymore. I don't want them to exist as a military organization." He continued, "Once they are gone, be prepared to continue the attack to Baghdad because there isn't going to be anything else out there."

Opening Situation on G-Day, Sunday, 24 February 1991, the 1st Cavalry Division still in the Hafar al-Batin area showed Saddam's forces a feint up the wadi, the 1st Infantry Division to the left of them would hit the bulk of Saddam's forces head on, and the 1st and 3rd Armored Divisions and the 3rd Armored Cavalry Regiment would be even further to the west. On VII Corps' west would be XVIII Airborne Corps. The two Corps collectively created a huge pincer that would move north into Iraq and then move clockwise toward Kuwait, crushing and destroying the Republican Guard in eastern Iraq and Kuwait. The US Navy and Marines would give the Iraqis the impression that there would be an amphibious assault making them commit four divisions in the defense at the sea. The 1st Marine Expeditionary Force with Arab allies along with the 2nd Armored Division would make their attack from Saudi Arabia into Kuwait.

Damon Beaird, a friend for about fifteen years, was with Alpha Company, 1st Battalion, 37th Armor, attached to 3rd Brigade of the 1st Armored Division (Old Ironsides) during the Gulf War and the first unit to deploy out of Vilseck, Germany. Damon arrived in theatre late in December 1990 with their equipment streaming in between the 4th and 12th of January, 1991. Beaird was an Abrams M1-A1 turret mechanic during Desert Storm, and shadowed their tanks closely throughout the ground war in M113 Armored Personnel Carriers (APC).

On G-Day, 2nd ACR (Armored Cavalry Regiment) was VII Corps' lead scout in front of the 1st and 3rd Armored Divisions. Their mission was to find the Republican Guard's T-72s so our armor could adjust their large formations toward them. The size and scope of just one of our armored divisions is mind boggling. There are approximately 22,000 soldiers, 350 tanks, 285 Bradleys, 115 howitzers, 36 MLRS (multiple launch rocket systems) and 80 helicopters (36 of those were Apaches). The desert wedge formation could be from twenty-five to forty-five kilometers wide and eighty to one hundred fifty kilometers deep. General Griffith's 1st Armored Division was spread over a twenty-six kilometer front. Damon's 3rd Brigade was behind and to the right of the 1st as they rolled into Iraq on the 24th. On the 25th, the lead brigade of the division reached the Iraqi 806th Infantry Brigade, 26th Infantry Division south of al-Busayyah. The weather worsened on G+1 (25 February) shutting down close air support. Griffith moved his lead brigade west of the Iraqis which put the enemy right in front of Damon's brigade. After the 3-1st Field Artillery bombardment, 3rd Brigade moved into position. When the Iraqis saw they were in a "lose-lose situation", they began to surrender. The remainder of the division easily took al-Busayyah the next day after division's Apache helicopters, MLRS, and artillery prepped the battlefield ahead of the direct fire tanks and Bradleys.

Moving past al-Busayyah to meet General Frank's quick VII Corps timetable, the division again turned its sights toward the Republican Guard. During the afternoon of the 26th, Griffith redirected his division's 6,000 vehicles to the east with the Iraqis just fifty kilometers away. In a sandstorm, the Corps (comprised of seven armored and mechanized brigades) now had an eighty kilometer front. Facing four heavy Iraqi brigades, the largest tank battle in the United States history was about to begin.

At G-Day + 2 on the 26th of February, 1-37th Armor moved toward the Tawakalna Division, one of the same divisions that threatened us at Hafar al-Batin. The 3-1st Field Artillery fired the initial shots of the battle. Damon made note there was a minefield that was cleared by the engineers as they made their approach. His unit started engaging at 2,000 meters out. Beaird watched as the forty-one Abrams tanks' sabot rounds quickly decimated the T-72s. They then moved towards four Iraqi battalions with over one hundred fifty armored vehicles and two tank battalions. In a short time, several dozen T-72s and BMPs were ablaze. 1-37th moved over a crest of a hill and observed a row of well dug-in enemy tanks within 1,000 meters. After cresting the ridge an Abrams was hit. The design of the tank and the blast escaping through the blow-out panels on top of the turret along with the Halon suppression system saved the lives of the crew. 1-37th lost four tanks in the battle but killed seventy-six T-72s, eighty-four BMPs, howitzers, command vehicles, and trucks. Damon said EPWs were taken and disarmed during their four day march. As Iraqi soldiers surrendered, the engineers behind the lead element would round them up, giving them water and rations.

On the morning of 27 February, 3rd Brigade made contact with the Iraqi 14th Mechanized Brigade and 10th Armored. However, the main fight was with the Medina Division to the north. The 2nd Brigade, 1st Armored Division stretched four armored battalions ten kilometers from north to south with two hundred tanks and Bradleys. From two miles away, Abrams tanks picked off the Medina, leaving them in a smoking pile of rubble. Counter-battery radars from Division Artillery also got into the action by pinpointing Iraqi guns along the unit border with XVIII Airborne Corps. Over a twenty-four hour period, MLRS destroyed seventy-two guns. When an Iraqi gun fired, DIVARTY would fire back with pinpoint accuracy knocking out the guns within two minutes. A-10s and F-16s were also on station as the Medina Division went down in flames. Air and artillery pummeled Medina Ridge for a few hours until the enemy was annihilated.

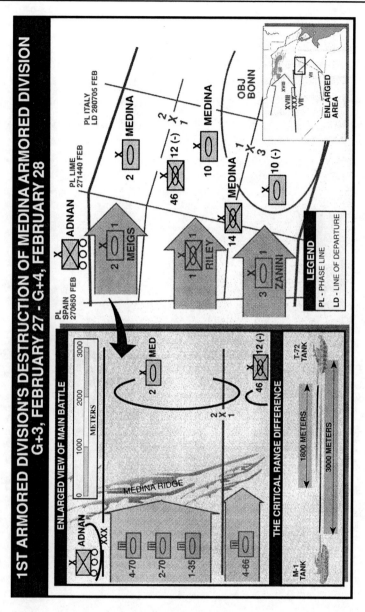

On the morning of 28 February, 1st Armored Division was just short of the Kuwaiti border when at 0723 hrs, VII Corps ordered the cease fire. The Republican Guard was destroyed.

The four days following the cease-fire, Damon and the 1-37th camped in Kuwait near the oil well fires that were set by Iraqi soldiers before their escape. He said that some days you could see the sun, and other days you couldn't. The light of day was contingent on which way the wind was blowing. Soldiers were told to stay in their vehicles or makeshift hooches to avoid the black, toxic environment. They only came out from under cover to retrieve rations or instructions from the First Sergeant. Over six hundred oil wells were set ablaze by the order of Saddam Hussein. The smoke billowed high in the atmosphere. There were days when the conditions forced the smoke along the ground surrounding everyone.

Oil well fires, Kuwait, March 1991
Courtesy of the U.S. Army

After moving away from the fires, 1-37th made camp in Iraq for a few weeks waiting for further orders. There wasn't much activity during that time. Damon told me they were spread out and were given instructions on how to deal with a lost Iraqi soldier if a straggler came into their AO. Cease-fire had some privileges such as the Australian shower hung from the 50 caliber which brought some immediate comfort and relief. From the day we left port, showers were basically nonexistent beyond getting one shower a month. "After the war was over, we were in a camp that had showers manned and guarded by the National Guard," said Beaird. "They didn't want us to come into the tent area with our weapons, and refused to let us shower. Since we lived with our weapons 24/7, we convinced the attendants to let us in."

The VII Corps under the leadership of General Fred Franks, Jr. did a remarkable job of executing the enormous end around. Saddam and his generals were expecting a small wheel up the Wadi al-Batin and into Kuwait, and thus had their divisions positioned accordingly. They were not expecting the "Great Wheel" that came in from the far west through their own country. Iraqi divisions were out of position and on their heels as VII Corps exploited them with an armored blitz unparalleled in history.

The enemy was not expecting us to be as deep as we were cutting supply routes, lines of communication, routes of escape, and threatening a lethal strike against their capital.

In an operation as large as Desert Shield _and_ Desert Storm, as with all wars and training exercises, there were many lessons learned. The after action reports that honestly review what was done well and the areas that need improvement are valuable documents that can be used for future war planning and training. Twenty years after the Gulf War, I am still impressed with our leadership and their ability to put together a meaningful coalition with a common purpose. Without the coalition, the war would have taken on a completely different tone. I was in awe of our generals and their ability to successfully execute their plans using the Air-Land Battle doctrine of initiative, depth, agility, and synchronization. We had professional, competent leadership and well trained highly motivated soldiers. Technology and superior weaponry alone did not win the Gulf War. The overwhelming success was also due to our soldiers from the top down being able to think independently and adapt to the conditions they faced. Soldiers knew their jobs. It was a tremendous honor to have served with them.

Hooah !!

*"The Air Force and armor were the thunder
of Desert Storm, while the 101ˢᵗ was
the lightning."*

---H. Norman Schwarzkopf

APPENDIX

Symbols

▓	Coalition Forces
▒	Iraqi Forces
▓	Republican Guard Forces
⊠	Infantry Units
⊗	Mechanized Infantry Units
⬭	Armor Units
⬭	Armored Cavalry Units
⌒	Air Defense Units
•	Field Artillery Units
●⋈●	Chemical Units
⊓	Engineer Units
▶◀	Attack Helicopter Units
Y	Air Assault Units
⊠	Motorized Units

☐	Combat Service Support Supply Units
⌒	Airborne Units
☐ oo	Coalition Support Units
☐ ooo	Iraqi Motorized Units
☐	Temporary Grouping of Units Battalion Company Teams or Task Force
⋯ ☐	Platoon
I ☐	Company
II ☐	Battalion
III ☐	Regiment
X ☐	Brigade
XX ☐	Division
XXX ☐	Corps

⇒ Single arrowhead for supporting direction of attack and supporting axis of advance

- - - - - - - - ⇢ Proposed axis of advance

⇒ Double arrowhead for direction of main attack and axis of advance for the main attack

⇒ General movement for aircraft

⇒ General movement for aircraft with assaulting troops

⇒ Movement of Army attack aircraft

217

Maps

ACRONYMS

AA	Assembly area
AAA	Antiaircraft artillery
AAR	After-action review
AASLT	Air assault
ABN	Airborne
ACL	Allowable cargo load
ACP	Assault command post
ACR	Armored cavalry regiment
AD	Armored division
ADA	Air defense artillery
ADC (O)	Assistant division commander for operations
ADC (S)	Assistant division commander for support
ADVON	Advance party
AFN	Armed Forces Network
AH-1S	Attack helicopter (Cobra)
AH-64	Attack helicopter (Apache)
ALO	Air liaison officer
ANVIS	Aviation night vision goggles
AO	Area of operations
AOC	Army Operations Center
APC	Armored personnel carrier
APO	Army post office
ARAMCO	Arabian-American Oil Company
ARCENT	Army Central Command
ARTEP	Army Training and Evaluation Program
ARVN	Army of the Republic of Vietnam
ASP	Ammunition supply point

Audible	Option play that commanders can call on the move to accommodate the enemy's reactions
AUSA	Association of the United States Army
AWACS	Airborne warning and control system
BAI	Battle air interdiction
BDA	Bomb damage assessment
BDE	Brigade
BDU	Battle dress uniform
BG	Brigadier general
Blackhawk	UH-60 utility helicopter
BMP	Boevaya mashina pekhoty (Russian tracked APC)
BN	Battalion
BP	Battle position
Bradley	M-2 infantry fighting vehicle or M-3 cavalry fighting vehicle
BRDM	Russian LAV
Buff	Big ugly fat fellow, or a USAF B-52 bomber
CA	Civil affairs
CAB	Combat aviation brigade
Camel meat	An unappetizing entree
CAS	Close air support
CAV	Cavalry
CD	Cavalry division
C-Day	Commencement of deployment, August 7, 1990
CENTAF	Central Air Force Command
CEO	Chief Executive Officer
CEV	Combat engineer vehicle

CFA	Covering force area
CG	Commanding general
Chinook	CH-47 cargo helicopter
CINC	Commander-in-chief
CINCCENT	Commander-in-chief, Central Command
CINCFOR	Commander-in-chief, Forces Command
Closes	The arrival of a unit's deploying personnel and equipment at a specified destination
COL	Colonel
CONPLAN	Contingency plan
CONUS	Continental United States
CP	Command post
CPT	Captain
CSA	Corps support area
CSAR	Combat search and rescue
DA	Department of the Army
DBDU	Desert battle dress uniform
Desert One	Site of failed 1979 rescue attempt in Iranian desert
DIA	Defense Intelligence Agency
DMA	Defense Mapping Agency
DOD	Department of Defense
Dog him out	To chide or find fault with
DPICM	Dual-purpose improved conventional munitions
DRB	Division ready brigade
EA	Engagement area
EG	Egypt
Emerald City	King Khalid Military City
EPW	Enemy prisoners of war

FAA	Forward assembly area'
FAC	Forward air controller
Fast movers	High-performance jet aircraft
FEBA	Forward edge of the battle area
"First Team"	Nickname for the 1st Cavalry Division
FIST	Fire support team
FISTV	Fire support team vehicle
FLIR	Forward-looking infrared
FM	Field manual
FO	Forward observer
FOB	Forward operating base
FORSCOM	United States Army Forces Command
FR	French
FRAGO	Fragmentary order
FRAGPLAN	Fragmentary plan
FROG	Free rocket over ground
FSCL	Fire support coordination line
FSE	Fire support element
G2	Intelligence staff officer / section
G3	Operations and plans staff officer / section
G4	Logistics staff officer / section
G-Day	February 24, beginning of the ground phase of the campaign
GEN	General
GHQ	General headquarters
Good to go	Ready to perform admirably
GPS	Global Positioning System
HAM	Hammurabi
HARM	High-speed antiradiation missile
HEAT	High-explosive antitank

Hellfire	Laser-guided antitank missile
HEMTT	Heavy expanded mobility tactical truck
HET	Heavy equipment transporter
H-Hour	The specific hour on D-Day at which a particular operation commences
HMMWV	High-mobility, multipurpose wheeled vehicle
HNS	Host nation support
HQ	Headquarters
Huey	UH-1 Iroquois utility helicopter
HUMINT	Human intelligence or human resources intelligence
HWY	Highway
ICBM	Intercontinental ballistic missile
ID	Infantry division
IN	Infantry
INTERNAL LOOK 2	A joint training exercise
"Ironsides"	Nickname for 1ˢᵗ Armored Division
IRR	Individual Ready Reserve
J2	Intelligence staff officer / staff section at joint headquarters
J5	Operations and plans officer / section at joint headquarters
JAAT	Joint air attack team
"Jayhawk"	Nickname for VII Corps
JCS	Joint Chiefs of Staff
JFACC	Joint forces air component commander
JFC-E	Joint Forces Command – East
JFC-N	Joint Forces Command – North

JIC	Joint Intelligence Center
JLO	Joint Liaison Organization
JRTC	Joint Readiness Training Center
JSOTF	Joint Special Operations task force
JSTARS	Joint Surveillance Target Attack Radar System
JTF	Joint task force
Just Cause	December 1989 operation in Panama
KFIA	King Fahd International Airport
KKMC	King Khalid Military City
KM	Kilometers
KTF	Kuwaiti task force
KTO	Kuwaiti theater of operations
KU	Kuwait
LD	Line of departure
LT	Lieutenant
LTC	Lieutenant colonel
LTG	Lieutenant general
M1	Abrams tank
MBA	Main battle area
MEB	Marine Expeditionary Brigade
Mech	Mechanized
MED	Medina
MEDEVAC	Medical evacuation
METT-T	Mission, enemy, terrain, troops, and time available
MG	Major general
MHD	Material handling device
MI	Military intelligence
MiG	Common model designation for Russian- or Chinese- built fighter planes

MILES	Multiple Integrated Laser Engagement System
MLRS	Multiple-Launch Rocket System
MP	Military police
MRE	Meals, ready to eat
MSR	Main supply route
NBC	Nuclear, biological, chemical
NCO	Noncommissioned officer
NCOES	Noncommissioned Officer Education System
NEB	Nebuchadnezzar
NTC	National Training Center
NVA	North Vietnamese Army
OBJ	Objective
OCS	Officer Candidate School
OPFOR	Opposing force
OPLAN	Operations plan
PDF	Panamanian Defense Force
PL	Phase line
POG	Psychological Operations Group
POW	Prisoners of war
PSYOP	Psychological operations
RC	Reserve component
REFORGER	Return of forces to Germany
RES	Reserves
RGFC	Republican Guard Forces Command
RP	Release point
RPG	Rocket-propelled grenade
SA	Saudi Arabia
Sabkha	A coastal salt flat
Sabot	Type of armor-piercing projectile

SACEUR	Supreme Allied Commander, Europe
Sagger	Soviet-manufactured wire-guided antitank missile
SANG	Saudi Army National Guard
SATCOM	Satellite communications
Scud	Ballistic missile
SF	Special Forces
Shamal	A seasonal windstorm often associated with blowing dust and rain
SMA	United States Sergeant Majors Academy
SO	Special Operations
SOC	Sector Operations Center
SOCCENT	Special Operations Command Central
SOCOM	Special Operations Command
SOF	Special Operations forces
Spectre	Air Force AC-130 aircraft
Stinger	Antiaircraft infrared missile
SY	Syria
TAA	Tactical or Taskforce assembly area
TAACOM	Theater army area command
TAC	Tactical command post
TACSAT	Tactical satellite (communications)
TAW	Tawakalna
TF	Task force
TOC	Tactical operations center
TOW	Tube-launched, optically tracked, wire-guided antitank missile

TPFDD	Time-phased force deployment data
TRADOC	US Army Training and Doctrine Command
TSA	Theater support area
UK	United Kingdom
USAF	United States Air Force
USAREUR	US Army Europe
USTRANSCOM	US Transportation Command
VULCAN	Model designation for 20mm antiaircraft cannon/gun system
XO	Executive officer
YFC	Yakima Firing Center
YTC	Yakima Training Center
ZSU	Model designation for Soviet-style antiaircraft gun system

Gulf War Chronology

August 2, 1990   Iraq invades Kuwait.

August 6   The United Nations Security Council imposes economic sanctions against Iraq.

August 7   President George H.W. Bush ordered U.S. armed forces into Saudi Arabia to prevent further aggression.

August 8   U.S. Air Force elements from the 1st Tactical Fighter Wing arrive in theater.

August 9   U.S. Army elements from the 82nd Airborne Division arrive in theater.

August 10   FORSCOM issues its deployment order to the 101st Airborne Division (Air Assault). The division's Assault Command Post (ACP) personnel begin processing for deployment.

August 13   First ship – FSS Capella – departs Savannah with the 24th Infantry Division (Mech) equipment.

August 14	The first five 101st Airborne Division (Air Assault) soldiers deploy to Saudi Arabia. The Advon Party arrives in Saudi Arabia on 15 August.
	82nd Airborne DRB-1 closes at the KTO and moves to secure ports.
August 15	First Marine MPS-2 arrives in Saudi Arabia.
August 17	101st Airborne Division (Air Assault) DRB-1 (Division Ready Brigade) equipment departs Campbell Army Airfield.
	By 30 August, all of the DRB-1 personnel and equipment are in Saudi Arabia.
August 19	The American Eagle, one of ten ships carrying 101st equipment departs Jacksonville for Ad Damman, Saudi Arabia. The ship also carried the division's equipment to Vietnam.
August 22	Presidential Executive Order #12727 authorizes first use of 200K Selected Reserve call-up and limited implementation of Stop Loss Program.
August 23	Secretary of Defense authorizes call-up of 25,000 Army National Guardsmen and Army Reservists in combat and combat service support units.
August 27	Army activates first Reserve units.
	First FSS arrives in Saudi Arabia and begins off-loading; first M1 Abrams tanks arrive in theater.

August 29	82nd Airborne Division closes in theater.
September 1/2	Stop Loss Program goes into effect.
	101st Airborne Division (Air Assault) deploys aviation task force to the vicinity of An Nuayriyah to establish a forward operating base to support covering force operations. On 2 September, the division named the base FOB Bastogne.
September 2	I Corps designated to replace XVIII Airborne Corps as primary contingency corps for worldwide operations.
September 4	The 101st Airborne Division (Air Assault) assumes control of FOB Bastogne from the 82nd Airborne Division.
September 5	Over a twenty day period, the bulk of the 101st manpower is deployed from Campbell Army Airfield to Saudi Arabia.
September 6/7	Marine MPS 2 and 3 complete off-loading.
September 11	The 101st issues its first operation plan (OPLAN) of Operation Desert Shield, OPLAN 90-1 (Eagle Defense). "When directed 101st Airborne Division (Air Assault) defends King Fahd International Airport (KFIA) to protect the airport and key facilities."
September 12	Major combat elements of 24th Infantry Division (Mech) close in theater.
October 6, 1990	101st Airborne Division (Air Assault) closes in theater.

October 15	The 101st published OPLAN 90-3 (Operation Desert Destiny). This was the division's mature theater OPLAN for the defense of Saudi Arabia.
October 18	"Sandfill 27" forward observers arrive at King Fahd International Airport (KFIA) from Fort Campbell, Kentucky.
October 22	1st Cavalry Division closes in theater.
October 24	1/320th Field Artillery and 1/502nd return from covering force mission at FOB Oasis.
November 8	VII Corps and 1st Infantry Division alerted for deployment.
November 13	Presidential Executive Order #12733 extends selected Reserve call-up to 180 days.
November 14	Secretary of Defense increases Army selected Reserve call-up authority to 80,000 and authorizes call-up of Reserve combat units.
November 16	1/502nd moves to FOB Bastogne from Camp Eagle II in covering force mission. At all times, two thirds of the division was deployed forward in the covering force area, while the other one third was refitting at Camp Eagle II.
November 21	1/502nd moves from FOB Bastogne to FOB Oasis in covering force mission. VII Corps begins deployment to Saudi Arabia.
November 22	Thanksgiving Day at FOB Oasis.

November 30   First Army National Guard roundout brigades
               called to active duty.

December 1   XVIII Airborne Corps closes in theater.

               Secretary of Defense increases Army selected
               Reserve call-up authority to 115,000.

December 6   First ship carrying VII Corps equipment arrives
               in theater.

December 11   1/502nd departs FOB Oasis, arrives King Fahd
               International Airport (KFIA) by C-130s for rest
               and refit at Camp Eagle II.

Holiday Season Visits from celebrities Bob Hope, Johnny Bench,
               Jay Leno, and Steve Martin help keep the
               morale high with the soldiers.

December 25   Christmas Day at Camp Eagle II, soldiers are
               entertained by Bob Hope and Johnny Bench.

January 10, 1991 502nd Infantry Regiment and 1/320th Field
               Artillery move from Camp Eagle II to Al
               Qaysumah airfield at Hafar al Batin. With the
               January 15 deadline for Saddam's withdrawal
               from Kuwait drawing near, planners were
               concerned that Iraq would strike preemptively
               down the Wadi al Batin attacking Saudi Arabia
               and King Khalid Military City.

               The 502nd Infantry Regiment and 1/320th FA
               becomes tactically controlled by the 1st Cavalry
               Division under VII Corps.

January 13	Colonel Thomas Purdom, 502nd Infantry Regiment Commander receives an intelligence message about an imminent Iraqi attack down the Hafar al-Batin wadi complex.
January 15	UN deadline for Iraqi withdrawal.
January 17	Operation Desert Storm begins. Destroying key radar sites, 101st Airborne Division Apache helicopters fire the first shots of the war.
January 18	Presidential Executive Order #12743 declares partial mobilization.
January 18/19	Iraq fires first Scud missiles at Israel and Saudi Arabia.
January 20	XVIII Airborne and VII Corps begin movement to forward assembly areas for ground phase of the campaign (G-Day).
January 26	The 502nd Infantry Regiment is released from 1st Cavalry Division's control at Hafar al-Batin and moves northwest to TAA Campbell in preparation for G-Day.
January 31	"Spirit 03", an AC-130 Spectre gunship shot down by a surface to air missile in the Kuwaiti Theater of Operation (KTO) with no survivors.
February 3, 1991	XVIII Airborne and VII Corps (minus elements of 3d Armored Division) complete movement to forward assembly areas.
February 5	The 502nd receives Warning Order for G-Day operations and Forward Operating Base Cobra

February 6	VII Corps closes in theater with the arrival of last elements of 3d Armored Division.
February 17	Charlie Company 1/502nd starts probing ahead of LD (Line of Departure). The first 26 EPWs of the war were taken.
February 23	G-Day (Ground Operations Day) eve. The 1/502nd co-locates with Blackhawks that will take them to FOB Cobra the next morning.
February 24	G-Day. LTC James E. Donald's 1/502nd with forward observers from 1/320th FA makes the initial ninety mile air assault into FOB Cobra with Colonel James T. Hill's 1st Brigade. The establishment of FOB Cobra was the largest air assault ever conducted in a single day.
	Coalition forces begin ground phase of campaign (G-Day).
February 25	Third Brigade's Rakassans air assault to the Euphrates River (LZ Sand) to cut off Highway 8.
February 27	The 502nd (Second Brigade TF) with one battalion (3-327) from the First Brigade make ninety three mile air assault east into FOB Viper. Second Brigade TF establishes a FARP (forward air refueling point) for 101st attack helicopters to attack enemy forces in EA (Engagement Area) Thomas, northwest of Basrah.
February 28	Temporary cease-fire initiated. During the one hundred hours of ground combat, the 101st Airborne Division (Air Assault) cut the enemy's lines of communications, struck deep into Iraq in three directions, and threatened a lethal strike against Baghdad.

March 3, 1991	Cease-fire terms accepted by Iraq at Safwan Airfield.
March 5	The 502nd with fire support teams from 1/320th FA leaves FOB Viper by Blackhawk and returns to TAA Campbell near Rafha.
March 6	Units from the 502nd Infantry Regiment departs TAA Campbell by C-130 to King Fahd International Airport and Camp Eagle II. After the 502nd Infantry Regiment departure, forward observers and fire support teams are re-attached to the 1/320th Field Artillery.
March 8	Nine hundred and five riflemen from the 502nd Infantry Regiment depart Camp Eagle II and King Fahd International Airport for their return to Fort Campbell, Kentucky.
March 12	1/320th FA soldiers fly by C-130 transports from Rafha (TAA Campbell) to King Fahd International Airport and Camp Eagle II.
March 25	The last element of the 101st Airborne Division (Air Assault) leaves Iraq and returns to Saudi Arabia.
March 31	Easter Sunday. 1/320th FA departs KFIA at 0600 local time by PAN AM 747. Layovers were in Rome and New York's, JFK arriving at Campbell Army Airfield, 1750 hrs local time.
April 3-15	The bulk of the 101st Airborne Division (Air Assault) returns to Campbell Army Airfield. The division colors returned with General Peay on 12 April 1991.

April 7, 1991   Iraq accepts United Nations cease-fire conditions and resolutions.

May 1, 1991   The last 101st soldier departs Saudi Arabia.

Nose art that was on the front of our Blackhawk helicopter,
sketched by Martin McPherson on the eve of G-Day.
Courtesy of Martin McPherson

G-DAY

February 24, 1991
(First Lift - Forward Operating Base Cobra)

"WHITE LIGHTNING"
Soldiers and Crew

Blackhawk Pilots 4/101

CW2 James A. Owenby
CW2 E. Joyce Strait
Sgt. Philip J. Barbera, Crew Chief

Charlie Company 1-502nd, "First Strike" Soldiers

Lt. Lee A. Rysewyk, 2nd Platoon Leader
Charlie Company 1st Sgt., William K. Batie
Sgt. Stephen D. Wiehe, Forward Observer
Pfc. Martin L. McPherson, FO/RTO
Sp4 Bryan Nelson, RTO
Sgt. Scott Charlesworth
Cpl. James T. "Doc" Slater
Sgt. Lonnie J. Hood
Sgt. Robert L. Haigler
Sp4 William W. Hill
Sp4 Cedric Smith
Sp4 Richard D. Athen
Pfc. Rodolfo A. Morales
Pfc. James A Root
Pfc. L. Patrick Kacho
Sp4 Whiteford C. McWaters

History of the 101ˢᵗ Airborne Division
Rendezvous with Destiny

General Order Number Five: The Birth of a Division

"The 101st Airborne Division, activated at Camp Claiborne, has no history, but it has a rendezvous with destiny. Like the early American pioneers whose invincible courage was the foundation stone of this nation, we have broken with the past and its traditions in order to establish our claim to the future. Due to the nature of our armament, and the tactics in which we shall perfect ourselves, we shall be called upon to carry out operations of far-reaching military importance and we shall habitually go into action when the need is immediate and extreme. Let me call your attention to the fact that our badge is the great American eagle. This is a fitting emblem for a division that will crush its enemies by falling upon them like a thunderbolt from the skies. The history we shall make, the record of high achievement we hope to write in the annals of the American Army and the American people, depends wholly and completely on the men of this division. Each individual, each officer and each enlisted man, must therefore regard himself as a necessary part of a complex and powerful instrument for the overcoming of the enemies of the nation. Each, in his job, must realize that he is not only a means, but an indispensable means for obtaining the goal of victory. It is, therefore, not

243

too much to say that the future itself, in whose molding we expect to have our share, is in the hands of the Soldiers of the 101st Airborne Division."

Major General William C. Lee
101ˢᵗ Airborne Division's First Commander
His First Address to Soldiers,
August 16, 1942 at Camp Claiborne, Louisiana

The origination of the 101ˢᵗ Airborne Division —the "Screaming Eagles"—traces its roots to the early 20ᵗʰ Century. The 101ˢᵗ Division was formed on July 23, 1918 and was demobilized shortly thereafter on December 11, 1918 due to the Armistice and the end of WW I. The 101ˢᵗ was reconstituted in 1921 as a reserve unit with their headquarters in Milwaukee, Wisconsin.

In 1938 the Germans formulated an elite parachute force, the 7ᵗʰ Flieger (Air) Division with three parachute rifle regiments. The division had significant roles during the Wehrmacht operations in 1940. In that same year, Major William C. Lee suggested to the U.S. Army that they should form a parachute test platoon. The platoon was made up of volunteers from the 29ᵗʰ Infantry Regiment. The test platoon was successful and led to the expansion of the Army's parachute capabilities in the following years.

After in-depth research into the British Army's use of parachute regiments in the early months of 1942, then Brigadier General Lee initiated the expansion of the Army's use of these regiments into divisions. Shortly after, the formulation of the 82ⁿᵈ Airborne Division and the 101ˢᵗ Airborne Division took place.

On August 16, 1942, the 101ˢᵗ Infantry Division became the United States Army's 101ˢᵗ Airborne Division. The new division was activated at Camp Claiborne, Louisiana under the command of Major General William C. Lee. The 101ˢᵗ Airborne Division's first regiment was the 502ⁿᵈ Parachute Infantry, two glider regiments (the 327ᵗʰ and the 401ˢᵗ Glider Infantry), and three artillery battalions (the 377ᵗʰ Parachute Field Artillery, the 321ˢᵗ Glider Field Artillery, the 907th Glider Field Artillery). Support units included the 326ᵗʰ Engineer Battalion, the 101ˢᵗ Signal

Company, and the 326ᵗʰ Airborne Medical Company. Just two months after the division's formulation, the 101ˢᵗ began training at Ft. Bragg, North Carolina.

In June 1943, the 506ᵗʰ Parachute Infantry Regiment (PIR) Currahee (Cherokee for "stands alone") from Camp Toccoa, Georgia joined the 101ˢᵗ. After the 101ˢᵗ Airborne Division's training at Ft. Bragg, the division moved by ships to England in September 1943. In England, the division opened a jump school and trained six days a week. While the division was training in England, General Lee suffered a heart attack and was replaced by Brigadier General Maxwell Taylor. In January 1944, the 501ˢᵗ Parachute Infantry Regiment joined the 101ˢᵗ. While training, the allies began their invasion plans for Northern France, code-named "Operation Overlord."

General Eisenhower speaking with the men of E, 502ⁿᵈ PIR
on the eve of D-Day, June 5, 1944.

Normandy
June 6, 1944

On the 5ᵗʰ of June, 1944 C-47 transports of the IX Troop Carrier Command lined runways in England preparing to deliver six thousand paratroopers, pathfinders and equipment of the 101ˢᵗ

Airborne Division to its objective in Normandy. Paratroopers staged by their cargo planes that would carry them into France. The first combat mission of the 101st was to secure the flank of the American invasion force and to occupy bridges and terrain features in the Carentan area. The action would keep the Germans at bay while the 4th Infantry Division landed on Utah Beach.

At 0015 hrs on June 6, 1944, 101st Airborne Division Pathfinders jumped into occupied France followed by the six thousand paratroopers. The C-47s, in making their jump run, ran into heavy German flak. Many were lost and/or steered off course resulting in the paratroopers being dropped over a wide area. That night, barely half of the invasion force had linked up with their units. It wasn't unusual to have members of the 82nd and 101st linking up with each other. Following the paratroopers were 52 gliders. Most of the landing zones were unsuitable due to hedgerows and trees. Five soldiers were killed in the initial glider landings, including Brigadier General Pratt, the assistant Division Commander.

During the first few days following D-Day, there were fierce battles between the 101st and the Germans. Behind enemy lines, the 101st was instrumental in seizing key objectives and not allowing the Germans to drive the allies back into the sea. After seizing causeways to the beachhead, the 101st turned their attention to the capture of Carentan. A planned link-up between American forces that landed on Utah and Omaha beach, Carentan was a critical objective for the invasion forces. The battle for Carentan was fierce; it took five days for the 101st to defeat the German 6th Parachute Division. Lieutenant Colonel Robert G. Cole, commander of the 3rd Battalion 502nd PIR led an assault on the Germans, which resulted in his winning the first Congressional Medal of Honor for the division.

On July 13, after seizing division objectives and continuous combat since D-Day, the division was pulled back to England for a brief rest and refit. There was a heavy price to pay in Normandy in that almost half of the division was a casualty. The

101st began receiving replacements in England and preparing for their next mission.

Operation Market-Garden
Holland
September 17, 1944

Between July 13 and September 17, 1944, the 101st rehearsed and trained for missions and possible objectives. In August 1944, the 1st Allied Airborne Corps was formed and consisted of the American's 18th Airborne Corps (82nd and 101st Airborne Divisions) and the British 1st Airborne Division. On the 17th of September, the 101st was part of Operation Market-Garden (code-named 'Market' for airborne operations and 'Garden' for ground operations). The operation included the newly formed 1st Allied Airborne Corps. The Airborne Corp's job was to secure bridges between Son, Holland and Arnhem, Holland in advance of The British XXX (30th) Corps thrust from the city of Neerpelt to Arnhem on a narrow road or corridor named "The Highway from Hell." The specific objectives for the 101st were three bridges in Holland. The four 101st drop zones were between the towns of Son and Veghel. There was heavy opposition and fierce fighting along this corridor.

Glider operations played a key roll in the operation by bringing in additional materials and men. It took two days for elements from the British Armored Division to reach the 101st at Eindhoven, the first link up between 'Market' and 'Garden'. The Americans continued to fight the Germans who had a superior force for almost two months along the narrow sixteen mile front. The division was relieved in late November and sent to Mourmelon-le-Grand near Reims in France for rest and refitting. In Operation Market-Garden (the second combat assault for the division), almost 3,000 casualties were taken.

During the battle of Market-Garden, Private First Class Joe E. Mann of the 3rd Battalion 502nd PIR became the second member of the 101st Airborne Division to be awarded the Congressional

Medal of Honor. At the cost of his own life, PFC Mann shielded his squad from an exploding grenade.

The Ardennes Offensive
Bastogne
December 16, 1944 – January 25, 1945

The division was resting, refitting, and preparing for Christmas celebrations when the Germans began a large offensive in Belgium at the Ardennes. On the 16th of December the Germans had broken through Allied lines held by the American VIII Corp and the Americans were in jeopardy of losing their front line.

The 101st received orders on the 17th of December to proceed as quickly as possible to the broken front line. General Anthony McAuliffe was the acting commanding general as General Taylor was in Washington at the time. The division made their way to the Ardennes in open trucks, and by the 19th of December, the division had arrived at Bastogne. The 101st was ill-prepared for the harsh winter conditions as winter clothing was in short supply.

The Germans massed their forces in and around Bastogne and on the 20th had surrounded the area. It was the 101st Airborne Division's mission to defend Bastogne and a key road junction. On the 20th of December, Bastogne was cut off. German armored units attempted to break through Allied lines and were beaten back each time.

On the 22nd of December, German commander Lieutenant General Heinrich von Luttwitz demanded the surrender of the 101st. Brigadier General Anthony C. McAuliffe sent back his famous one word reply. "Nuts." The division continued to fight and hold until December 26th when the 3rd Army's 4th Armored Division broke through and saved the 101st and Bastogne. Intense fighting continued until the 18th of January when VIII Corps relieved the 101st.

For the first time in U.S. history the Presidential Unit Citation was awarded to an entire division. The 101st had received this historic award for their heroic defense of Bastogne.

Berchtesgaden
May 5, 1945

The 101ˢᵗ Airborne Division pursued retreating German forces into Bavaria. In the spring of 1945 the division liberated the Landsberg concentration camp and captured Hitler's retreat at Berchtesgaden. The 101ˢᵗ Airborne Division and the Third Infantry Division completed the mission, accepted surrender from major German units, and captured high ranking Nazis.

Inactivation
November 30, 1945

The 101ˢᵗ Airborne Division moved to Auxerre, France and began training for the invasion of Japan. But within weeks, Japan had surrendered, and on the 30ᵗʰ of November the division was disbanded. In the division's last bulletin, Colonel Kinnard wrote:

"To those of you left to read this last daily bulletin, do not dwell on the disintegration of our great unit but rather be proud that you are of the old guard of the greatest division ever to fight for our country. Carry with you the memory of its greatness wherever you may go, being always assured of respect when you say, I served with the 101ˢᵗ."

Pentomic Division
September 21, 1956

For eleven years, the division was activated and inactivated three times as a training unit, and was transferred to Fort Campbell, Kentucky in March 1956. With the threat of nuclear weapons, the army had to develop divisions that could react and fight on the nuclear battlefield. On September 21, 1956, the 101ˢᵗ Airborne Division became the Army's first pentomic division, divided into five battle groups that could quickly respond to world-wide threats and emergencies. With the 101ˢᵗ Airborne Division's new nuclear quick response capabilities, the division was placed on alert during the Cuban missile crisis in 1962. President Kennedy was able to stare down the Russians in their attempt to bring nuclear weapons into Cuba, and thus the 101st did not have to be used.

Responding to a racially charged Little Rock, Arkansas in September 1957, 1-327 Infantry was sent to aid local law enforcement in maintaining order. The mission was not to conduct military operations against an enemy of the United States, but to maintain law and order during the integration of Central High School in Little Rock. Had it not been for the show of force by the 101st, the situation could have been a disaster for Little Rock and our country.

Vietnam
April 1965

The 101st Airborne Division's involvement in Vietnam began in April 1965 when the 101st Aviation Battalion was the first unit to be sent to Vietnam, and the first combat unit to see action since WWII. In this same year, Washington made the decision to escalate our nation's involvement in the war. The 1st brigade of the 101st arrived by ship to Vietnam's Cam Ranh Bay on July 29, 1965. The brigade earned the nickname "Nomads of Vietnam."

The 101st was active in Vietnam for almost seven years operating against the Vietnam People's Army's (NVA) infiltration routes through Laos and the A Shau Valley. The 101st participated in fifteen campaigns, including Operation Highland, Operation Hawthorne, Operation Wheeler, Operation Eagle Thrust, the Tet Offensive of 1968, Operation Nevada Eagle, A Shau Valley, and the Battle of Hamburger Hill in 1969.

In March of 1970, the 3rd Brigade of 101st rebuilt the abandoned Fire Support Base Ripcord to be used for a covert planned offensive by the 101st to destroy NVA supply bases in the mountains above the A Shau Valley. During the subsequent twenty-three day siege, seventy-five U.S. servicemen were killed in action, including Colonel Andre Lucas, the 2nd Battalion, 506th Infantry commanding officer (posthumously awarded the Medal

250

of Honor), and the only American professional athlete to be killed during the war, 1st Lt. Bob Kalsu.

Parts of the division supported the ARVN Operation Lam Son 719, which was the 1971 invasion of southern Laos, but only aviation units actually entered Laos. The Viet Cong had never seen a bald eagle, so they called the 101st Infantry Division "Chicken Men." Their commanders regularly told their soldiers to avoid the "Chicken Men" unless they wanted to be defeated.

The division was involved with numerous campaigns during the Vietnamization process which involved handing over all combat operations to the South Vietnamese and the withdrawal of all U.S. forces. In 1968, the 101st changed its designation to the 101st Airborne Division (Airmobile). However, the division kept the "Airborne" tab to honor the Screaming Eagle's history. In 1972, the 101st withdrew from Vietnam and returned to Fort Campbell.

In those seven years of combat in Vietnam, the division suffered 4,011 Killed in Action and 18,259 Wounded in Action, with the division incurring the third highest casualty rate of all divisions fighting in the war. Soldiers from the 101st were awarded seventeen Congressional Medals of Honor. The division earned the following decorations for its service in Vietnam:

Presidential Unit Citation (Army) for Dak To, Vietnam 1966

Valorous Unit Award for Tuy Hoa

Meritorious Unit Commendation (Army) for Vietnam 1965-1966

Republic of Vietnam Cross of Gallantry with Palm for
Vietnam 1966-1967

Republic of Vietnam Cross of Gallantry with Palm for
Vietnam 1971

Republic of Vietnam Civil Action Honor Medal,
First Class for Vietnam 1968-1970

Air Assault
October 1974

In October 1974, two years after the division's return to the Fort Campbell, the division was re-designated the 101st Airborne Division (Air Assault). On January 20, 1978, retroactive to April 1, 1974, those that demonstrated professional knowledge and skills through the Air Assault School could now wear the new Air Assault Badge.

Following numerous training exercises like Gallant Shield and Reforger in Europe, the division began training with NATO (North Atlantic Treaty Organization) units, and the "One Army" concept received emphasis. The division trained in Alaska, and at the Jungle Operations Training Center in Panama. In June 1979, the 101st started to receive the new UH-60 Blackhawk helicopters and combined them with the Vietnam era UH-1 Hueys.

In 1980, the division began joint exercises with foreign allies in Joint Task Force Bright Star. The training gave the division experience in desert operations and coordination of effort with allies. In March 1982, 1-502 Infantry was sent to the Sinai Peninsula in Egypt for a six month rotation with the Multinational Force and Observers (MFO). The mission was to provide a peace-keeping force as per the 1979 Egypt-Israeli peace treaty. The division participated in fifteen major exercises that included trips to Germany, Honduras, and Egypt.

In 1982, the division reorganized into three brigades. The 1st brigade was made up of the 327th, the 2nd was made up of the 502nd, and the 3rd was made up of the 187th. The 2nd brigade's 3-502nd suffered loss upon their return from MFO peacekeeping duty in the Sinai. On December 12, 1985, Arrow Flight Number 1285 carrying two hundred forty-eight members from the 3rd Battalion 502nd crashed near Gander, Newfoundland killing all on board. President Ronald Reagan and his wife Nancy flew to Ft. Campbell to be with grieving family members.

Gulf War - Desert Shield / Desert Storm
August 1990

After the fall of the Berlin Wall in 1989, the world was once again lulled into thinking about sustained peace throughout the world and the possibility of a world without wars crept into the minds of many. Following a long dispute between Iraq and Kuwait, Iraqi forces invaded Kuwait on August 2, 1990. This invasion immediately jeopardized U.S. security interests in the region. On the 10th of August 1990, the 101st Airborne Division received its orders to join a massive build up in the region and to immediately defend Saudi Arabia from further attacks.

Several units of the division were spread out due to various training exercises, and had to be recalled to Ft. Campbell for the 101st Airborne Division's deployment to Saudi Arabia. The first combat force to deploy from Ft. Campbell was the first Division Ready Brigade (DRB-1). The DRB -1 was made up of an aviation task force and the Second Air Assault Brigade Task Force which included the 502nd Infantry Regiment ("Strike" brigade) and the 1-320th Field Artillery Battalion.

When the 502nd arrived in Saudi Arabia, their first mission was to provide a covering force north along the Kuwaiti-Saudi border and establish forward operating bases, defending President H.W. Bush's "Line in the Sand." The first bases to be established in Desert Shield were Forward Operating Base (FOB) Bastogne and FOB Oasis. The complete division was in theatre by October 1990. Iraqi forces had massed along the border and were poised to attack into the Saudi Arabian industrial complex.

As the mid-January UN deadline approached, Iraqi forces amassed five divisions along the border between Iraq and Saudi Arabia at the Wadi al-Batin. Intelligence sources confirmed that Iraqi divisions had established command and control in the area and were to cross the border and blitz down the wadi towards King Khalid Military City, Saudi Arabia no later than January 14, 1991. To defend the Iraqi approach, General H. Norman Schwarzkopf ordered General J.H. Binford Peay, III to send one brigade task force to provide a covering force in the vicinity of Hafar al-Batin. General Peay sent the 502nd Infantry Regiment under the command of Colonel Ted Purdom to the area on January 10, 1991. Once the 502nd arrived, the brigade fell under the command and control of the 1st Cavalry Division. In what some call "The greatest battle that never was," Iraqi forces bogged down in their approach to Saudi Arabia following a rain and were unable to execute their planned attack.

The air war began January 17, 1991 and Desert Shield, a mission of defense, became Desert Storm, a mission on the offense. Code-named Normandy, the 101st Airborne Division fired the first shots of the war. Using Apache gunships (AH-64), the 101st attack helicopters eliminated key radar facilities inside Iraq allowing for a twenty mile wide corridor of undetected airspace. The elimination of these radar units allowed coalition aircraft to go deep into Iraq undetected.

After the Iraqis were blinded by the constant bombardment from coalition air power and superiority, the coalition's ground forces moved west. Saddam and his generals did not see the build up of forces to the west that included the 101st Airborne Division (Air Assault). What was to be called the "Hail Mary", the 101st Airborne Division under the leadership of General Peay, made an historic thrust into Forward Operating Base Cobra (Iraq) on February 24, 1991 (G-Day). Called a "bold and bodacious action", the early morning air assault led by Tom Hill's 1st Brigade (three battalions) along with the 1st Battalion of the 502nd (First Strike) made the ninety-three mile push into FOB Cobra (the largest air assault ever conducted in a single day). Colonel Hill paraphrased William Shakespeare, "Cry Havoc. Let loose the dogs of war," as the four battalions thundered toward its LZ (landing zone).

FOB Cobra was a base of critical tactical and operational importance. It served as a forward operating base from which the division could support operations to cut the enemy's lines of communications and supply. The FOB also positioned the division to cut the Iraqi escape route through follow-on missions by the third brigade along Highway 8, and offered the threat of a Screaming Eagle attack against Baghdad.

To further tighten the noose around Saddam Hussein's neck, the 101st Airborne Division launched yet another 93 mile air assault east of Cobra on 27 February 1991. Led by Colonel Theodore (Ted) Purdom's 502nd Infantry Regiment (2nd Brigade) and one battalion from the 1st Brigade (3-327th), FOB Viper would serve as a base for yet another assault, this one by attack helicopters striking 120 miles northeast from Viper into Engagement Area (EA) Thomas. In EA Thomas, the 101st and 12th Aviation Brigades destroyed Iraqi forces trying to escape north from Basrah and damaged a major bridge across the Euphrates. Once FOB Viper was secured, the 101st Aviation Brigade began screening the XVIII Airborne Corps' northern flank.

On the 28th of February, 1991 the Iraqis surrendered and subsequently agreed to the terms of the United Nations. Over the next two months, the division returned to Ft. Campbell, Kentucky.

-General H. Norman Schwarzkopf

"The Air Force and armor were the thunder of Desert Storm, while the 101st was the lightning."

Post Cold War
The 1990s

With the collapse of the Soviet Union, the 101st Airborne Division's missions were diverse. The division was called on to provide assistance in Bosnia and Kosovo, guarding Patriot Air Defense batteries in Saudi Arabia, as well as domestic duties such as hurricane relief efforts and fire fighting duties in Montana. The United Nations called on the United States to assist in restoring order in the hunger-stricken, war-torn nation of Somalia. As the relief effort expanded, the division sent air assets as well as an evacuation hospital and a graves registration unit. The graves unit was responsible for handling the bodies of those lost during Task Force Ranger October 3-4, 1993.

In 1994, 3rd Battalion 502nd Infantry formulated task force "Safe Passage" for over 3,500 Cubans that were fleeing the Castro regime. After formulating the joint operation, Cuban immigrants were able to be safely processed for processing at Guantanamo Bay rather than attempting to enter the United States using dangerous makeshift rafts tied together in a flotilla. In an attempt to get rid of hundreds of criminals and to reduce their prison population, the Cuban government sent them to sink or swim to the U.S. The legal and illegal immigrants had to be processed at Guantanamo Bay for U.S. Visas or extradition back to Cuba.

In August 2000, the 2nd Battalion 327th Infantry helped secure the peace in Kosovo and support elections for the formulation of a new Kosovo government. While 2nd Battalion was stabilizing Kosovo in 2000, the 3rd Battalion 327 Infantry was fighting fires in Montana. In 2001, Task Force Eagle made up of the second brigade 502nd and soldiers throughout the division relieved 2nd Battalion 327 Infantry and assumed responsibility in the region.

Global War on Terror
September 11, 2001

The 101st Airborne Division and the world changed on September 11, 2001. New York's World Trade Center's towers and America was attacked by Al Qaeda trained terrorists, and the attacks were broadcast on live television. Immediately, 5th Special Forces Group and Task Force 160th Special Operations Aviation Regiment stationed at Fort Campbell were deployed to Afghanistan. Intelligence gathering, identification of targets, and the connection to the Northern Alliance proved beneficial to the 101st and their follow-on missions.

Operation Enduring Freedom
January 2002

After the September 11th attacks in 2001, the 3rd Brigade Rakkasans assumed the 101st Airborne Division's DRB-1 status and deployed to Afghanistan to participate in Operation

Anaconda. The 3ʳᵈ Brigade along with the 10ᵗʰ Mountain Division targeted the large Taliban force in the Shahi-Kot region of eastern Afghanistan. Operation Anaconda and the 5ᵗʰ Special Forces Group's actions led to the establishment of a new government replacing the Taliban regime in five months. The 3ʳᵈ Brigade redeployed to Ft. Campbell in June after completing a six month tour in Afghanistan.

Operation Iraqi Freedom
February 6, 2003

Under the leadership of Major General David H. Petraeus, the entire division including trucks and equipment deployed to Kuwait in February, 2003. The deployment only took ten days. On March 21ˢᵗ, the 101ˢᵗ Airborne Division moved five hundred seventy-one kilometers into Iraq through a sandstorm and hostile enemy territory to establish two critical refueling points. The action allowed V Corps to destroy enemy targets deep into Iraq. Critical to V Corps communications and major road networks, the 101ˢᵗ decisively engaged the enemy in spite of poor weather and enemy resistance. The division liberated the cities of An Najaf, Karbala, Al Hillah, and cleared South Baghdad. Conducting the longest air assault in history, breaking the record set in Operation Desert Storm, the division arrived in northern Iraq on April 22, 2003. The division ultimately occupied the northern region of Iraq, designated AO North.

Once in AO North, the 101ˢᵗ became active in restoring basic services and improving quality of life for the Iraqi towns. The division was responsible for the construction of new wells, restoration of schools, increasing electrical capacity, in total spending over fifty-seven million dollars on over five thousand projects. The 101ˢᵗ Airborne directly employed over fifteen thousand civilians and set up a veteran's employment office to assist Iraq's veterans with jobs to help rebuild their country.

While conducting operations in their AO, elements of the 101ˢᵗ cornered Saddam's two sons, Uday and Qusay Hussein. The division constantly pursued members of the previous regime and foreign fighters. Using Mosul as the division base, the 1st Brigade (327th Infantry Regiment) guarded the Qayarrah Airfield, the 2nd Brigade (502nd Infantry Regiment) and the 3rd Battalion of the 327th Infantry Regiment were responsible for Mosul, and the 3rd Brigade (187th Infantry Regiment) controlled Tal Afar north of Mosul.

After securing their area of operation, the division was replaced by Stryker Brigade and redeployed to Ft. Campbell in February, 2004.

Reorganization and Deployment
October 2005

Upon the division's return in 2004, the 101st added a fourth infantry brigade and a second aviation brigade formulating brigade combat teams (BCT). The fourth brigade was the 506th Infantry which rejoined the division after thirty years and all brigades were reduced to two battalions each. The division began re-deployment to Iraq in October 2005.

Once in theatre, the 101st Airborne's area of operation was northern Iraq. By December, the entire northern half of Iraq (about the size of Ohio) was under their care and responsibility. The 101st mission was to train Iraqi security forces, protect Iraq's infrastructure, neutralize anti-Iraqi forces, and establish local governments. As a result, the division assisted in its first national election and the people of Iraq were allowed to participate in the democratic process.

The division worked with four Iraqi Army Divisions by training them and helping them earn the trust of the Iraqi people. Once trained, the Iraqi soldiers worked with U.S. Army Special Forces units resulting in the capture of insurgents and high value targets. Thirty-five Iraqi Army battalions finally assumed control of their areas of operation during the Screaming Eagles 2005-2007 deployment.

The 2005-2007 deployment deployed the Division HQ to Afghanistan to lead the Combined Joint Task Force (CJTF) 101 which had the 4ᵗʰ Brigade Combat Team (506ᵗʰ) assigned to it, and the three remaining brigade combat teams were in Iraq. It was very difficult having the division split and under four different division headquarters.

Operations in Afghanistan were under the control of the International Security and Assistance Force (ISAF) directed by NATO. U.S. Forces were assigned to control all ISAF forces in Regional Command East (RC-E). The 101ˢᵗ was to control RC-E and was designated the Combined Joint Task Force 101. The mission of the 101ˢᵗ was to secure the Afghan people, promote a capable governance, and defeat terrorists and insurgents.

During the 2007-2009 deployment to Iraq, the 1ˢᵗ, 2ⁿᵈ, and 3ʳᵈ Brigade Combat Teams (BCT) executed the surge. The 1ˢᵗ BCT was assigned to the 1ˢᵗ Armored Division which AO was in northern Iraq, 2ⁿᵈ BCT was assigned to the 4ᵗʰ Infantry Division in Baghdad, and the 3ʳᵈ BCT was assigned to the 10ᵗʰ Mountain Division in the center of Iraq.

In 2009, the division consolidated at Ft. Campbell and began the preparation process for re-deployment to Afghanistan. The 101ˢᵗ Airborne Division Headquarters redeployed again as CJTF-101, and three of the four brigade Combat Teams are currently in Afghanistan fighting a fierce battle with Taliban insurgents. The division under the leadership of Major General John F. Campbell is maintaining control in the volatile border region between Afghanistan and Pakistan, as well as the Hindu Kush and Afghan Control Highlands.

The soldiers of the 101ˢᵗ Airborne Division are not only soldiers but diplomats, helping to improve the government of Afghanistan, restoring the peoples' confidence while training the Afghan National Security Forces (ANSF). The division's fight in Afghanistan continues to this day.

John O'Connor (far right), WWII

Acknowledgments

Early in 2010, being the pack-rat and old softy that I am regarding my Army days, I started pulling out the old memories, as I had done every year for nineteen years. As I was looking at the small three inch by six inch planner I used as my journal during Desert Shield and Desert Storm, the year leaped off the page. It's 2010, and Desert Shield was in 1990! My, how time flies. This year will be twenty-one years since I got the call at Fort Lewis to join the 101st Airborne Division in Desert Shield and February, 2011 was the 20th Anniversary of G-Day (the commencement of ground operations for Desert Storm). The second thought was not far from the first, "I really need to write a book about my time with the 101st." While I still have my mind, I need to get some of this stuff written so that my kids and hopefully, grandkids someday can see what happened to Grand-dad.

Now with the seed of the book planted in my mind, I began talking to my wife, Sue, Mom and Dad, Kristen, and Clay about my Army days and my vision for writing the book. With Sue being my wife, she took the brunt of the initial concept. Sue O'Connor grew up in a well-grounded, patriotic, Catholic family that is knowledgeable about the military. Her Dad, John O'Connor, a Purple Heart recipient during World War II, served with the historic 350th Fighter Group in the Mediterranean Theatre of Operations (North Africa, Sicily, and Italy). John returned home following the war to his fiancé, Mary Whitmore in Addison, New York where they were married and had seven children. Sue's older brothers all served their country. Jim served with United States

Army in Korea, Steve served as a U.S. Army Military Policeman in Germany, and Mike served in the Air Force in Thailand (all three serving during the Vietnam era). Younger brother, Tim served in the Air Force Reserve. Her sister, Cindy's husband, Richard Eyster served in the US Air Force Security Police, also serving during the Vietnam era. I want to thank Tim and Joe O'Connor for serving as a sounding board during the early days of the project. Sue was a God-send throughout this project. I want to thank her for always being there, re-living and reading about my Gulf War days, and lending direct support to this project for the past year. Without her friendship, love, and encouragement, this would not have been possible.

I attempted and failed miserably for years to re-connect with guys that I had served with, but I was determined to make this 20th year different. I was thinking if I connect with just one or two this year, it would be great. The first one was not of my own making. Dave Gurley found my telephone number and contacted me in 2010. When he called, he started by saying, "This is a voice from 20 years ago and I don't know if you'll remember me, this is Dave Gurley." Of course I remembered Dave and was excited to re-connect with him, re-living "our" story from our training days to the time at Fort Lewis. After catching each other up on our kids and families, the 20 year gap disappeared. I want to thank Dave for sharing with me through numerous emails and phone calls, his time with me, the 2/75th Ranger Battalion at Fort Lewis, and his storied career in the Army.

Through a military connection website, I found Matt Huff who posted a reunion coming to Fort Campbell, Kentucky of 1-320th Field Artillery Gulf War veterans. The connection with Matt gave me even more connections with guys that I served with in the battalion. Matt has spent years coordinating and working on reunions that have kept the guys together. I want to thank Matt for submitting his Desert Shield – Desert Storm stories, 1-320th photographs, emails, and phone calls about the battalion and our time in the desert, 20 years ago.

Kalub Duggins was Command Sergeant Major of the 1-320th Field Artillery Battalion, 101st Airborne Division during Desert Shield – Desert Storm and one of my first reconnections in 2010. CSM Duggins was a soldiers' soldier and always had his soldier's welfare at heart. Duggins' almost 24 year history in the Army began with B Btry 2-19 FA, 1st Air Cavalry Division in Vietnam where he saw intense combat and was awarded two Bronze Stars with V devices. When asked about the Bronze Stars, he told me he received the awards for "Just doing my job." Duggins served as Drill Sergeant at Ft. Sill, Oklahoma, helping to start "One Station Unit Training." He also was selected to be an advisor to the 1st Rock Army Headquarters in 78-79 while serving with the USA Combat Support Coordination Team #1, United Nations Command in Korea, where he was awarded the Joint Services Medal. CSM Duggins was selected to activate the 11th ACR Combat Support Squadron in Fulda, Germany where he served as the 1st Command Sergeant Major of the unit. Throughout his career, Duggins held many senior leadership positions before being assigned to the 101st. We were fortunate to have his combat experience and leadership skills going into the Gulf War. CSM Duggins retired on 1 Feb 92.

Kal worked with me on this project from beginning to completion and was a tremendous asset when it came to filling in the blanks. He got me up to speed on the Army, past and present, helping me see how the Army and the 101st evolved and adapted from Vietnam to the current day. He was very helpful in providing 1-320th deployment information from Ft. Campbell to Saudi Arabia and movements of the battalion as we made our way from Camp Eagle II to the forward operating bases in the defense of Saudi Arabia, and ultimately, the attack into Iraq. His knowledge of the 101st, The Army, and the world's geopolitical situation was very beneficial. When I was lacking photographs, Kal spent hours pouring over images at the Fort Campbell Museum that could be included. Over the past six months, I have been able to talk to Kal Duggins for hours about a wide range of subjects including post traumatic stress disorders, to family support groups and how the rear detachment personnel handled the unit while we were deployed. Once I shared a particular subject matter or chapter I was working on, behind the scenes he would be researching and providing information. As the months went by, there was no subject that could not be addressed, and as a result of those conversations, I consider him a good friend. To this day, Kal continues to be a soldier's advocate when it comes to veteran's issues and concerns. He truly loves his daughter, Alison, his departed wife, Barbara, the soldier, the Army, and his Country. He is still steadfast in his beliefs with a Command Sergeant Major's heart, and for these things, I am an admirer. His daughter Alison was also a major contributor to this book. Her recollections and insights as a 19 year old working with her Mother, Barbara on the home front gave me insight into how families held down the fort while we were away. Alison was Barbara's "right hand" and worked with her Mom on many initiatives aimed at helping the morale of soldiers and their families. Her unpublished essay was used in Chapter 11, The Military Family.

Ian Berkowitz, an infantry squad leader in 2nd platoon, Charlie Company, 1-502nd was one of my best friends in the 101st Airborne Division. Ian was a professional Non-Commissioned Officer that knew his job and knew how to lead soldiers. Ian and I worked side-by-side in Desert Shield-Desert Storm, and being his forward observer, we developed a great working relationship. During the Gulf War, Ian instilled confidence and demanded perfection from his soldiers. He also was smart and brave enough to lighten the burden in life-or-death situations with humor. Ian's knowledge of Arabic that he learned at the Defense Language Institute prior to the Gulf War was a valuable commodity for our unit during the war. Ian was one of my many friends that made a career in the Army; honorably discharged in 1995. During his career he served as Company First Sergeant, Division S-3 Plans and Operations NCO, NCO Academy Instructor (Instructor of the month and Instructor of the quarter, 2nd Infantry Division NCO Academy), Drill Sergeant (Distinguished Honor Graduate), Platoon Sergeant, and Squad Leader. Some deployments included

264

the evacuation of Vietnamese refugees in Operation New Life, two overseas tours to the Republic of South Korea with over one hundred combat patrols in the Korean DMZ, Operation Wildfire (firefighting in northern California), and with the 101ˢᵗ Airborne Division in Desert Shield and Desert Storm. In addition to his service with the 1-502ⁿᵈ at Fort Campbell, Ian served with the 25ᵗʰ Infantry Division at the Schofield Barracks in Hawaii, 7ᵗʰ Infantry Division at Ft. Ord, California, 197ᵗʰ Infantry Brigade at Ft. Benning, 2ⁿᵈ Infantry Training Brigade, Ft. Benning, 2ⁿᵈ Infantry Division, 38ᵗʰ Infantry Regiment, 503ʳᵈ Infantry Regiment, 2ⁿᵈ ID NCO Academy in the Republic of South Korea. Before coming to the 101ˢᵗ in 1990, Ian was with the 4ᵗʰ Infantry Division, 12ᵗʰ Infantry Regiment at Ft. Carson, Colorado. After his return from the Persian Gulf War, Ian had a one year tour at the 8ᵗʰ Army NCO Academy, Republic of South Korea and then returned to the 101ˢᵗ where he finished his career. Some of his awards include the Meritorious Service Medal, 11 Army Commendation Medals, two Army Achievement Medals, Good Conduct Medal (six awards), Humanitarian Service Medal with one bronze star, National Defense Service Medal with bronze star, Southwest Asia Service Medal with two bronze stars, Non Commissioned Officer's Professional Development Ribbon with numeral 3, Army Service Ribbon, Overseas Service Ribbon (3ʳᵈ award), Liberation of Kuwait/Saudi Arabia Medal, Korean Defense Ribbon, Combat Infantryman's Badge, Parachutists Badge, Air Assault Badge, Rappel Master, Expert Marksman Badge, Driver's Badge, and Imjim Scout Award.

Ian worked with me on this project from the beginning, contributing 2ⁿᵈ platoon and 1-502ⁿᵈ movements, details regarding those movements, verifying my recollections, contributing photographs, and assisting in reconnections with other soldiers from the Gulf War. Ian made himself available at any time, visiting with me through numerous phone calls and emails. To this day, Ian is still active in military affairs and all veterans' organizations. He is Commander and Life Member of the Wilfred Bank Orange County Post 413 of the Jewish War Veterans Of America, Senior

Vice-Commander of the John T. Kenney Post 973 Veterans of Foreign Wars (VFW), Life Member of Chapter 152, Disabled American Veterans (DAV), Vice Commander of the American Legion, Newburgh Township Post 1420, involved with District 9 American Legion Baseball, and President of the Vietnam Veterans of America, Hudson Valley Chapter 537.

Martin L. McPherson (Marty) was my radio telephone operator in Operation Desert Shield and Desert Storm and always by my side. Martin was born in Portland, Oregon in 1971 and after graduating from high school, joined the Army with a buddy. After going through basic and advanced individual training at Ft. Sill, Oklahoma in 1989, he was assigned to the 1st Battalion, 320th Field Artillery Regiment, 101st Airborne Division (Air Assault) as a Fire Support Specialist. Martin was one of the first Screaming Eagle boots to hit the ground in August, 1990 as he was with the Division's Ready Brigade. Being a Fire Support Specialist with the 1-320th, McPherson was attached to Charlie Company, 1/502nd Infantry Regiment as a forward observer and my assistant during Desert Shield and Desert Storm. Martin's dedication and superior performance while at war with Iraq earned him a recommendation for promotion from me on 17 March 1991, just four days after our return to Camp Eagle II following the war. I want to thank Martin for sharing in detail his Gulf War experience through numerous emails and telephone conversations. I also want to thank him for sharing the actual sketch he made on G-Day eve of "White Lightning", the nose art that was on the front of the Blackhawk that took us into Forward Operating Base Cobra on 24 February 1991. Since Martin and I ate the same dirt in a time of war, I will never forget his loyalty and support. Martin got out of the Army in 1992 and currently lives happily in Oregon with his wife and two kids.

I was very fortunate in my research to have reconnected with seven other forward observers and old friends, and all were contributors to G-Day. Three of the seven were from the Ft. Lewis "Sandfill 27" and all three came out of 1-11 FA. Both Frank Giger and Ernie Swindle are retired Army. Ernie, Frank, and I spent more than one or two evenings at the mess tent at Camp Eagle II drinking coffee, writing letters, and solving the world's problems. I want to thank Ernie for sharing his recollections and photographs, Walter Hein for numerous phone calls and emails, and Frank Giger for his Camp Eagle II recollections and the submission of his unpublished essay, "Friendliest of Fire" that was included in the chapter, "After the Storm."

Frank Giger was the only one of us to get shot. If the infantry private's misfire at Task Force Assembly Area Campbell had been discharged at a different angle, we might be reflecting on Frank in a little different way today. I'll never forget Frank and I coming up with the idea of sending President Bush a letter during one of our evenings at the mess tent. I have always felt the letter I received from the President a month later is his also. Frank is the son of German immigrants, spent his childhood as an Army brat, and was rumored to have grown up while in the Regular Army. A year after Desert Storm, he was transferred to Recruiting Command, where he spent the remainder of his career. Retiring after twenty-two years, he presently resides in Alabama with his bride of seventeen years and fifteen year old son. Frank is enjoying his retirement these days, building his own World War I replica airplane, and being a pilot.

I want to thank Blain Mamiya who worked with me on the original concept of the book and gave me some helpful advice on how to get started. Blain was the friend and catalyst who erased my doubts as to being able to put my story into print. Blain holds a Doctorate Degree in Medicinal Chemistry, Masters of Science Degree in Organic Chemistry and Bachelors of Science Degree in Chemistry. Blain is currently a professor at a local college and experienced in motivating and nurturing a lifelong love of knowledge in his students. He has a proven track record of student achievement at the secondary and post-secondary levels of education. Whenever I had a question, Blain was there. I can honestly say that without Blain's knowledge and encouragement, G-Day, Rendezvous with Eagles would have just remained an idea and a dream.

I want to thank my sister's husband, Mark Woodbridge, who in the final days of the project rolled up his sleeves and acted as a proofreader. Mark served as one of my readers of the final manuscript. When I felt like I was finished, he encouraged me to elaborate on key facts and thoughts making the book a little more readable for those not familiar with military terminology.

All writers need sounding boards, and my friend Doug Nelle served as mine. Doug is a true American Patriot that loves America, soldiers, and veterans. I want to thank Doug for his friendship, encouragement, and "daily" support during this project.

I am truly blessed to have so many friends and neighbors who love the veteran and love America. These friends made a point to keep up with the project over the past year and were my cheerleaders. I want to thank them for being there and pushing me to go forward.

Selected Bibliography

Private Papers, Letters, and Communications

Baskin, Fred. E-mail and Telephone Interviews.

Beaird, Sergeant Damon. E-mail and Telephone Interviews.

Berkowitz, SFC. (Ret) Ian M. E-mail and Telephone Interviews, Photographs and Biographical Sketch.

Bush, President George H.W. "A Gulf War Exclusive: President Bush Talking With David Frost." 12 Dec. 1995: 1-40. Print.

Ceurvels, David, AC-130 Gunner. Spirit 03 Photograph taken December 25, 1990. Message to the author. E-mail.

Department of the Army and Chafin, James S. Message to the Author. E-mail. Approval to use the 101st Airborne Division SSI. December 15, 2010.

Don F. Pratt Museum, and LTC (Ret) John O'Brien. "Forward Operating Base Cobra Photographs."

Duggins, Alison C. "The Military Family." E-mail and Telephone Interview. Unpublished Essay, Undated.

Duggins, Command Sergeant Major (Ret) Kalub D. E-mail and Telephone Interviews, Photographs, and Biographical Sketch.

Giger, SFC (Ret) Frank. E-mail Interview. Unpublished Essay, "The Friendliest of Fire – Or the luckiest unlucky affair of my career." Undated. Biographical Sketch.

Godwin, Lauren E. *Photo Restoration.* Austin.

Gurley, David D. Email and Telephone Interviews.

Hein, Walter A. E-mail and Telephone Interviews. Photographs.

Huff, SPC. Matthew C. E-mail and Telephone Interviews. *Wardogs on the Move.* Unpublished Essay, Undated.

McGee, Senior Master Sergeant (Ret) Patrick. "The A-10 and the 2951st Combat Logistics Support Squadron." E-mail interview.

McPherson, Martin L. "White Lightning Sketch - G-Day." Message to the Author. E-mail. E-mail and Telephone Interviews. Biographical Sketch.

Peay, III, General (Ret) J.H. Binford. *Command Report: 101st Airborne Division (Air Assault) for Operation Desert Shield and Desert Storm, 2 August 1990 through 1 May 1991.* dated July 1, 1991. Print.

Potomac Books, Inc., and Sam Dorrance. "Maps." Message to the author. 13 Dec. 2010. E-mail.

Sizemore, Vernon E. E-mail Interview.

Swindle, Ernest D. E-mail Interview. Photographs.

Walter, CMSGT (Ret) Bill. E-mail interview.

<u>Websites</u>

AUSA. *Association of the United States Army.*
Web.<http://www.ausa.org/>.

Bush, President George H.W. "Archives." *George Bush Presidential Library and Museum.* Texas A&M University.
Web. <http://bushlibrary.tamu.edu/>.

101st Airborne Division (Air Assault). *Fort Campbell, Kentucky.* United States Army. Web. <http://campbell.army.mil/>.

The 101st Airborne Division Association. Web.
<http://www.screamingeagle.org>.

Gulf Link. *Office of the Special Assistant for Gulf War Illnesses.*
Web. <http://www.gulflink.com>.

Library of Congress. *The Library of Congress Veterans History Project.*
Web. <http://www.loc.gov/vets>.

McGee, Senior Master Sergeant (Ret) Patrick. "The A-10 in Desert Storm." *2951st Combat Logistics Support Squadron.*
Web. <http://www.2951clss-gulfwar.com/>.

National Military Family Organization. Web.
<http://www.militaryfamily.org/>.

Spectre Association. Web. <http://www.spectre-association.org>.

U.S. Army. *Army Family Readiness Group.*
Web. <http://www.armyfrg.org/>.

The VA. *United States Department of Veterans Affairs.*
Web. <http://www.va.gov/>.

Wounded Warrior Project. *WWP.* The Wounded Warrior Project.
Web. <http://www.woundedwarriorproject.org/>.

Military documents

Bolt, Col William J. *Command Report: 101st Airborne Division (Air Assault) for Operation Desert Shield and Desert Storm, 2 August 1990 through 1 May 1991. Dated July 1, 1991.* Print.

Department of the Air Force. *Air Performance in Desert Storm.* dated April 1991. Print.

Department of the Army - U.S. Army Center of Military History. *Air Assault in the Gulf, An Interview with MG J.H. Binford Peay, III, Commanding General, 101st Airborne Division (Air Assault).* dated 5 June 1991. Print.

Department of the Army - U.S. Army Center of Military History. *XVIII Airborne Corps in Operations Desert Shield and Desert Storm, An Annotated Chronology, Updated 9 April, 1998.* Print.

United States Central Command. *Operation Desert Shield and Desert Storm, Executive Summary, (unclassified).* dated 11 July 1991. Print.

U.S. Army Combined Arms Training Activity (CATA). *Newsletter No. 90-7 Special Edition, Winning in the Desert, August 1990.* Print.

Magazines

Air Force Magazine. "More Data from the Desert, January 1996." Print.

Brown, BG (Ret) John S. "Historically Speaking, Desert Storm at 20." *Army - Association of the United States Army.* Published in Army Magazine in three parts. January 2011 through March 2011. Print.

Department of Veterans Affairs. "Gulf War Review." Print.

Published Sources

The 101st Airborne Division (Air Assault). *North to the Euphrates -
  101st Airborne Division (Air Assault) - Operations Desert Shield
  and Desert Storm.* Tennessee-Kentucky Chapter of the United
  States Army, 1991. Print.

The 101st Airborne Division Association. *The History of the 101st
  Airborne Division (Air Assault).* Oct. 2009. Fort Campbell,
  Kentucky. Print.

"Day One." *Czech Chemical Detection Units in the Gulf War.* ABC News.
  New York. Television.

Flanagan, E. M. *Lightning: the 101st in the Gulf War.* Washington, D.C.
  Potomac, 1994. Print.

Scales, Robert H. *Certain Victory.* Washington, D.C. Potomac, 1994. Print.

Schwarzkopf, H. Norman, and Peter Petre. *It Doesn't Take a Hero:
  General H. Norman Schwarzkopf, the Autobiography.* New York.
  Bantam, 1992. Print.

Taylor, Thomas. *Lightning in the Storm: the 101st Air Assault Division in
  the Gulf War.* New York. Hippocrene, 1994. Print.

About The Editors

Douglas Dean Wiehe, DME.

I was blessed to have a circle of remarkable people who worked with me on this story about the 101st Airborne Division. My inner-circle begins with my family who has always been devoted to the service of their country and to the service of others. As with the generations of Wiehes and Weirs that proceeded us, Mom and Dad instilled in us a love for God, family, country, and the military.

My parents worked with me on this project from the beginning. In our first telephone conversation regarding the book, I told them about my desire to tell the story for our family and my comrades. They were immediately on board and embraced the concept. In the same conversation I told Dad that I was going to make an attempt to contact my commanding general at the time, General J.H. Binford Peay, III (Retired), Commander, 101st Airborne Division (Air Assault) during the Gulf War. I could tell by my Dad's voice that he felt this was a lofty goal, but he felt I should make the effort. One week after my letter to General Peay, I received a response along with his command report for Operations Desert Shield and Desert Storm. We were off and running. Dad immediately staffed up his "war room" along with my competent, computer savvy assistant, Mom.

My Dad, Douglas D. Wiehe, was born in Centralia, Illinois in 1926 to Lawrence and Thelma Wiehe. From a very early age, he and his brother, Larry exhibited a talent and appreciation for music. Their dad sold their home during the depression, moving in with grandparents so they would have enough money to pay for weekly trips to St. Louis and music lessons. Young Douglas and his brother excelled in music. The boys were required to practice three hours every day except Christmas.

During Doug's high school years, World War II was raging. He didn't want to miss out on the opportunity to serve his country. He attempted to enlist before coming of age, but his Dad, like many others, would not sign for their sons to go to war. In 1944, after graduating from Centralia Township High School, he enrolled in the Eastman School of Music in Rochester New York, where he studied trumpet. While in Rochester he worked part time

275

at the rail yard loading artillery munitions for the war effort. Later that year he enlisted in the Army Air Corps. When the Air Corps discontinued pilot training he volunteered for jump school with parachute and glider training at Fort Benning, Georgia. As a paratrooper in postwar Germany, he was assigned to the 508th Parachute Infantry Regiment. After he returned to Ft. Bragg, he was assigned to the 82nd Airborne Division Band.

After serving with the 82nd, Douglas enrolled in North Texas State University in Denton, Texas where he studied music and played in the band and orchestra. While at North Texas he met my Mom, Donna Miller, an oboist. They married on December 28, 1951 in Crane, Texas. After completing their master's degrees in music, Doug was hired in Beeville, Texas as director of both high school and junior high bands and the high school choir while Donna taught elementary music. In addition to his regular duties he gave every student free private lessons. His bands excelled and won many accolades.

In 1957 Douglas accepted the high school band director's position in Big Spring, Texas. In 1964 the Big Spring Band had 12 wind and percussion students win positions in the Texas All-State Band and Orchestra, more than any other school in Texas. His band earned sweepstakes awards for six consecutive years. The band performed in the New Orleans Mardi Gras and the World's Fair in Seattle, Washington. In addition to elevating the music program to a new level of performance and winning many awards, he began working on his doctorate at the University of Colorado. In 1966, with Doug's notoriety as an elite music educator, he was offered and accepted a position at North Texas State University as assistant director of bands. In addition to directing the bands, he taught music history, band methods and brass methods classes. He later finished his doctorate at the University of Oklahoma. In 1971 he was named director of bands at Southwest Texas State University in San Marcos, Texas. In 1974 he became Supervisor of Fine Arts in the Brazosport Independent School District. He served on the State of Texas textbook committee for all subjects, served as Texas Music Educators Association region chairman. For more than twenty years he was executive secretary for University Interscholastic League Music Region 17. Douglas Dean Wiehe was voted into the Texas Bandmasters Hall of Fame in 2006.

After retiring from the public schools, Doug and Donna moved to Seguin, Texas where they continue their involvement in music, church activities and golf. They also judge instrumental solo and ensemble contests for the Texas University Interscholastic League. They were performing regularly with the San Antonio Municipal Band until recently. My parents continue to be involved in the lives of their three children and five grandchildren. My dad is also a student of history and continues to consume books written about our country and its founders.

A special thanks go to my mom and dad for always being there for me and for their commitment to this book. I consider Dad to be my best friend and will cherish forever his gentle red pen strokes and notes on G-Day Rendezvous with Eagles.

Marc D. Felman, Colonel, USAF (ret)

Recognizing early that there would be a need for a content editor, someone familiar with military terminology, the Middle East, and the world's past and current geo-political situation, I chose Colonel Marc Felman for help with the final manuscript. Marc, being a decorated Air Force Colonel and my cousin, the choice was not a hard one.

Marc D. Felman was born in Biloxi, Mississippi, at Keesler Air Force Base, to Air Force Captain Harold Felman and his wife Vivian Knox Felman. Marc was the youngest of three siblings and the only boy. Some might say Marc was destined to be an Air Force pilot. His father was a Master Navigator and an Electronics Warfare Officer (EWO) in B-29's and flew combat missions in the Korean War. His eldest sister Francine married a B-52 Pilot, when Marc was eleven years old. When Marc was a cadet at the United States Air Force Academy, his sister Sharon married an Air Force F-4 Weapons Systems Officer. But the moment where his fate was probably sealed was in 1962 when as a second grader his family was traveling from Harold's military station in Izmir, Turkey, to visit the sites in Rome, Italy. During flight in the Douglas DC-3 Gooney Bird, Marc visited the cockpit to get a drink of water when the pilot invited him to sit in the empty copilot's seat who had just excused himself to use the "honey bucket." Without hesitation Marc took the controls, the autopilot was disengaged and the aircraft began a gentle climb and descent plus or minus one hundred feet. Upon returning to his seat in the back, his sister, not knowing what had just taken place in the cockpit, quipped: "It felt like you were flying the plane." With a sheepish grin Marc proclaimed; "I Did!"

Marc's school years were characterized by mid-year moves from Biloxi to Izmir and Stewart Air Force Base (AFB) in Newburgh, New York. In Newburg, there were visits to the nearby West Point Military Academy and his parents were pretty transparent about how one day they would like to see him get appointed to the Academy. Later when his Dad retired from the Air Force and took up employment as a Defense Contractor in Washington, D.C., Marc became the first of three children to have the privilege of attending one school for the entirety of junior high school and senior high school respectively. The Naval Academy was recruiting Marc to play soccer but living in Maryland, there was a long line of applicants for nearby Annapolis. Marc was unable to land a coveted Congressional appointment and just when he thought his chances were over, and had been accepted to a pre-dentistry program at the University of Maryland, the "fat" envelope came from the United States Air Force Academy (USAFA) in Colorado Springs, Colorado. Marc had received one of President Nixon's rare 90 nationwide appointments to USAFA.

After enduring the four year curriculum and 186 credit hours of engineering focused coursework Marc graduated on June 2, 1976 with a Bachelor of Science. At one minute past midnight on the 2nd, Marc's Dad proudly took his son Marc's commissioning oath. Just a year later, Marc's Dad pinned silver pilot wings on Marc's chest after a grueling and highly competitive Undergraduate Pilot Training course at Columbus AFB, MS. There was a short four month stint at the Strategic Air Command's Combat Crew Training Squadron (CCTS) at Castle AFB, in Merced, California. In March of 1978, Marc and his wife of only three weeks flew to Okinawa where Marc served as an Emergency War Order (EWO) (Cold War nuclear deterrence) certified crewmember in the venerable Strategic Air Command (SAC). Marc would be away from home for one week out of the month for the next eight years of his life, serving alert at an isolated facility near the end of a SAC runway.

After two years of overwater flying in and out of remote island destinations and distant locations like: Osan AB, Korea; Clark Air Base, Philippines; Diego Garcia, British Indian Ocean Territory; Ohakea, New Zealand; Darwin, Australia; Guam, Wake and Midway islands; and Hawaii; Marc attended then CCTS in California again and was a distinguished graduate from Aircraft Commander upgrade. As Aircraft Commander Marc commanded a crew of four on numerous higher headquarters directed and operational missions refueling reconnaissance, bomber, and fighter aircraft from the Air Force, Navy, U.S. Marine Corps, and even allies from the Royal Australian Air Force and Royal Singaporean Air Force. While in Okinawa, he was fortunate to earn a Master of Science in Systems Management from the University of Southern California. In off duty time, Marc completed a rigorous curriculum taught by USC Professors who traveled to various military bases to make these extension programs possible.

Marc returned to the States at the end of 1982 and began flying with the 911th Air Refueling Squadron, at Seymour Johnson Air Force Base SJAFB), North Carolina. A month after arrival, his son David (Marc Jr.) entered the world. In order for Marc to be there for the birth of his son, another pilot had to substitute for him on SAC alert because the base hospital was beyond the authorized alert crew travel area. A week later, Marc's new crew of four received an in-flight evaluation from SAC's 1ˢᵗ Combat Evaluation Group and Marc brought home a seldom seen "Highly Qualified" grade at every crew position. Marc upgraded to Instructor Pilot in the next available Combined Flight Instructor Course taught at Carswell AFB, in Fort Worth, Texas. Subsequently he attended SAC's Instrument Flight Instructor Course and over the next five years was the Officer in Charge of teaching hundreds of pilots the annual instrument flight refresher course. At the time, Marc was selected as the youngest Flight Commander in SAC. Marc deployed to the European Tanker Task Force and spent several tours in Riyadh, Saudi Arabia, supporting the Elf One training mission, refueling Saudi AWACS and F-15 aircraft over the Gulf of Hormuz during the Iran-Iraq war.

When the SJAFB KC-135s were reassigned to a northern tier SAC base in Michigan, the Air Force placed a brand new KC-10 squadron in its place and elected to retain a few board selected crewmembers to stay at SJAFB in the new McDonnell Douglas KC-10s being delivered from the factory as they were coming off the assembly line over the course of the next several years. Marc was fortunate to be selected to check out as the first new KC-10 aircraft commander at SJAFB and join a cadre of veteran KC-10 crewmembers reassigned from the other two KC-10 bases in Louisiana and California. Marc and several copilots completed American Airlines Training at March AFB, in Riverside, California and just three months after their last KC-135 flight, they were flying a qualification check ride in the KC-10. The wing had only received three KC-10'of its 20 aircraft final complement so actual stick time was limited so that every crewmember could remain current and qualified. After just a few rides and a check, Marc was watched by an Instructor Pilot for a few training missions but then released to fly without an instructor on his first KC-10 Operational overwater air refueling mission. These overwater "fighter drags" are pretty common and take place almost every day as small fighter aircraft capable of carrying only a couple of hours of fuel must fly across the pond with tanker aircraft and refuel many times to make the long journey. On March 6, 1986, Marc was tanking a flight of USMC A-4 camels from the East Coast of the United States to a stopover at Lajes Field situated in the tiny Portuguese islands about half way across the Atlantic; and an ultimate destination of Bodo, Norway for an annual NATO exercise.

When the weather rapidly and unexpectedly deteriorated at Lajes, Marc's flight of KC-10s and A-4s had to divert from landing at Lajes Field and find the Portugese Island of Santa Maria, 100 miles further east. Marc successfully guided his fighters through the weather and they all safely landed. Unfortunately a follow on sister flight of KC-10s and A-4s was not so lucky. One A-4 crashed and with nowhere to land the remaining airborne aircraft had nothing left to do but prepare to ditch in the icy waters of the Atlantic.

Marc had his crew preparing for such a contingency and was refueled and ready to take off and save the day. Taking off in front of the wrecked A-4 at a runway intersection Marc was airborne in minutes and was credited for saving 15 lives and $76 million worth of aircraft. The Air Force and the National Aeronautics Association dubbed this flight the most meritorious of 1986 and award Marc and his crew the Mackay Trophy, displayed in the Smithsonian Air and Space Museum in Washington, D.C. Previous winners of the oldest national aviation trophy have included Chuck Yeager, Jimmy Doolittle, and Hap Arnold to name just a few. The Air Force Academy awarded Marc the Jabara Award for the greatest contribution in aviation. This trophy was recently awarded to Captain "Sully" Sullenberger for his miracle airline landing on the Hudson River.

Marc later upgraded to Instructor Pilot again and eventually was selected as a Standardization and Evaluation Pilot. During this period he flew in support of Operation Earnest Will, the Reflagging of Kuwaiti Oil Tankers in the Gulf of Hormuz. Marc attended Air Command and Staff College at Maxwell Air Force Base, Montgomery, Alabama. He was subsequently drafted to be a faculty member for the next class before being handpicked to be a member of the inaugural class of the School of Advanced Air and Space Studies (SAASS), earning a Master of Airpower Art and Science. Marc's thesis was one of the first published by Air University entitled "The Military Media Clash and the New Principle of War: Media Spin." A year earlier, not knowing he was going to be selected for SAASS, he began pursuing his Doctorate of Public Administration from the University of Alabama. He completed all but dissertation even as he was beginning the rigorous curriculum at SAASS and getting married to his wife Pamela.

Marc returned to flying and his old 911th Air Refueling Squadron. The assignment culminated with his command of a squadron he had been a member of an aggregate of nine years and in two different aircraft. During this tour, he supported Southern Watch Missions out of the United Arab Emirates, enforcing the United Nations No Fly Zones in Southern Iraq; he flew humanitarian relief cargo into austere Mogadishu, Somalia for Operation Restore Hope; and he refueled aircraft for Operation Restore Democracy in Haiti. His squadron was the best KC-10 unit in the AF, winning the Ellis Trophy.

The Chairman of the Joint Chiefs staff is competitively selected by law, and Marc made the cut. Assigned as a J-5 Strategy and Policy Advisor, Marc authored seminal Defense and National Security Documents. Marc returned to USAFA as the 34th Operations Group Commander where he was in charge of all the airmanship programs at the busiest visual flight rules airport in the world. Leading from the front, he earned his free fall parachute wings.

Under his watch, the Academy had a perfect safety record, the "Wings of Blue" Parachute Team recaptured the NCAA championship from West Point, the soaring team won a National Best Award and the flying team won the regional championship and came in second nationally to an aviation only college.

For Marc's War College or Senior Service Professional Military Education, the Air Force sent him to Harvard University's Weatherhead Center for International Affairs. He held his own alongside 19 classmates that were career diplomats, ambassadors, and journalists from around the world. During the year, he authored the manuscript "10 Propositions of Coalition Warfare." Marc is a lifetime Harvard Fellow.

Following Harvard Marc and his family moved to Naples, Italy where he served as Deputy Assistant Chief of Staff for Plans, Policy, Programs, Exercises, and Partnership for Peace, for NATO's Air Forces Southern Region (AIRSOUTH). In this capacity he was Deputy to a Spanish General and led a staff of 70 people from 14 nations. Later he was promoted to Director of Staff with 300 officers, enlisted and civilian from 14 different nations. Marc was the Commander of AIRSOUTH's personal representative on the ground as "Air Forward" in Kosovo serving the Kosovo Stabilization Forces NATO commander.

Shortly after 9/11 Marc was whisked into command of the 39th Wing in Incirlik, Turkey and given leadership responsibility for 7,000 people in seven geographically separate locations in Turkey, including Izmir, where Marc had attended first through third grade. While in command, Marc's wing was unique in that it was the first time in history more than one major operation was conducted from a single base. Marc shouldered three different command responsibilities simultaneously: Operation Northern Watch, the NATO allied support of the Northern Iraq United Nations No-Fly zone sanctions; Operations Enduring Freedom and Iraqi Freedom for Central Command; and a 24/7/365 nuclear surety mission for United States Air Forces in Europe.

Marc culminated his Air Force career as the Air Force's Deputy Director for Operational Plans and Joint Matters. His decorations include the Defense Superior Service Medal, the Legion of Merit with one oak leaf cluster, and the Distinguished Flying Cross. After leaving the Air Force, Marc became a Booz Allen Hamilton Associate, consulting for clients like: the National Guard Bureau; the National Geospatial-Intelligence Agency; the Federal Emergency Management Agency; and the Department of Homeland Security. He lives in Woodbridge, Virginia with his lovely wife Pamela, and his son Marc Jr., is a Webpage Designer living in Pittsburgh, Pennsylvania with his wife Kristyn.

9 780983 436102